Author's National Edition

THE WRITINGS OF
MARK TWAIN
VOLUME XXII

This is the authorized
Uniform Edition of all
my books.

Mark Twain

MARK TWAIN
From a Photograph taken in 1899 by H. W. Barnett, London

HOW TO TELL A STORY

AND OTHER ESSAYS

By MARK TWAIN

ILLUSTRATED

NEW YORK AND LONDON

HARPER & BROTHERS PUBLISHERS

ILLUSTRATIONS

CONTENTS

Acknowledgment is hereby made to Harper & Brothers, The Century Company, The Cosmopolitan, and S. S. McClure & Co., for courtesy shown in allowing the reprint in this volume of a number of their articles.

HOW TO TELL A STORY

AND

OTHER ESSAYS

HOW TO TELL A STORY

The Humorous Story an American Development.— Its
Difference from Comic and Witty Stories.

I DO not claim that I can tell a story as it ought to
be told. I only claim to know how a story
ought to be told, for I have been almost daily in the
company of the most expert story-tellers for many
years.

There are several kinds of stories, but only one
difficult kind — the humorous. I will talk mainly
about that one. The humorous story is American,
the comic story is English, the witty story is French.
The humorous story depends for its effect upon the
manner of the telling; the comic story and the witty
story upon the *matter*.

The humorous story may be spun out to great
length, and may wander around as much as it
pleases, and arrive nowhere in particular; but the
comic and witty stories must be brief and end with
a point. The humorous story bubbles gently along,
the others burst.

The humorous story is strictly a work of art —
high and delicate art — and only an artist can tell it;

but no art is necessary in telling the comic and the witty story; anybody can do it. The art of telling a humorous story — understand, I mean by word of mouth, not print — was created in America, and has remained at home.

The humorous story is told gravely; the teller does his best to conceal the fact that he even dimly suspects that there is anything funny about it; but the teller of the comic story tells you beforehand that it is one of the funniest things he has ever heard, then tells it with eager delight, and is the first person to laugh when he gets through. And sometimes, if he has had good success, he is so glad and happy that he will repeat the " nub " of it and glance around from face to face, collecting applause, and then repeat it again. It is a pathetic thing to see.

Very often, of course, the rambling and disjointed humorous story finishes with a nub, point, snapper, or whatever you like to call it. Then the listener must be alert, for in many cases the teller will divert attention from that nub by dropping it in a carefully casual and indifferent way, with the pretence that he does not know it is a nub.

Artemus Ward used that trick a good deal; then when the belated audience presently caught the joke he would look up with innocent surprise, as if wondering what they had found to laugh at. Dan Setchell used it before him, Nye and Riley and others use it to-day.

But the teller of the comic story does not slur the nub; he shouts it at you — every time. And when he prints it, in England, France, Germany, and Italy, he italicizes it, puts some whooping exclamation-points after it, and sometimes explains it in a parenthesis. All of which is very depressing, and makes one want to renounce joking and lead a better life.

Let me set down an instance of the comic method, using an anecdote which has been popular all over the world for twelve or fifteen hundred years. The teller tells it in this way:

THE WOUNDED SOLDIER.

In the course of a certain battle a soldier whose leg had been shot off appealed to another soldier who was hurrying by to carry him to the rear, informing him at the same time of the loss which he had sustained; whereupon the generous son of Mars, shouldering the unfortunate, proceeded to carry out his desire. The bullets and cannon-balls were flying in all directions, and presently one of the latter took the wounded man's head off — without, however, his deliverer being aware of it. In no long time he was hailed by an officer, who said:

"Where are you going with that carcass?"

"To the rear, sir — he's lost his leg!"

"His leg, forsooth?" responded the astonished officer; "you mean his head, you booby."

Whereupon the soldier dispossessed himself of his

burden, and stood looking down upon it in great
perplexity.　At length he said:

"It is true, sir, just as you have said."　Then
after a pause he added, "*But he* TOLD *me* IT WAS
HIS LEG! ! ! ! !"

Here the narrator bursts into explosion after explosion of thunderous horse-laughter, repeating that
nub from time to time through his gaspings and
shriekings and suffocatings.

It takes only a minute and a half to tell that in its
comic-story form; and isn't worth the telling, after
all.　Put into the humorous-story form it takes ten
minutes, and is about the funniest thing I have ever
listened to — as James Whitcomb Riley tells it.

He tells it in the character of a dull-witted old
farmer who has just heard it for the first time, thinks
it is unspeakably funny, and is trying to repeat it to
a neighbor.　But he can't remember it; so he gets
all mixed up and wanders helplessly round and
round, putting in tedious details that don't belong
in the tale and only retard it; taking them out con-
scientiously and putting in others that are just as
useless; making minor mistakes now and then and
stopping to correct them and explain how he came
to make them; remembering things which he forgot
to put in in their proper place and going back to
put them in there; stopping his narrative a good
while in order to try to recall the name of the soldier
that was hurt, and finally remembering that the
soldier's name was not mentioned, and remarking

placidly that the name is of no real importance, anyway — better, of course, if one knew it, but not essential, after all — and so on, and so on, and so on.

The teller is innocent and happy and pleased with himself, and has to stop every little while to hold himself in and keep from laughing outright; and does hold in, but his body quakes in a jelly-like way with interior chuckles; and at the end of the ten minutes the audience have laughed until they are exhausted, and the tears are running down their faces.

The simplicity and innocence and sincerity and unconsciousness of the old farmer are perfectly simulated, and the result is a performance which is thoroughly charming and delicious. This is art — and fine and beautiful, and only a master can compass it; but a machine could tell the other story.

To string incongruities and absurdities together in a wandering and sometimes purposeless way, and seem innocently unaware that they are absurdities, is the basis of the American art, if my position is correct. Another feature is the slurring of the point. A third is the dropping of a studied remark apparently without knowing it, as if one were thinking aloud. The fourth and last is the pause.

Artemus Ward dealt in numbers three and four a good deal. He would begin to tell with great animation something which he seemed to think was wonderful; then lose confidence, and after an

apparently absent-minded pause add an incongru-
ous remark in a soliloquizing way; and that was
the remark intended to explode the mine — and
it did.

For instance, he would say eagerly, excitedly, " I
once knew a man in New Zealand who hadn't a
tooth in his head "— here his animation would die
out; a silent, reflective pause would follow, then he
would say dreamily, and as if to himself, " and yet
that man could beat a drum better than any man I
ever saw."

The pause is an exceedingly important feature in
any kind of story, and a frequently recurring feature,
too.   It is a dainty thing, and delicate, and also uncertain and treacherous; for it must be exactly the
right length — no more and no less — or it fails of
its purpose and makes trouble.   If the pause is too
short the impressive point is passed, and the audience have had time to divine that a surprise is
intended — and then you can't surprise them, of
course.

On the platform I used to tell a negro ghost story
that had a pause in front of the snapper on the end,
and that pause was the most important thing in the
whole story.   If I got it the right length precisely,
I could spring the finishing ejaculation with effect
enough to make some impressible girl deliver a
startled little yelp and jump out of her seat — and
that was what I was after.   This story was called
" The Golden Arm," and was told in this fashion.

You can practise with it yourself — and mind you look out for the pause and get it right.

THE GOLDEN ARM.

Once 'pon a time dey wuz a monsus mean man, en he live 'way out in de prairie all 'lone by hisself, 'cep'n he had a wife. En bimeby she died, en he tuck en toted her way out dah in de prairie en buried her. Well, she had a golden arm — all solid gold, fum de shoulder down. He wuz pow'ful mean — pow'ful; en dat night he couldn't sleep, caze he want dat golden arm so bad.

When it come midnight he couldn't stan' it no mo'; so he git up, he did, en tuck his lantern en shoved out thoo de storm en dug her up en got de golden arm; en he bent his head down 'gin de win', en plowed en plowed en plowed thoo de snow. Den all on a sudden he stop (make a considerable pause here, and look startled, and take a listening attitude) en say: "My *lan*', what's dat!"

En he listen — en listen — en de win' say (set your teeth together and imitate the wailing and wheezing singsong of the wind), "Bzzz-z-zzz" — en den, way back yonder whah de grave is, he hear a *voice*! — he hear a voice all mix' up in de win' — can't hardly tell 'em 'part — "Bzzz-zzz — W-h-o — g-o-t — m-y — g-o-l-d-e-n *arm?* — zzz — zzz — W-h-o g-o-t m-y g-o-l-d-e-n *arm?*" (You must begin to shiver violently now.)

En he begin to shiver en shake, en say, "Oh,

2E

my! *Oh,* my lan'!'' en de win' blow de lantern
out, en de snow en sleet blow in his face en mos'
choke him, en he start a-plowin' knee-deep towards
home mos' dead, he so sk'yerd — en pooty soon
he hear de voice agin, en (pause) it 'us comin'
after him! "Bzzz — zzz — zzz — W-h-o — g-o-t —
m-y — g-o-l-d-e-n — *arm?*"

When he git to de pasture he hear it agin —
closter now, en a-*comin'!* — a-comin' back dah in
de dark en de storm — (repeat the wind and the
voice). When he git to de house he rush up-stairs
en jump in de bed en kiver up, head and years, en
lay dah shiverin' en shakin' — en den way out dah
he hear it *agin!* — en a-*comin'!* En bimeby he
hear (pause — awed, listening attitude) — pat — pat
— pat —*hit's a-comin' up-stairs!* Den he hear de
latch, en he *know* it's in de room!

Den pooty soon he know it's a-*stannin'* *by
de bed!* (Pause.) Den — he know it's a-*bendin'
down over him* — en he cain't skasely git his
breath! Den — den — he seem to feel someth'n
c-o-l-d, right down 'most agin his head!
(Pause.)

Den de voice say, *right at his year* — " W-h-o —
g-o-t — m-y — g-o-l-d-e-n *arm?*'' (You must wail
it out very plaintively and accusingly; then you
stare steadily and impressively into the face of the
farthest-gone auditor — a girl, preferably — and let
that awe-inspiring pause begin to build itself in the
deep hush. When it has reached exactly the right

length, jump suddenly at that girl and yell, "*You've got it!*"

If you've got the *pause* right, she'll fetch a dear little yelp and spring right out of her shoes. But you *must* get the pause right; and you will find it the most troublesome and aggravating and uncertain thing you ever undertook.)

IN DEFENCE OF HARRIET SHELLEY

I

I HAVE committed sins, of course; but I have not committed enough of them to entitle me to the punishment of reduction to the bread and water of ordinary literature during six years when I might have been living on the fat diet spread for the righteous in Professor Dowden's *Life of Shelley*, if I had been justly dealt with.

During these six years I have been living a life of peaceful ignorance. I was not aware that Shelley's first wife was unfaithful to him, and that that was why he deserted her and wiped the stain from his sensitive honor by entering into soiled relations with Godwin's young daughter. This was all new to me when I heard it lately, and was told that the proofs of it were in this book, and that this book's verdict is accepted in the girls' colleges of America and its view taught in their literary classes.

In each of these six years multitudes of young people in our country have arrived at the Shelley-reading age. Are these six multitudes unacquainted with this life of Shelley? Perhaps they are; indeed, one may feel pretty sure that the great bulk of them are. To these, then, I address myself, in the hope that some account of this romantic historical fable and the fabulist's manner of constructing and adorning it may interest them.

First, as to its literary style. Our negroes in America have several ways of entertaining themselves which are not found among the whites anywhere. Among these inventions of theirs is one which is particularly popular with them. It is a competition in elegant deportment. They hire a hall and bank the spectators' seats in rising tiers along the two sides, leaving all the middle stretch of the floor free. A cake is provided as a prize for the winner in the competition, and a bench of experts in deportment is appointed to award it. Sometimes there are as many as fifty contestants, male and female, and five hundred spectators. One at a time the contestants enter, clothed regardless of expense in what each considers the perfection of style and taste, and walk down the vacant central space and back again with that multitude of critical eyes on them. All that the competitor knows of fine airs and graces he throws into his carriage, all that he knows of seductive expression he throws into his countenance. He may use all the helps he can devise: watch-chain to twirl with his fingers, cane to do graceful things with, snowy handkerchief to flourish and get artful effects out of, shiny new stovepipe hat to assist in his courtly bows; and the

2*₊*₊

colored lady may have a fan to work up *her* effects with, and smile over and blush behind, and she may add other helps, according to her judgment. When the review by individual detail is over, a grand review of all the contestants in procession follows, with all the airs and graces and all the bowings and smirkings on exhibition at once, and this enables the bench of experts to make the necessary comparisons and arrive at a verdict. The successful competitor gets the prize which I have before mentioned, and an abundance of applause and envy along with it. The negroes have a name for this grave deportment-tournament; a name taken from the prize contended for. They call it a Cake-Walk.

This Shelley biography is a literary cake-walk. The ordinary forms of speech are absent from it. All the pages, all the paragraphs, walk by sedately, elegantly, not to say mincingly, in their Sunday-best, shiny and sleek, perfumed, and with *boutonnieres* in their button-holes; it is rare to find even a chance sentence that has forgotten to dress. If the book wishes to tell us that Mary Godwin, child of sixteen, had known afflictions, the fact saunters forth in this nobby outfit: " Mary was herself not unlearned in the lore of pain " — meaning by that that she had not always traveled on asphalt; or, as some authorities would frame it, that she had " been there herself," a form which, while preferable to the book's form, is still not to be recommended. If the book wishes to tell us that Harriet Shelley hired a wet-nurse, that commonplace fact gets turned into a dancing-master, who does his professional bow before us in pumps and knee-breeches, with his fiddle under one arm and his crush-hat under the other, thus: "The beauty of Harriet's motherly relation to her babe was marred in Shelley's eyes by the introduction into his house of a hireling nurse to whom was delegated the mother's tenderest office."

This is perhaps the strangest book that has seen the light since Frankenstein. Indeed, it is a Frankenstein itself; a Frankenstein with the original infirmity supplemented by a new one; a Frankenstein with the reasoning faculty wanting. Yet it believes it can reason, and is always trying. It is not content to leave a mountain of fact standing in the clear sunshine, where the simplest reader can perceive its form, its details, and its relation to the rest of the landscape, but thinks it must help him examine it and understand it; so its drifting mind settles upon it with that intent, but always with one and the same result: there is a change of temperature and the mountain is hid in a fog. Every time it sets up a premise and starts to reason from it, there is a surprise in store for the reader. It is strangely near-sighted, cross-eyed, and purblind. Sometimes when a mastodon walks across the field of its vision it takes it for a rat; at other times it does not see it at all.

B*.*.

The materials of this biographical fable are facts, rumors, and poetry. They are connected together and harmonized by the help of suggestion, conjecture, innuendo, perversion, and semi-suppression.

The fable has a distinct object in view, but this object is not acknowledged in set words. Percy Bysshe Shelley has done something which in the case of other men is called a grave crime; it must be shown that in his case it is not that, because he does not think as other men do about these things.

Ought not that to be enough, if the fabulist is serious? Having proved that a crime is not a crime, was it worth while to go on and fasten the responsibility of a crime which was not a crime upon somebody else? What is the use of hunting down and holding to bitter account people who are responsible for other people's innocent acts?

Still, the fabulist thinks it a good idea to do that. In his view Shelley's first wife, Harriet, free of all offense as far as we have historical facts for guidance, must be held unforgivably responsible for her husband's innocent act in deserting her and taking up with another woman.

Any one will suspect that this task has its difficulties. Any one will divine that nice work is necessary here, cautious work, wily work, and that there is entertainment to be had in watching the magician do it. There is indeed entertainment in watching him. He arranges his facts, his rumors, and his poems on his table in full view of the house, and shows you that everything is there — no deception, everything fair and above board. And this is apparently true, yet there is a defect, for some of his best stock is hid in an appendix-basket behind the door, and you do not come upon it until the exhibition is over and the enchantment of your mind accomplished — as the magician thinks.

There is an insistent atmosphere of candor and fairness about this book which is engaging at first, then a little burdensome, then a trifle fatiguing, then progressively suspicious, annoying, irritating, and oppressive. It takes one some little time to find out that phrases which seem intended to guide the reader aright are there to mislead him; that phrases which seem intended to throw light are there to throw darkness; that phrases which seem intended to interpret a fact are there to misinterpret it; that phrases which seem intended to forestall prejudice are there to create it; that phrases which seem anti-dotes are poisons in disguise. The naked facts arrayed in the book establish Shelley's guilt in that one episode which disfigures his otherwise super-latively lofty and beautiful life; but the historian's careful and methodical misinterpretation of them transfers the responsibility to the wife's shoulders — as he persuades himself. The few meagre facts of Harriet Shelley's life, as furnished by the book, acquit her of offense; but by calling in the for-bidden helps of rumor, gossip, conjecture, insinua-tion, and innuendo he destroys her character and rehabilitates Shelley's — as he believes. And in truth his unheroic work has not been barren of the results he aimed at; as witness the assertion made to me that girls in the colleges of America are taught that Harriet Shelley put a stain upon her husband's honor, and that that was what stung him into repurifying himself by deserting her and his child and entering into scandalous relations with a school-girl acquaintance of his.

If that assertion is true, they probably use a re-duction of this work in those colleges, maybe only a sketch outlined from it. Such a thing as that could be harmful and misleading. They ought to cast it out and put the whole book in its place. It would not deceive. It would not deceive the janitor.

All of this book is interesting on account of the sorcerer's methods and the attractiveness of some of his characters and the repulsiveness of the rest, but no part of it is so much so as are the chapters wherein he tries to think he thinks he sets forth the causes which led to Shelley's desertion of his wife in 1814.

Harriet Westbrook was a school-girl sixteen years old. Shelley was teeming with advanced thought. He believed that Christianity was a degrading and selfish superstition, and he had a deep and sincere desire to rescue one of his sisters from it. Harriet was impressed by his various philosophies and looked upon him as an intellectual wonder — which indeed he was. He had an idea that she could give him valuable help in his scheme regarding his sister; therefore he asked her to correspond with him. She was quite willing. Shelley was not thinking of love, for he was just getting over a passion for his cousin, Harriet Grove, and just getting well steeped in one for Miss Hitchener, a school-teacher. What might happen to Harriet Westbrook before the letter-writing was ended did not enter his mind. Yet an older person could have made a good guess at it, for in person Shelley was as beautiful as an angel, he was frank, sweet, winning, unassuming, and so rich in unselfishness, generosities, and magnanimities that he made his whole generation seem poor in these great qualities by comparison. Besides, he was in distress. His college had expelled him for writing an atheistical pamphlet and afflicting the reverend heads of the university with it, his rich father and grandfather had closed their purses against him, his friends were cold. Necessarily, Harriet fell in love with him; and so deeply, indeed, that there was no way for Shelley to save her from suicide but to marry her. He believed himself to blame for this state of things, so the marriage took place. He was pretty fairly in love with Harriet, although he loved Miss Hitchener better. He wrote and explained the case to Miss Hitchener after the wedding, and he could not have been franker or more *naïve* and less stirred up about the circumstance if the matter in issue had been a commercial transaction involving thirty-five dollars.

Shelley was nineteen. He was not a youth, but a man. He had never had any youth. He was an erratic and fantastic child during eighteen years, then he stepped into manhood, as one steps over a door-sill. He was curiously mature at nineteen in his ability to do independent thinking on the deep questions of life and to arrive at sharply definite decisions regarding them, and stick to them — stick to them and stand by them at cost of bread, friendships, esteem, respect, and approbation.

For the sake of his opinions he was willing to sacrifice all these valuable things, and did sacrifice them; and went on doing it, too, when he could at any moment have made himself rich and supplied himself with friends and esteem by compromising with his father, at the moderate expense of throwing overboard one or two indifferent details of his cargo of principles.

He and Harriet eloped to Scotland and got married. They took lodgings in Edinburgh of a sort answerable to their purse, which was about empty, and there their life was a happy one and grew daily more so. They had only themselves for company, but they needed no additions to it. They were as cozy and contented as birds in a nest. Harriet sang evenings or read aloud; also she studied and tried to improve her mind, her husband instructing her in Latin. She was very beautiful, she was modest, quiet, genuine, and, according to her husband's testimony, she had no fine lady airs or aspirations about her. In Matthew Arnold's judgment, she was " a pleasing figure."

The pair remained five weeks in Edinburgh, and then took lodgings in York, where Shelley's college mate, Hogg, lived. Shelley presently ran down to London, and Hogg took this opportunity to make love to the young wife. She repulsed him, and reported the fact to her husband when he got back. It seems a pity that Shelley did not copy this creditable conduct of hers some time or other when under temptation, so that we might have seen the author of his biography hang the miracle in the skies and squirt rainbows at it.

At the end of the first year of marriage — the most trying year for any young couple, for then the mutual failings are coming one by one to light, and the necessary adjustments are being made in pain and tribulation — Shelley was able to recognize that his marriage venture had been a safe one. As we have seen, his love for his wife had begun in a rather shallow way and with not much force, but now it was become deep and strong, which entitles his wife to a broad credit mark, one may admit. He addresses a long and loving poem to her, in which both passion and worship appear:

Exhibit A

" O thou
Whose dear love gleamed upon the gloomy path
Which this lone spirit travelled,

.   .   .   .

. . . wilt thou not turn

> Those spirit-beaming eyes and look on me,
> Until I be assured that Earth is Heaven
> And Heaven is Earth ?
> .   .   .   .   .   .
> Harriet ! let death all mortal ties dissolve,
> But ours shall not be mortal."

Shelley also wrote a sonnet to her in August of this same year in celebration of her birthday :

Exhibit B

> " Ever as now with Love and Virtue's glow
>   May thy unwithering soul not cease to burn,
> Still may thine heart with those pure thoughts o'erflow
>   Which force from mine such quick and warm return."

Was the girl of seventeen glad and proud and happy? We may conjecture that she was.

That was the year 1812. Another year passed — still happily, still successfully — a child was born in June, 1813, and in September, three months later, Shelley addresses a poem to this child, Ianthe, in which he points out just when the little creature is most particularly dear to him :

Exhibit C

> " Dearest when most thy tender traits express
>   The image of thy mother's loveliness."

Up to this point the fabulist counsel for Shelley and prosecutor of his young wife has had easy sailing, but now his trouble begins, for Shelley is getting ready to make some unpleasant history for himself, and it will be necessary to put the blame of it on the wife.

Shelley had made the acquaintance of a charming

gray-haired, young-hearted Mrs. Boinville, whose face " retained a certain youthful beauty "; she lived at Bracknell, and had a young daughter named Cornelia Turner, who was equipped with many fascinations. Apparently these people were sufficiently sentimental. Hogg says of Mrs. Boinville:

" The greater part of her associates were odious. I generally found there two or three sentimental young butchers, an eminently philosophical tinker, and several very unsophisticated medical practitioners or medical students, all of low origin and vulgar and offensive manners. They sighed, turned up their eyes, retailed philosophy, such as it was," etc.

Shelley moved to Bracknell, July 27th (this is still 1813) purposely to be near this unwholesome prairie-dogs' nest. The fabulist says: " It was the entrance into a world more amiable and exquisite than he had yet known."

" In this acquaintance the attraction was mutual " — and presently it grew to be very mutual indeed, between Shelley and Cornelia Turner, when they got to studying the Italian poets together. Shelley, " responding like a tremulous instrument to every breath of passion or of sentiment," had his chance here. It took only four days for Cornelia's attractions to begin to dim Harriet's. Shelley arrived on the 27th of July; on the 31st he wrote a sonnet to Harriet in which " one detects already the little rift in the lover's lute which had seemed to be healed or never to have gaped at all when the later and happier sonnet to Ianthe was written " — in September, we remember:

Exhibit D

"EVENING. TO HARRIET

" O thou bright Sun !   Beneath the dark blue line
Of western distance that sublime descendest,
And, gleaming lovelier as thy beams decline,
Thy million hues to every vapor lendest,
And over cobweb, lawn, and grove, and stream
Sheddest the liquid magic of thy light,
Till calm Earth, with the parting splendor bright,
Shows like the vision of a beauteous dream;
What gazer now with astronomic eye
Could coldly count the spots within thy sphere ?
Such were thy lover, Harriet, could he fly
The thoughts of all that makes his passion dear,
And turning senseless from thy warm caress
Pick flaws in our close-woven happiness."

I cannot find the " rift "; still it may be there.
What the poem *seems* to say is, that a person would
be coldly ungrateful who could consent to count and
consider little spots and flaws in such a warm, great,
satisfying sun as Harriet is.   It is a " little rift
which had seemed to be healed, *or* never to have
gaped at all."   That is, " one *detects* " a little rift
which perhaps had never existed.   How does one
do that ?   How does one see the invisible?   It is the
fabulist's secret; he knows how to detect what does
not exist, he knows how to see what is not seeable;
it is his gift, and he works it many a time to poor
dead Harriet Shelley's deep damage.

" As yet, however, if there was a speck upon
Shelley's happiness it was no more than a speck "
—meaning the one which one detects where " it

may never have gaped at all '' — '' nor had Harriet cause for discontent.''

Shelley's Latin instructions to his wife had ceased. '' From a teacher he had now become a pupil.'' Mrs. Boinville and her young married daughter Cornelia were teaching him Italian poetry; a fact which warns one to receive with some caution that other statement that Harriet had no '' cause for discontent.''

Shelley had stopped instructing Harriet in Latin, as before mentioned. The biographer thinks that the busy life in London some time back, and the intrusion of the baby, account for this. These were hindrances, but were there no others? He is always overlooking a detail here and there that might be valuable in helping us understand a situation. For instance, when a man has been hard at work at the Italian poets with a pretty woman, hour after hour, and responding like a tremulous instrument to every breath of passion or of sentiment in the meantime, that man is dog-tired when he gets home, and he *can't* teach his wife Latin; it would be unreasonable to expect it.

Up to this time we have submitted to having Mrs. Boinville pushed upon us as ostensibly concerned in these Italian lessons, but the biographer drops her now, of his own accord. Cornelia '' perhaps '' is sole teacher. Hogg says she was a prey to a kind of sweet melancholy, arising from causes purely imaginary; she required consolation, and found it

3ᴇ

in Petrarch. He also says, " Bysshe entered at once fully into her views and caught the soft infection, breathing the tenderest and sweetest melancholy, as every true poet ought."

Then the author of the book interlards a most stately and fine compliment to Cornelia, furnished by a man of approved judgment who knew her well " in later years." It is a very good compliment indeed, and she no doubt deserved it in her " later years," when she had for generations ceased to be sentimental and lackadaisical, and was no longer engaged in enchanting young husbands and sowing sorrow for young wives. But why is that compliment to that old gentlewoman intruded there? Is it to make the reader believe she was well-chosen and safe society for a young, sentimental husband? The biographer's device was not well planned. That old person was not present — it was her other self that was there, her young, sentimental, melancholy, warm-blooded self, in those early sweet times before antiquity had cooled her off and mossed her back.

" In choosing for friends such women as Mrs. Newton, Mrs. Boinville, and Cornelia Turner, Shelley gave good proof of his insight and discrimination." That is the fabulist's opinion — Harriet Shelley's is not reported.

Early in August, Shelley was in London trying to raise money. In September he wrote the poem to the baby, already quoted from. In the first week of October Shelley and family went to Warwick, then to Edinburgh, arriving there about the middle of the month.

" Harriet was happy." Why? The author furnishes a reason, but hides from us whether it is history or conjecture; it is because " *the babe had borne the journey well*." It has all the aspect of one of his artful devices — flung in in his favorite casual way — the way he has when he wants to draw one's attention away from an obvious thing and amuse it with some trifle that is less obvious but more useful — in a history like this. The obvious thing is, that Harriet was happy because there was much territory between her husband and Cornelia Turner now; and because the perilous Italian lessons were taking a rest; and because, if there chanced to be any respondings like a tremulous instrument to every breath of passion or of sentiment in stock in these days, she might hope to get a share of them herself; and because, with her husband liberated, now, from the fetid fascinations of that sentimental retreat so pitilessly described by Hogg, who also dubbed it " Shelley's paradise " later, she might hope to persuade him to stay away from it permanently; and because she might also hope that his brain would cool, now, and his heart become healthy, and both brain and heart consider the situation and resolve that it would be a right and manly thing to stand by this girl-wife and her child and see that they were honorably dealt with, and cherished and protected and loved by the man that had promised these things, and so be made happy and kept so. And because, also — may we conjecture this? — we may hope for the privilege of taking up our cozy Latin lessons again, that used to be so pleasant, and brought us so near together — so near, indeed, that often our heads touched, just as heads do over Italian lessons; and our hands met in casual and unintentional, but still most delicious and thrilling little contacts and momentary clasps, just as they inevitably do over Italian lessons. Suppose one should say to any young wife: " I find that your husband is poring over the Italian poets and being instructed in the beautiful Italian language by the lovely Cornelia Robinson " — would that cozy picture fail to rise before her mind? would its possibilities fail to suggest themselves to her? would there be a pang in her heart and a blush on her face? or, on the contrary, would the remark give her pleasure, make her joyous and gay? Why, one needs only to make the experiment — the result will not be uncertain.

However, we learn — by authority of deeply reasoned and searching conjecture — that the baby bore the journey well, and that that was why the young wife was happy. That accounts for two per cent. of the happiness, but it was not right to imply that it accounted for the other ninety-eight also.

Peacock, a scholar, poet, and friend of the Shelleys, was of their party when they went away. He used to laugh at the Boinville menagerie, and " was

not a favorite.'' One of the Boinville group, writing
to Hogg, said, '' The Shelleys have made an addition to their party in the person of a cold scholar,
who, I think, has neither taste nor feeling. This,
Shelley will perceive sooner or later, for his warm
nature craves sympathy.'' True, and Shelley will
fight his way back there to get it — there will be no
way to head him off.

Towards the end of November it was necessary
for Shelley to pay a business visit to London, and
he conceived the project of leaving Harriet and the
baby in Edinburgh with Harriet's sister, Eliza Westbrook, a sensible, practical maiden lady about thirty
years old, who had spent a great part of her time
with the family since the marriage. She was an
estimable woman, and Shelley had had reason to
like her, and did like her; but along about this time
his feeling towards her changed. Part of Shelley's
plan, as he wrote Hogg, was to spend his London
evenings with the Newtons — members of the Boinville Hysterical Society. But, alas, when he arrived
early in December, that pleasant game was partially
blocked, for Eliza and the family arrived *with* him.
We are left destitute of conjectures at this point by
the biographer, and it is my duty to supply one. I
chance the conjecture that it was Eliza who inter-
fered with that game. I think she tried to do what
she could towards modifying the Boinville connection, in the interest of her young sister's peace and
honor.

3*₊*₊

If it was she who blocked that game, she was not strong enough to block the next one. Before the month and year were out — no date given, let us call it Christmas — Shelley and family were nested in a furnished house in Windsor, " at no great distance from the Boinvilles " — these decoys still residing at Bracknell.

What we need, now, is a misleading conjecture. We get it with characteristic promptness and depravity:

"But Prince Athanase found not the aged Zonoras, the friend of his boyhood, in any wanderings to Windsor. Dr. Lind had died a year since, and with his death Windsor must have lost, for Shelley, its chief attraction."

Still, not to mention Shelley's wife, there was Bracknell, at any rate. While Bracknell remains, all solace is not lost. Shelley is represented by this biographer as doing a great many careless things, but to my mind this hiring a furnished house for three months in order to be with a man who has been dead a year, is the carelessest of them all. One feels for him — that is but natural, and does us honor besides — yet one is vexed, for all that. He could have written and asked about the aged Zonoras before taking the house. He may not have had the address, but that is nothing — any postman would know the aged Zonoras; a dead postman would remember a name like that.

And yet, why throw a rag like this to us ravening wolves? Is it seriously supposable that we will stop to chew it and let our prey escape? No, we are getting to expect this kind of device, and to give it merely a sniff for certainty's sake and then walk around it and leave it lying. Shelley was not after the aged Zonoras; he was pointed for Cornelia and the Italian lessons, for his warm nature was craving sympathy.

II

THE year 1813 is just ended now, and we step into 1814.

To recapitulate, how much of Cornelia's society has Shelley had, thus far? Portions of August and September, and four days of July. That is to say, he has had opportunity to enjoy it, more or less, during that brief period. Did he want some more of it? We must fall back upon history, and then go to conjecturing.

"In the early part of the year 1814, Shelley was a frequent visitor at Bracknell."

"Frequent" is a cautious word, in this author's mouth; the very cautiousness of it, the vagueness of it, provokes suspicion; it makes one suspect that this frequency was more frequent than the mere common everyday kinds of frequency which one is in the habit of averaging up with the unassuming term "frequent." I think so because they fixed up a bedroom for him in the Boinville house. One

C*.*.*

doesn't need a bedroom if one is only going to run over now and then in a disconnected way to respond like a tremulous instrument to every breath of passion or of sentiment and rub up one's Italian poetry a little.

The young wife was not invited, perhaps. If she was, she most certainly did not come, or she would have straightened the room up; the most ignorant of us knows that a wife would not endure a room in the condition in which Hogg found this one when he occupied it one night. Shelley was away — why, nobody can divine. Clothes were scattered about, there were books on every side: "Wherever a book could be laid was an open book turned down on its face to keep its place." It seems plain that the wife was not invited. No, not that; I think she was invited, but said to herself that she could not bear to go there and see another young woman touching heads with her husband over an Italian book and making thrilling hand-contacts with him accidentally.

As remarked, he was a frequent visitor there, "where he found an easeful resting-place in the house of Mrs. Boinville — the white-haired Maimuna — and of her daughter, Mrs. Turner." The aged Zonoras was deceased, but the white-haired Maimuna was still on deck, as we see. "Three charming ladies entertained the mocker (Hogg) with cups of tea, late hours, Wieland's Agathon, sighs and smiles, and the celestial manna of refined sentiment."

"Such," says Hogg, "were the delights of Shelley's paradise in Bracknell."

The white-haired Maimuna presently writes to Hogg:

"I will not have you despise home-spun pleasures. Shelley is making a trial of them with us —"

A trial of them. It may be called that. It was March 11, and he had been in the house a month. She continues:

Shelley "likes them so well that he is resolved to leave off rambling —"

But he has *already* left it off. He has been there a month.

"And begin a course of them himself."

But he has already begun it. He has been at it a *month*. He likes it so well that he has forgotten all about his wife, as a letter of his reveals.

"Seriously, I think his mind and body want rest."

Yet he has been resting both for a month, with Italian, and tea, and manna of sentiment, and late hours, and every restful thing a young husband could need for the refreshment of weary limbs and a sore conscience, and a nagging sense of shabbiness and treachery.

"His journeys after what he has never found have racked his purse and his tranquillity. He is resolved to take a little care of the former, in pity to the latter, which I applaud, and shall second with all my might."

But she does not say whether the young wife, a

stranger and lonely yonder, wants another woman
and her daughter Cornelia to be lavishing so much
inflamed interest on her husband or not. That
young wife is always silent — we are never allowed
to hear from her. She must have opinions about
such things, she cannot be indifferent, she must be
approving or disapproving, surely she would speak
if she were allowed — even to-day and from her
grave she would, if she could, I think — but we
get only the other side, they keep her silent always.

" He has deeply interested us. In the course of your intimacy he
must have made you feel what we now feel for him. He is seeking a
house close to us —"

Ah! he is not close enough yet, it seems —

" and if he succeeds we shall have an additional motive to induce you
to come among us in the summer."

The reader would puzzle a long time and not
guess the biographer's comment upon the above
letter. It is this:

" These sound like words of a considerate and judicious friend."

That is what he thinks. That is, it is what he
thinks he thinks. No, that is not quite it: it is what
he thinks he can stupefy a particularly and unspeakably dull reader into thinking it is what he thinks.
He makes that comment with the knowledge that
Shelley is in love with this woman's daughter, and
that it is because of the fascinations of these two
that Shelley has deserted his wife — for this month,
considering all the circumstances, and his new pas-

sion, and his employment of the time, amounted to desertion; that is its rightful name. We cannot know how the wife regarded it and felt about it; but if she could have read the letter which Shelley was writing to Hogg four or five days later, we could guess her thought and how she felt. Hear him:

.   .   .   .

" I have been staying with Mrs. Boinville for the last month; I have escaped, in the society of all that philosophy and friendship combine, from the dismaying solitude of myself."

It is fair to conjecture that he was feeling ashamed.

" They have revived in my heart the expiring flame of life. I have felt myself translated to a paradise which has nothing of mortality but its transitoriness; my heart sickens at the view of that necessity which will quickly divide me from the delightful tranquillity of this happy home — for it has become my home.

.   .   .   .

" Eliza is still with us — not here! — but will be with me when the infinite malice of destiny forces me to depart."

Eliza is she who blocked that game — the game in London — the one where we were purposing to dine every night with one of the " three charming ladies " who fed tea and manna and late hours to Hogg at Bracknell.

Shelley could send Eliza away, of course; could have cleared her out long ago if so minded, just as he had previously done with a predecessor of hers whom he had first worshiped and then turned against; but perhaps she was useful there as a thin excuse for staying away himself.

" I am now but little inclined to contest this point. I certainly hate her with all my heart and soul. . . .

" It is a sight which awakens an inexpressible sensation of disgust and horror, to see her caress my poor little Ianthe, in whom I may hereafter find the consolation of sympathy. I sometimes feel faint with the fatigue of checking the overflowings of my unbounded abhorrence for this miserable wretch. But she is no more than a blind and loathsome worm, that cannot see to sting.

" I have begun to learn Italian again. . . . Cornelia assists me in this language. Did I not once tell you that I thought her cold and reserved? She is the reverse of this, as she is the reverse of everything bad. She inherits all the divinity of her mother. . . . I have sometimes forgotten that I am not an inmate of this delightful home — that a time will come which will cast me again into the boundless ocean of abhorred society.

" I have written nothing but one stanza, which has no meaning, and that I have only written in thought:

> " Thy dewy looks sink in my breast;
>   Thy gentle words stir poison there;
> Thou hast disturbed the only rest
>   That was the portion of despair.
> Subdued to duty's hard control,
>   I could have borne my wayward lot:
> The chains that bind this ruined soul
>   Had cankered then, but crushed it not.

" This is the vision of a delirious and distempered dream, which passes away at the cold clear light of morning. Its surpassing excellence and exquisite perfections have no more reality than the color of an autumnal sunset."

Then it did not refer to his wife. That is plain; otherwise he would have said so. It is well that he explained that it has no meaning, for if he had not done that, the previous soft references to Cornelia and the way he has come to feel about her now would make us think she was the person who had inspired it while teaching him how to read the warm and ruddy Italian poets during a month.

The biography observes that portions of this letter " read like the tired moaning of a wounded creature." Guesses at the nature of the wound are permissible; we will hazard one.

Read by the light of Shelley's previous history, his letter seems to be the cry of a tortured conscience. Until this time it was a conscience that had never felt a pang or known a smirch. It was the conscience of one who, until this time, had never done a dishonorable thing, or an ungenerous, or cruel, or treacherous thing, but was now doing all of these, and was keenly aware of it. Up to this time Shelley had been master of his nature, and it was a nature which was as beautiful and as nearly perfect as any merely human nature may be. But he was drunk now, with a debasing passion, and was not himself. There is nothing in his previous history that is in character with the Shelley of this letter. He had done boyish things, foolish things, even crazy things, but never a thing to be ashamed of. He had done things which one might laugh at, but the privilege of laughing was limited always to the thing itself; you could not laugh at the motive back of it — that was high, that was noble. His most fantastic and quixotic acts had a purpose back of them which made them fine, often great, and made the rising laugh seem profanation and quenched it; quenched it, and changed the impulse to homage.

Up to this time he had been loyalty itself, where his obligations lay — treachery was new to him; he had never done an ignoble thing — baseness was new to him; he had never done an unkind thing — that also was new to him.

This was the author of that letter, this was the man who had deserted his young wife and was lamenting, bcause he must leave another woman's house which had become a " home " to him, and go away. Is he lamenting *mainly* because he must go back to his wife and child? No, the lament is mainly for what he is to leave behind him. The physical comforts of the house? No, in his life he had never attached importance to such things. Then the thing which he grieves to leave is narrowed down to a person — to the person whose " dewy looks " had sunk into his breast, and whose seducing words had " stirred poison there."

He was ashamed of himself, his conscience was upbraiding him. He was the slave of a degrading love; he was drunk with his passion, the real Shelley was in temporary eclipse. This is the verdict which his previous history must certainly deliver upon this episode, I think.

One must be allowed to assist himself with conjectures like these when trying to find his way through a literary swamp which has so many misleading finger-boards up as this book is furnished with.

We have now arrived at a part of the swamp where the difficulties and perplexities are going to be greater than any we have yet met with — where, indeed, the finger-boards are multitudinous, and the most of them pointing diligently in the wrong direction. We are to be told by the biography why Shelley deserted his wife and child and took up with Cornelia Turner and Italian. It was not on account of Cornelia's sighs and sentimentalities and tea and manna and late hours and soft and sweet and industrious enticements; no, it was because " his happiness in his home had been wounded and bruised almost to death."

It had been wounded and bruised almost to death in this way:

1st. Harriet persuaded him to set up a carriage.

2d. After the intrusion of the baby, Harriet stopped reading aloud and studying.

3d. Harriet's walks with Hogg " commonly conducted us to some fashionable bonnet-shop."

4th. Harriet hired a wet-nurse.

5th. When an operation was being performed upon the baby, " Harriet stood by, narrowly observing all that was done, but, to the astonishment of the operator, betraying not the smallest sign of emotion."

6th. Eliza Westbrook, sister-in-law, was still of the household.

The evidence against Harriet Shelley is all in; there is no more. Upon these six counts she stands indicted of the crime of driving her husband into that sty at Bracknell; and this crime, by these helps, the biographical prosecuting attorney has set himself the task of proving upon her.

Does the biographer *call* himself the attorney for the prosecution? No, only to himself, privately; publicly he is the passionless, disinterested, impartial judge on the bench. He holds up his judicial scales before the world, that all may see; and it all tries to look so fair that a blind person would sometimes fail to see him slip the false weights in.

Shelley's happiness in his home had been wounded and bruised almost to death, first, because Harriet had persuaded him to set up a carriage. I cannot discover that any evidence is offered that she asked him to set up a carriage. Still, if she did, was it a heavy offence? Was it unique? Other young wives had committed it before, others have committed it since. Shelley had dearly loved her in those London days; possibly he set up the carriage gladly to please her; affectionate young husbands do such things. When Shelley ran away with another girl, by-and-by, this girl persuaded him to pour the price of many carriages and many horses down the bottomless well of her father's debts, but this impartial judge finds no fault with that. Once she appeals to Shelley to raise money — necessarily by borrowing, there was no other way — to pay her father's debts with at a time when Shelley was in danger of being arrested and imprisoned for his own debts; yet the good judge finds no fault with her even for this.

First and last, Shelley emptied into that rapacious mendicant's lap a sum which cost him — for he borrowed it at ruinous rates — from eighty to one hundred thousand dollars. But it was Mary Godwin's papa, the supplications were often sent through Mary, the good judge is Mary's strenuous friend, so Mary gets no censures. On the Continent *Mary rode in her private carriage*, built, as Shelley boasts, "by one of the best makers in Bond Street," yet the good judge makes not even a passing comment on this iniquity. Let us throw out Count No. 1 against Harriet Shelley as being far-fetched and frivolous.

Shelley's happiness in his home had been wounded and bruised almost to death, secondly, because Harriet's studies "had dwindled away to nothing, Bysshe had ceased to express any interest in them." At what time was this? It was when Harriet "had fully recovered from the fatigue of her first effort of maternity,. . . and was now in full force, vigor, and effect." Very well, the baby was born two days before the close of June. It took the mother a month to get back her full force, vigor, and effect; this brings us to July 27th and the deadly Cornelia. If a wife of eighteen is studying with her husband and he gets smitten with another woman, isn't he likely to lose interest in his wife's studies for *that* reason, and is not his wife's interest in her studies likely to languish for the *same* reason? Would not the mere sight of those books of hers sharpen the

4E

pain that is in her heart? This sudden breaking down of a mutual intellectual interest of two years' standing is coincident with Shelley's re-encounter with Cornelia; and we are allowed to gather from that time forth for nearly two months he did all his studying in that person's society. We feel at liberty to rule out Count No. 2 from the indictment against Harriet.

Shelley's happiness in his home had been wounded and bruised almost to death, thirdly, because Harriet's walks with Hogg commonly led to some fashionable bonnet-shop. I offer no palliation; I only ask why the dispassionate, impartial judge did not offer one himself — merely, I mean, to offset his leniency in a similar case or two where the girl who ran away with Harriet's husband was the shopper. There are several occasions where she interested herself with shopping — among them being walks which ended at the bonnet-shop — yet in none of these cases does she get a word of blame from the good judge, while in one of them he covers the deed with a justifying remark, she doing the shopping that time to find easement for her mind, her child having died.

Shelley's happiness in his home had been wounded and bruised almost to death, fourthly, by the introduction there of a wet-nurse. The wet-nurse was introduced at the time of the Edinburgh sojourn, immediately after Shelley had been enjoying the two months of study with Cornelia which broke up his wife's studies and destroyed his personal interest in them. Why, by this time, nothing that Shelley's wife could do would have been satisfactory to him, for he was in love with another woman, and was never going to be contented again until he got back to her. If he had been still in love with his wife it is not easily conceivable that he would care much who nursed the baby, provided the baby was well nursed. Harriet's jealousy was assuredly voicing itself now, Shelley's conscience was assuredly nagging him, pestering him, persecuting him. Shelley needed excuses for his altered attitude towards his wife; Providence pitied him and sent the wet-nurse. If Providence had sent him a cotton doughnut it would have answered just as well; all he wanted was something to find fault with.

Shelley's happiness in his home had been wounded and bruised almost to death, fifthly, because Harriet narrowly watched a surgical operation which was being performed upon her child, and, "to the astonishment of the operator," who was watching Harriet instead of attending to his operation, she betrayed "not the smallest sign of emotion." The author of this biography was not ashamed to set down that exultant slander. He was apparently not aware that it was a small business to bring into his court a witness whose name he does not know, and whose character and veracity there is none to vouch for, and allow him to strike this blow at the mother-heart of this friendless girl. The biographer says, "We may not infer from this that Harriet did not feel" — why put it in, then? — "but we learn that those about her could believe her to be hard and insensible." Who were those who were about her? Her husband? He hated her now, because he was in love elsewhere. Her sister? Of course that is not charged. Peacock? Peacock does not testify. The wet-nurse? She does not testify. If any others were there we have no mention of them. "Those about her" are reduced to one person — her husband. Who reports the circumstance? It is Hogg. Perhaps he was there — we do not know. But if he was, he still got his information at second-hand, as it was the operator who noticed Harriet's lack of emotion, not himself. Hogg is not given to saying kind things when Harriet is his subject. He may have said them the time that he tried to tempt her to soil her honor, but after that he mentions her usually with a sneer. "Among those who were about her" was one witness well equipped to silence all tongues, abolish all doubts, set our minds at rest; one witness, not called, and not callable, whose evidence, if we could but get it, would outweigh the oaths of whole battalions of hostile Hoggs and nameless surgeons — the baby. I wish we had the baby's testimony; and yet if we had it it would not do us any good — a furtive conjecture, a sly insinuation, a pious "if" or two, would be smuggled in, here and there, with a solemn air of judicial investigation, and its positiveness would wilt into dubiety.

The biographer says of Harriet, "If words of tender affection and motherly pride proved the reality of love, then undoubtedly she loved her first-born child." That is, if mere empty words can prove it, it stands proved — and in this way, without committing himself, he gives the reader a chance to infer that there isn't any extant evidence but words, and that he doesn't take much stock in them. How seldom he shows his hand! He is always lurking behind a non-committal "if" or something of that kind; always gliding and dodging around, distributing colorless poison here and there and everywhere, but always leaving himself in a position to say that his language will be found innocuous if taken to pieces and examined. He clearly exhibits a steady and never-relaxing purpose to make Harriet the scapegoat for her husband's first great sin — but it is in the general view that this is revealed, not in the details. His insidious literature is like blue water; you know what it is that makes it blue, but you cannot produce and verify any detail of the cloud of microscopic dust in it that does it. Your adversary can dip up a glassful and show you that it is pure white and you cannot deny it; and he can dip the lake dry, glass by glass, and show that every glassful is white, and prove it to any one's eye — and yet that lake *was* blue and you can swear it. This book is blue — with slander in solution.

Let the reader examine, for example, the paragraph of comment which immediately follows the

4*.*.*

letter containing Shelley's self-exposure which we
have been considering. This is it. One should in-
spect the individual sentences as they go by, then
pass them in procession and review the cake-walk as
a whole:

" Shelley's happiness in his home, as is evident from this pathetic
letter, had been fatally stricken; it is evident, also, that he knew where
duty lay; he felt that his part was to take up his burden, silently and
sorrowfully, and to bear it henceforth with the quietness of despair.
But we can perceive that he scarcely possessed the strength and fortitude
needful for success in such an attempt. And clearly Shelley himself was
aware how perilous it was to accept that respite of blissful ease which
he enjoyed in the Boinville household; for gentle voices and dewy looks
and words of sympathy could not fail to remind him of an ideal of
tranquillity or of joy which could never be his, and which he must
henceforth sternly exclude from his imagination."

That paragraph commits the author in no way.
Taken sentence by sentence it *asserts* nothing against
anybody or in favor of anybody, pleads for nobody,
accuses nobody. Taken detail by detail, it is as
innocent as moonshine. And yet, taken as a whole,
it is a design against the reader; its intent is to remove the feeling which the letter must leave with
him if let alone, and put a different one in its place
— to remove a feeling justified by the letter and
substitute one not justified by it. The letter itself
gives you no uncertain picture — no lecturer is
needed to stand by with a stick and point out its
details and let on to explain what they mean. The
picture is the very clear and remorsefully faithful
picture of a fallen and fettered angel who is ashamed
of himself; an angel who beats his soiled wings and

cries, who complains to the woman who enticed him
that he *could* have borne his wayward lot, he *could*
have stood by his duty if it had not been for her
beguilements; an angel who rails at the " boundless
ocean of abhorred society," and rages at his poor
judicious sister-in-law.   If there is any dignity about
this spectacle it will escape most people.

Yet when the paragraph of comment is taken as a
whole, the picture is full of dignity and pathos; we
have before us a blameless and noble spirit stricken
to the earth by malign powers, but not conquered;
tempted, but grandly putting the temptation away;
enmeshed by subtle coils, but sternly resolved to
rend them and march forth victorious, at any peril
of life or limb.   Curtain — slow music.

Was it the purpose of the paragraph to take the
bad taste of Shelley's letter out of the reader's
mouth?   If that was not it, good ink was wasted;
without that, it has no relevancy — the multiplica-
tion table would have padded the space as rationally.

We have inspected the six reasons which we are
asked to believe drove a man of conspicuous
patience, honor, justice, fairness, kindliness, and
iron firmness, resolution, and steadfastness, from
the wife whom he loved and who loved him, to a
refuge in the mephitic paradise of Bracknell.   These
are six infinitely little reasons; but there were six
colossal ones, and these the counsel for the destruction of Harriet Shelley persists in not considering
very important.

D*₊*₊

Moreover, the colossal six preceded the little six, and had done the mischief before they were born. Let us double-column the twelve; then we shall see at a glance that each little reason is in turn answered by a retorting reason of a size to overshadow it and make it insignificant:

1. Harriet sets up carriage.	1. CORNELIA TURNER.
2. Harriet stops studying.	2. CORNELIA TURNER.
3. Harriet goes to bonnet-shop.	3. CORNELIA TURNER.
4. Harriet takes a wet-nurse.	4. CORNELIA TURNER.
5. Harriet has too much nerve.	5. CORNELIA TURNER.
6. Detested sister-in-law.	6. CORNELIA TURNER.

As soon as we comprehend that Cornelia Turner and the Italian lessons happened *before* the little six had been discovered to be grievances, we understand why Shelley's happiness in his home had been wounded and bruised almost to death, and no one can persuade us into laying it on Harriet. Shelley and Cornelia are the responsible persons, and we cannot in honor and decency allow the cruelties which they practised upon the unoffending wife to be pushed aside in order to give us a chance to waste time and tears over six sentimental justifications of an offence which the six can't justify, nor even respectably assist in justifying.

Six? There were seven; but in charity to the biographer the seventh ought not to be exposed. Still, he hung it out himself, and not only hung it out, but thought it was a good point in Shelley's favor. For two years Shelley found sympathy and intellectual food and all that at home; there was enough for spiritual and mental support, but not enough for luxury; and so, at the end of the contented two years, this latter detail justifies him in going bag and baggage over to Cornelia Turner and supplying the rest of his need in the way of surplus sympathy and intellectual pie unlawfully. By the same reasoning a man in merely comfortable circumstances may rob a bank without sin.

III

IT is 1814, it is the 16th of March, Shelley has written his letter, he has been in the Boinville paradise a month, his deserted wife is in her husbandless home. Mischief had been wrought. It is the biographer who concedes this. We greatly need some light on Harriet's side of the case now; we need to know how she enjoyed the month, but there is no way to inform ourselves; there seems to be a strange absence of documents and letters and diaries on that side. Shelley kept a diary, the approaching Mary Godwin kept a diary, her father kept one, her half-sister by marriage, adoption, and the dispensation of God kept one, and the entire tribe and all its friends wrote and received letters, and the letters were kept and are producible when this biography needs them; but there are only three or four scraps of Harriet's writing, and no diary. Harriet wrote plenty of letters to her husband — nobody knows where they are, I suppose; she wrote plenty of letters to other people — apparently they have disappeared, too. Peacock says she wrote good letters, but apparently interested people had sagacity enough to mislay them in time. After all her industry she went down into her grave and lies silent there— silent, when she has so much need to speak. We can only wonder at this mystery, not account for it.

No, there is no way of finding out what Harriet's state of feeling was during the month that Shelley was disporting himself in the Bracknell paradise. We have to fall back upon conjecture, as our fabulist does when he has nothing more substantial to work with. Then we easily conjecture that as the days dragged by Harriet's heart grew heavier and heavier under its two burdens — shame and resentment: the shame of being pointed at and gossiped about as a deserted wife, and resentment against the woman who had beguiled her husband from her and now kept him in a disreputable captivity. Deserted wives — deserted whether for cause or without cause — find small charity among the virtuous and the discreet. We conjecture that one after another the neighbors ceased to call; that one after another they got to being " engaged " when Harriet called; that finally they one after the other cut her dead on the street; that after that she stayed in the house daytimes, and brooded over her sorrows, and nighttimes did the same, there being nothing else to do with the heavy hours and the silence and solitude and the dreary intervals which sleep should have charitably bridged, but didn't.

Yes, mischief had been wrought. The biographer arrives at this conclusion, and it is a most just one. Then, just as you begin to half hope he is going to discover the cause of it and launch hot bolts of wrath at the guilty manufacturers of it, you have to turn away disappointed. You are disappointed, and you sigh. This is what he says — the italics are mine:

"However the mischief may have been wrought — *and at this day no one can wish to heap blame on any buried head —*"

So it is poor Harriet, after all. Stern justice must take its course — justice tempered with delicacy, justice tempered with compassion, justice that pities a forlorn dead girl and refuses to strike her. Except in the back. Will not be ignoble and *say* the harsh thing, but only insinuate it. Stern justice knows about the carriage and the wet-nurse and the bonnet-shop and the other dark things that caused this sad mischief, and may not, *must* not blink them; so it delivers judgment where judgment belongs, but softens the blow by not seeming to deliver judgment at all. To resume — the italics are mine:

"However the mischief may have been wrought — and at this day no one can wish to heap blame on any buried head — *it is certain that some cause or causes of deep division between Shelley and his wife were in operation during the early part of the year 1814.*"

This shows penetration. No deduction could be more accurate than this. There were indeed some causes of deep division.   But next comes another disappointing sentence:

"To guess at the precise nature of these causes, in the absence of definite statement, were useless."

Why, he has already been guessing at them for several pages, and we have been trying to outguess him, and now all of a sudden he is tired of it and won't play any more.   It is not quite fair to us. However, he will get over this by-and-by, when Shelley commits his next indiscretion and has to be guessed out of it at Harriet's expense.

"We may rest content with Shelley's own words" — in a Chancery paper drawn up by him three years later.   They were these: "Delicacy forbids me to say more than that we were disunited by incurable dissensions."

As for me, I do not quite see why we should rest content with anything of the sort.   It is not a very definite statement.   It does not necessarily mean anything more than that he did not wish to go into the tedious details of those family quarrels.   Delicacy could quite properly excuse him from saying, "I was in love with Cornelia all that time; my wife kept crying and worrying about it and upbraiding me and begging me to cut myself free from a connection which was wronging her and disgracing us both; and I being stung by these reproaches retorted with fierce and bitter speeches — for it is my nature to do that when I am stirred, especially if the target of them is a person whom I had greatly loved and respected before, as witness my various attitudes towards Miss Hitchener, the Gisbornes, Harriet's sister, and others — and finally I did not improve this state of things when I deserted my wife and spent a whole month with the woman who had infatuated me."

No, he could not go into those details, and we excuse him; but, nevertheless, we do not rest content with this bland proposition to puff away that whole long disreputable episode with a single meaningless remark of Shelley's.

We do admit that " it is certain that some cause or causes of deep division were in operation." We would admit it just the same if the grammar of the statement were as straight as a string, for we drift into pretty indifferent grammar ourselves when we are absorbed in historical work; but we have to decline to admit that we cannot guess those cause or causes.

But guessing is not really necessary. There is evidence attainable — evidence from the batch discredited by the biographer and set out at the back door in his appendix-basket; and yet a court of law would think twice before throwing it out, whereas it would be a hardy person who would venture to offer in such a place a good part of the material which is placed before the readers of this book as " evidence," and so treated by this daring biographer. Among some letters (in the appendix-basket) from Mrs. Godwin, detailing the Godwinian share in the

Shelleyan events of 1814, she tells how Harriet
Shelley came to her and her husband, agitated and
weeping, to implore them to forbid Shelley the
house, and prevent his seeing Mary Godwin.

> " She related that last November he had fallen in love with Mrs.
> Turner and paid her such marked attentions Mr. Turner, the husband,
> had carried off his wife to Devonshire."

The biographer finds a technical fault in this;
" the Shelleys were in *Edinburgh* in November."
What of that? The woman is recalling a conversation which is more than two months old; besides,
she was probably more intent upon the central and
important fact of it than upon its unimportant date.
Harriet's quoted statement has some sense in it; for
that reason, if for no other, it ought to have been
put in the body of the book. Still, that would not
have answered; even the biographer's enemy could
not be cruel enough to ask him to let this real
grievance, this compact and substantial and picturesque figure, this rawhead-and-bloody-bones, come
striding in there among those pale shams, those
rickety spectres labeled WET-NURSE, BONNET-SHOP,
and so on — no, the father of all malice could not
ask the biographer to expose his pathetic goblins to
a competition like that.

The fabulist finds fault with the statement because
it has a technical error in it; and he does this at the
moment that he is furnishing us an error himself,
and of a graver sort. He says:

> " If Turner carried off his wife to Devonshire he brought her back,

and Shelley was staying with her and her mother on terms of cordial
intimacy in March, 1814.''

We accept the '' cordial intimacy'' — it was the
very thing Harriet was complaining of — but there
is nothing to show that it was Turner who brought
his wife back. The statement is thrown in as if it
were not only true, but was proof that Turner was
not uneasy. Turner's *movements* are proof of nothing. Nothing but a statement from Turner's mouth
would have any value here, and he made none.

Six days after writing his letter Shelley and his
wife were together again for a moment — to get
remarried according to the rites of the English
Church.

Within three weeks the new husband and wife
were apart again, and the former was back in his
odorous paradise. This time it is the wife who does
the deserting. She finds Cornelia too strong for
her, probably. At any rate, she goes away with
her baby and sister, and we have a playful fling at
her from good Mrs. Boinville, the '' mysterious
spinner Maimuna ''; she whose '' face was as a
damsel's face, and yet her hair was gray ''; she of
whom the biographer has said, '' Shelley was indeed
caught in an almost invisible thread spun around
him, but unconsciously, by this subtle and benignant
enchantress.'' The subtle and benignant enchantress writes to Hogg, April 18: '' Shelley is again a
widower; his beauteous half went to town on
Thursday.''

Then Shelley writes a poem — a chant of grief over the hard fate which obliges him now to leave his paradise and take up with his wife again. It seems to intimate that the paradise is cooling towards him; that he is warned off by acclamation; that he must not even venture to tempt with one last tear his friend Cornelia's ungentle mood, for her eye is glazed and cold and dares not entreat her lover to stay:

Exhibit E

.   .   .   .

" Pause not! the time is past!   Every voice cries ' Away!'
    Tempt not with one last tear thy friend's ungentle mood;
Thy lover's eye, so glazed and cold, dares not entreat thy stay:
    Duty and dereliction guide thee back to solitude."

Back to the solitude of his now empty home, that is!

    " Away! away! to thy sad and silent home;
        Pour bitter tears on its desolated hearth."

.   .   .   .

But he will have rest in the grave by-and-by. Until that time comes, the charms of Bracknell will remain in his memory, along with Mrs. Boinville's voice and Cornelia Turner's smile:

" Thou in the grave shalt rest — yet, till the phantoms flee
    Which that house and hearth and garden made dear to thee ere-
        while,
Thy remembrance and repentance and deep musings are not free
    From the music of two voices and the light of one sweet smile."

We *cannot* wonder that Harriet could not stand it. Any of us would have left. We would not even stay with a cat that was in this condition. Even the Boinvilles could not endure it; and so, as we have seen, they gave this one notice.

" Early in May, Shelley was in London. He did not yet despair of reconciliation with Harriet, nor had he ceased to love her."

Shelley's poems are a good deal of trouble to his biographer. They are constantly inserted as " evidence," and they make much confusion. As soon as one of them has proved one thing, another one follows and proves quite a different thing. The poem just quoted shows that he was in love with Cornelia, but a month later he is in love with Harriet again, and there is a poem to prove it.

" In this piteous appeal Shelley declares that he has now no grief but one — the grief of having known and lost his wife's love."

Exhibit F

" Thy look of love has power to calm
The stormiest passion of my soul."

But without doubt she had been reserving her looks of love a good part of the time for ten months, now — ever since he began to lavish his own on Cornelia Turner at the end of the previous July. He does really seem to have already forgotten Cornelia's merits in one brief month, for he eulogizes Harriet in a way which rules all competition out:

" Thou only virtuous, gentle, kind,
Amid a world of hate."

He complains of her hardness, and begs her to make the concession of a " slight endurance " — of his waywardness, perhaps — for the sake of " a

5ᴇ

fellow-being's lasting weal.''   But the main force of
his appeal is in his closing stanza, and is strongly
worded:

> " O trust for once no erring guide!
>   Bid the remorseless feeling flee;
> 'Tis malice, 'tis revenge, 'tis pride,
>   'Tis anything but thee;
> O deign a nobler pride to prove,
> And pity if thou canst not love."

This is in May — apparently towards the end of
it.   Harriet and Shelley were corresponding all the
time.   Harriet got the poem — a copy exists in her
own handwriting; she being the only gentle and
kind person amid a world of hate, according to
Shelley's own testimony in the poem, we are permitted to think that the daily letters would presently
have melted that kind and gentle heart and brought
about the reconciliation, if there had been time —
but there wasn't; for in a very few days — in fact,
before the 8th of June — Shelley was in love with
another woman.

And so — perhaps while Harriet was walking the
floor nights, trying to get *her* poem by heart — her
husband was doing a fresh one — for the other girl
— Mary Wollstonecraft Godwin — with sentiments
like these in it:

Exhibit G

> " To spend years thus and be rewarded,
>   As thou, sweet love, requited me
>   When none were near.
>   . . . thy lips did meet
>   Mine tremblingly; . . .

" Gentle and good and mild thou art,
    Nor can I live if thou appear
    Aught but thyself." . . .

And so on. " Before the close of June it was known
and felt by Mary and Shelley that each was inex-
pressibly dear to the other." Yes, Shelley had
found this child of sixteen to his liking, and had
wooed and won her in the graveyard. But that is
nothing; it was better than wooing her in her
nursery, at any rate, where it might have disturbed
the other children.

However, she was a child in years only. From
the day that she set her masculine grip on Shelley
he was to frisk no more. If she had occupied the
only kind and gentle Harriet's place in March it
would have been a thrilling spectacle to see her in-
vade the Boinville rookery and read the riot act.
That holiday of Shelley's would have been of short
duration, and Cornelia's hair would have been as
gray as her mother's when the services were over.

Hogg went to the Godwin residence in Skinner
Street with Shelley on that 8th of June. They
passed through Godwin's little debt-factory of a
book-shop and went up-stairs hunting for the proprietor. Nobody there. Shelley strode about the
room impatiently, making its crazy floor quake under
him. Then a door " was partially and softly opened.
A thrilling voice called ' Shelley!' A thrilling voice
answered, ' Mary!' And he darted out of the room
like an arrow from the bow of the far-shooting King.

A very young female, fair and fair-haired, pale, indeed, and with a piercing look, wearing a frock of tartan, an unusual dress in London at that time, had called him out of the room.''

This is Mary Godwin, as described by Hogg. The thrill of the voices shows that the love of Shelley and Mary was already upward of a fortnight old; therefore it had been born within the month of May — born while Harriet was still trying to get her poem by heart, we think. I must not be asked how I know so much about that thrill; it is my secret. The biographer and I have private ways of finding out things when it is necessary to find them out and the customary methods fail.

Shelley left London that day, and was gone ten days. The biographer conjectures that he spent this interval with Harriet in Bath. It would be just like him. To the end of his days he liked to be in love with two women at once. He was more in love with Miss Hitchener when he married Harriet than he was with Harriet, and told the lady so with simple and unostentatious candor. He was more in love with Cornelia than he was with Harriet in the end of 1813 and the beginning of 1814, yet he supplied both of them with love poems of an equal temperature meantime; he loved Mary and Harriet in June, and while getting ready to run off with the one, it is conjectured that he put in his odd time trying to get reconciled to the other; by-and-by, while still in love with Mary, he will make love to her half-sister by marriage, adoption, and the visitation of God, through the medium of clandestine letters, and she will answer with letters that are for no eye but his own.

When Shelley encountered Mary Godwin he was looking around for another paradise. He had tastes of his own, and there were features about the Godwin establishment that strongly recommended it. Godwin was an advanced thinker and an able writer. One of his romances is still read, but his philosophical works, once so esteemed, are out of vogue now; their authority was already declining when Shelley made his acquaintance — that is, it was declining with the public, but not with Shelley. They had been his moral and political Bible, and they were that yet. Shelley the infidel would himself have claimed to be less a work of God than a work of Godwin. Godwin's philosophies had formed his mind and interwoven themselves into it and become a part of its texture; he regarded himself as Godwin's spiritual son. Godwin was not without self-appreciation; indeed, it may be conjectured that from his point of view the last syllable of his name was surplusage. He lived serene in his lofty world of philosophy, far above the mean interests that absorbed smaller men, and only came down to the ground at intervals to pass the hat for alms to pay his debts with, and insult the man that relieved him. Several of his principles were out of the ordinary. For example, he was opposed to marriage. He was

5*.*.

not aware that his preachings from this text were but theory and wind; he supposed he was in earnest in imploring people to live together without marrying, until Shelley furnished him a working model of his scheme and a practical example to analyze, by applying the principle in his own family; the matter took a different and surprising aspect then. The late Matthew Arnold said that the main defect in Shelley's make-up was that he was destitute of the sense of humor. This episode must have escaped Mr. Arnold's attention.

But we have said enough about the head of the new paradise. Mrs. Godwin is described as being in several ways a terror; and even when her soul was in repose she wore green spectacles. But I suspect that her main unattractiveness was born of the fact that she wrote the letters that are out in the appendix-basket in the back yard — letters which are an outrage and wholly untrustworthy, for they say some kind things about poor Harriet and tell some disagreeable truths about her husband; and these things make the fabulist grit his teeth a good deal.

Next we have Fanny Godwin — a Godwin by courtesy only; she was Mrs. Godwin's natural daughter by a former friend. She was a sweet and winning girl, but she presently wearied of the Godwin paradise, and poisoned herself.

Last in the list is Jane (or Claire, as she preferred to call herself) Clairmont, daughter of Mrs. Godwin by a former marriage. She was very young and pretty and accommodating, and always ready to do what she could to make things pleasant. After Shelley ran off with her part-sister Mary, she became the guest of the pair, and contributed a natural child to their nursery — Allegra. Lord Byron was the father.

We have named the several members and advantages of the new paradise in Skinner Street, with its crazy book-shop underneath. Shelley was all right now, this was a better place than the other; more variety anyway, and more different kinds of fragrance. One could turn out poetry here without any trouble at all.

The way the new love-match came about was this: Shelley told Mary all his aggravations and sorrows and griefs, and about the wet-nurse and the bonnet-shop and the surgeon and the carriage, and the sister-in-law that blocked the London game, and about Cornelia and her mamma, and how they had turned him out of the house after making so much of him; and how he had deserted Harriet and then Harriet had deserted him, and how the reconciliation was working along and Harriet getting her poem by heart; and still he was not happy, and Mary pitied him, for she had had trouble herself. But I am not satisfied with this. It reads too much like statistics. It lacks smoothness and grace, and is too earthy and business-like. It has the sordid look of a trades-union procession out on strike. That is not the

E*.*.*

right form for it.   The book does it better; we will fall back on the book and have a cake-walk:

" It was easy to divine that some restless grief possessed him; Mary herself was not unlearned in the lore of pain.   His generous zeal in her father's behalf, his spiritual sonship to Godwin, his reverence for her mother's memory, were guarantees with Mary of his excellence.*   The new friends could not lack subjects of discourse, and underneath their words about Mary's mother, and ' Political Justice,' and ' Rights of Woman,' were two young hearts, each feeling towards the other, each perhaps unaware, trembling in the direction of the other.   The desire to assuage the suffering of one whose happiness has grown precious to us may become a hunger of the spirit as keen as any other, and this hunger now possessed Mary's heart; when her eyes rested unseen on Shelley, it was with a look full of the ardor of a ' soothing pity.' ' "

Yes, that is better and has more composure. That is just the way it happened. He told her about the wet-nurse, she told him about political justice; he told her about the deadly sister-in-law, she told him about her mother; he told her about the bonnet-shop, she murmured back about the rights of woman; then he assuaged her, then she assuaged him; then he assuaged her some more, next she assuaged him some more; then they both assuaged one another simultaneously; and so they went on by the hour assuaging and assuaging and assuaging, until at last what was the result? They were in love.   It will happen so every time.

" He had married a woman who, as he now persuaded himself, had never truly loved him, who loved only his fortune and his rank, and who proved her selfishness by deserting him in his misery."

* What she was after was guarantees of his excellence. That he stood ready to desert his wife and child was one of them, apparently.

I think that that is not quite fair to Harriet. We have no certainty that she knew Cornelia had turned him out of the house. He went back to Cornelia, and Harriet may have supposed that he was as happy with her as ever. Still, it was judicious to begin to lay on the whitewash, for Shelley is going to need many a coat of it now, and the sooner the reader becomes used to the intrusion of the brush the sooner he will get reconciled to it and stop fretting about it.

After Shelley's (conjectured) visit to Harriet at Bath — 8th of June to 18th — " it seems to have been arranged that Shelley should henceforth join the Skinner Street household each day at dinner."

Nothing could be handier than this; things will swim along now.

"Although now Shelley was coming to believe that his wedded union with Harriet was a thing of the past, he had not ceased to regard her with affectionate consideration ; he wrote to her frequently, and kept her informed of his whereabouts."

We must not get impatient over these curious inharmoniousnesses and irreconcilabilities in Shelley's character. You can see by the biographer's attitude towards them that there is nothing objectionable about them. Shelley was doing his best to make two adoring young creatures happy: he was regarding the one with affectionate consideration by mail, and he was assuaging the other one at home.

"Unhappy Harriet, residing at Bath, had perhaps never desired that the breach between herself and her husband should be irreparable and complete."

I find no fault with that sentence except that the "perhaps" is not strictly warranted. It should have been left out. In support — or shall we say extenuation? — of this opinion I submit that there is not sufficient evidence to warrant the uncertainty which it implies. The only "evidence" offered that Harriet was hard and proud and standing out against a reconciliation is a poem — the poem in which Shelley beseeches her to "bid the remorseless feeling flee" and "pity" if she "cannot love." We have just that as "evidence," and out of its meagre materials the biographer builds a cobhouse of conjectures as big as the Coliseum; conjectures which convince him, the prosecuting attorney, but ought to fall far short of convincing any fair-minded jury.

Shelley's love-poems may be very good evidence, but we know well that they are "good for this day and train only." We are able to believe that they spoke the truth for that one day, but we know by experience that they could not be depended on to speak it the next. The very supplication for a rewarming of Harriet's chilled love was followed so suddenly by the poet's plunge into an adoring passion for Mary Godwin that if it had been a check it would have lost its value before a lazy person could have gotten to the bank with it.

Hardness, stubbornness, pride, vindictiveness —

these may sometimes reside in a young wife and
mother of nineteen, but they are not charged against
Harriet Shelley outside of that poem, and one has
no right to insert them into her character on such
shadowy " evidence " as that.   Peacock knew Harriet well, and she has a flexible and persuadable
look, as painted by him:

" Her manners were good, and her whole aspect and demeanor such
manifest emanations of pure and truthful nature that to be once in her
company was to know her thoroughly.   She was fond of her husband,
and accommodated herself in every way to his tastes.   If they mixed
in society, she adorned it ; if they lived in retirement, she was satisfied ;
if they travelled, she enjoyed the change of scene."

" Perhaps " she had never desired that the breach
should be irreparable and complete.   The truth is,
we do not even know that there was any breach at
all at this time.   We know that the husband and
wife went before the altar and took a new oath on
the 24th of March to love and cherish each other
until death — and this may be regarded as a sort of
reconciliation itself, and a wiping out of the old
grudges.   Then Harriet went away, and the sister-
in-law removed herself from her society.   That was
in April.   Shelley wrote his " appeal " in May,
but the corresponding went right along afterwards.
We have a right to doubt that the subject of it was
a " reconciliation," or that Harriet had any suspicion that she needed to be reconciled and that her
husband was trying to persuade her to it — as the
biographer has sought to make us believe, with his

Coliseum of conjectures built out of a waste-basket
of poetry. For we have " evidence " now — not
poetry and conjecture. When Shelley had been
dining daily in the Skinner Street paradise fifteen
days and continuing the love-match which was
already a fortnight old twenty-five days earlier, he
forgot to write Harriet; forgot it the next day and
the next. During four days Harriet got no letter
from him. Then her fright and anxiety rose to
expression-heat, and she wrote a letter to Shelley's
publisher which seems to reveal to us that Shelley's
letters to her had been the customary affectionate
letters of husband to wife, and had carried no appeals for reconciliation and had not needed to:

"BATH (postmark July 7, 1814).

"MY DEAR SIR,—You will greatly oblige me by giving the enclosed
to Mr. Shelley. I would not trouble you, but it is now four days since
I have heard from him, which to me is an age. Will you write by return of post and tell me what has become of him ? as I always fancy
something dreadful has happened if I do not hear from him. If you
tell me that he is well I shall not come to London, but if I do not hear
from you or him I shall certainly come, as I cannot endure this dreadful
state of suspense. You are his friend and you can feel for me.

"I remain yours truly,

"H. S."

Even without Peacock's testimony that " her whole
aspect and demeanor were manifest emanations of a
pure and truthful nature," we should hold this to
be a truthful letter, a sincere letter, a loving letter;
it bears those marks; I think it is also the letter of
a person accustomed to receiving letters from her

husband frequently, and that they have been of a welcome and satisfactory sort, too, this long time back — ever since the solemn remarriage and reconciliation at the altar most likely.

The biographer follows Harriet's letter with a conjecture. He conjectures that she "would now gladly have retraced her steps." Which means that it is proven that she had steps to retrace — proven by the poem. Well, if the poem is better evidence than the letter, we must let it stand at that.

Then the biographer attacks Harriet Shelley's honor — by authority of random and unverified gossip scavengered from a group of people whose very names make a person shudder: Mary Godwin, mistress to Shelley; her part-sister, discarded mistress of Lord Byron; Godwin, the philosophical tramp, who gathers his share of it from a shadow — that is to say, from a person whom he shirks out of naming. Yet the biographer dignifies this sorry rubbish with the name of "evidence."

Nothing remotely resembling a distinct charge from a named person professing to know is offered among this precious "evidence."

1. "Shelley *believed*" so and so.

2. Byron's discarded mistress says that Shelley told Mary Godwin so and so, and *Mary* told *her*.

3. "Shelley said" so and so — and later "admitted over and over again that he had been in error."

4. The unspeakable Godwin "wrote to Mr. Bax-

ter '' that he knew so and so '' from unquestionable authority '' — name not furnished.

How any man in his right mind could bring himself to defile the grave of a shamefully abused and defenceless girl with these baseless fabrications, this manufactured filth, is inconceivable. How any man, in his right mind or out of it, could sit down and coldly try to persuade anybody to believe it, or listen patiently to it, or, indeed, do anything but scoff at it and deride it, is astonishing.

The charge insinuated by these odious slanders is one of the most difficult of all offences to prove; it is also one which no man has a right to mention even in a whisper about any woman, living or dead, unless he knows it to be true, and not even then unless he can also *prove* it to be true. There is no justification for the abomination of putting this stuff in the book.

Against Harriet Shelley's good name there is not one scrap of tarnishing evidence, and not even a scrap of evil gossip, that comes from a source that entitles it to a hearing.

On the credit side of the account we have strong opinions from the people who knew her best. Peacock says:

" I feel it due to the memory of Harriet to state my most decided conviction that her conduct as a wife was as pure. as true, as absolutely faultless, as that of any who for such conduct are held most in honor."

Thornton Hunt, who had picked and published

slight flaws in Harriet's character, says, as regards this alleged large one:

"There is not a trace of evidence or a whisper of scandal against her before her voluntary departure from Shelley."

Trelawney says:

"I was assured by the evidence of the few friends who knew both Shelley and his wife — Hookham, Hogg, Peacock, and one of the Godwins — that Harriet was perfectly innocent of all offence."

What excuse was there for raking up a parcel of foul rumors from malicious and discredited sources and flinging them at this dead girl's head? Her very defencelessness should have been her protection. The fact that all letters to her or about her, with almost every scrap of her own writing, had been diligently mislaid, leaving her case destitute of a voice, while every pen-stroke which could help her husband's side had been as diligently preserved, should have excused her from being brought to trial. Her witnesses have all disappeared, yet we see her summoned in her grave-clothes to plead for the life of her character, without the help of an advocate, before a disqualified judge and a packed jury.

Harriet Shelley wrote her distressed letter on the 7th of July. On the 28th her husband ran away with Mary Godwin and her part-sister Claire to the Continent. He deserted his wife when her confinement was approaching. She bore him a child at the end of November, his mistress bore him another one something over two months later. The truants were back in London before either of these events occurred.

On one occasion, presently, Shelley was so pressed for money to support his mistress with that he went to his wife and got some money of his that was in her hands — twenty pounds. Yet the mistress was not moved to gratitude; for later, when the wife was troubled to meet her engagements, the mistress makes this entry in her diary:

"Harriet sends her creditors here; nasty woman. Now we shall have to change our lodgings."

The deserted wife bore the bitterness and obloquy of her situation two years and a quarter; then she gave up, and drowned herself. A month afterwards the body was found in the water. Three weeks later Shelley married his mistress.

I must here be allowed to italicize a remark of the biographer's concerning Harriet Shelley:

"*That no act of Shelley's during the two years which immediately preceded her death tended to cause the rash act which brought her life to its close seems certain.*"

Yet her husband had deserted her and her children, and was living with a concubine all that time! Why should a person attempt to write biography when the simplest facts have no meaning to him? This book is littered with as crass stupidities as that one — deductions by the page which bear no discoverable kinship to their premises.

The biographer throws off that extraordinary remark without any perceptible disturbance to his serenity; for he follows it with a sentimental justification of Shelley's conduct which has not a pang of conscience in it, but is silky and smooth and undulating and pious — a cake-walk with all the colored brethren at their best. There may be people who can read that page and keep their temper, but it is doubtful.

Shelley's life has the one indelible blot upon it, but is otherwise worshipfully noble and beautiful. It even stands out indestructibly gracious and lovely from the ruck of these disastrous pages, in spite of the fact that they expose and establish his responsibility for his forsaken wife's pitiful fate — a responsibility which he himself tacitly admits in a letter to Eliza Westbrook, wherein he refers to his taking up with Mary Godwin as an act which Eliza " might excusably regard as the cause of her sister's ruin."

6E

FENIMORE COOPER'S LITERARY OFFENCES

The Pathfinder and *The Deerslayer* stand at the head of Cooper's novels as artistic creations. There are others of his works which contain parts as perfect as are to be found in these, and scenes even more thrilling. Not one can be compared with either of them as a finished whole.

The defects in both of these tales are comparatively slight. They were pure works of art. — *Prof. Lounsbury.*

The five tales reveal an extraordinary fulness of invention.

... One of the very greatest characters in fiction, Natty Bumppo. ...

The craft of the woodsman, the tricks of the trapper, all the delicate art of the forest, were familiar to Cooper from his youth up. — *Prof. Brander Matthews.*

Cooper is the greatest artist in the domain of romantic fiction yet produced by America. — *Wilkie Collins.*

IT seems to me that it was far from right for the Professor of English Literature in Yale, the Professor of English Literature in Columbia, and Wilkie Collins to deliver opinions on Cooper's literature without having read some of it. It would have been much more decorous to keep silent and let persons talk who have read Cooper.

Cooper's art has some defects. In one place in *Deerslayer*, and in the restricted space of two-thirds of a page, Cooper has scored 114 offences against

(78)

literary art out of a possible 115. It breaks the record.

There are nineteen rules governing literary art in the domain of romantic fiction — some say twenty-two. In *Deerslayer* Cooper violated eighteen of them. These eighteen require:

1. That a tale shall accomplish something and arrive somewhere. But the *Deerslayer* tale accomplishes nothing and arrives in the air.

2. They require that the episodes of a tale shall be necessary parts of the tale, and shall help to develop it. But as the *Deerslayer* tale is not a tale, and accomplishes nothing and arrives nowhere, the episodes have no rightful place in the work, since there was nothing for them to develop.

3. They require that the personages in a tale shall be alive, except in the case of corpses, and that always the reader shall be able to tell the corpses from the others. But this detail has often been overlooked in the *Deerslayer* tale.

4. They require that the personages in a tale, both dead and alive, shall exhibit a sufficient excuse for being there. But this detail also has been overlooked in the *Deerslayer* tale.

5. They require that when the personages of a tale deal in conversation, the talk shall sound like human talk, and be talk such as human beings would be likely to talk in the given circumstances, and have a discoverable meaning, also a discoverable purpose, and a show of relevancy, and remain in

the neighborhood of the subject in hand, and be
interesting to the reader, and help out the tale, and
stop when the people cannot think of anything more
to say. But this requirement has been ignored from
the beginning of the *Deerslayer* tale to the end of it.

6. They require that when the author describes
the character of a personage in his tale, the conduct
and conversation of that personage shall justify said
description. But this law gets little or no attention
in the *Deerslayer* tale, as Natty Bumppo's case will
amply prove.

7. They require that when a personage talks like
an illustrated, gilt-edged, tree-calf, hand-tooled,
seven-dollar Friendship's Offering in the beginning
of a paragraph, he shall not talk like a negro min-
strel in the end of it. But this rule is flung down
and danced upon in the *Deerslayer* tale.

8. They require that crass stupidities shall not be
played upon the reader as '' the craft of the woodsman, the delicate art of the forest,'' by either the
author or the people in the tale. But this rule is
persistently violated in the *Deerslayer* tale.

9. They require that the personages of a tale shall
confine themselves to possibilities and let miracles
alone; or, if they venture a miracle, the author
must so plausibly set it forth as to make it look
possible and reasonable. But these rules are not
respected in the *Deerslayer* tale.

10. They require that the author shall make the
reader feel a deep interest in the personages of his

tale and in their fate; and that he shall make the reader love the good people in the tale and hate the bad ones. But the reader of the *Deerslayer* tale dislikes the good people in it, is indifferent to the others, and wishes they would all get drowned together.

11. They require that the characters in a tale shall be so clearly defined that the reader can tell beforehand what each will do in a given emergency. But in the *Deerslayer* tale this rule is vacated.

In addition to these large rules there are some little ones. These require that the author shall

12. *Say* what he is proposing to say, not merely come near it.

13. Use the right word, not its second cousin.

14. Eschew surplusage.

15. Not omit necessary details.

16. Avoid slovenliness of form.

17. Use good grammar.

18 Employ a simple and straightforward style.

Even these seven are coldly and persistently violated in the *Deerslayer* tale.

Cooper's gift in the way of invention was not a rich endowment; but such as it was he liked to work it, he was pleased with the effects, and indeed he did some quite sweet things with it. In his little box of stage properties he kept six or eight cunning devices, tricks, artifices for his savages and woodsmen to deceive and circumvent each other with, and he was never so happy as when he was working

6*.*.*

these innocent things and seeing them go. A favorite one was to make a moccasined person tread in the tracks of the moccasined enemy, and thus hide his own trail. Cooper wore out barrels and barrels of moccasins in working that trick. Another stage-property that he pulled out of his box pretty frequently was his broken twig. He prized his broken twig above all the rest of his effects, and worked it the hardest. It is a restful chapter in any book of his when somebody doesn't step on a dry twig and alarm all the reds and whites for two hundred yards around. Every time a Cooper person is in peril, and absolute silence is worth four dollars a minute, he is sure to step on a dry twig. There may be a hundred handier things to step on, but that wouldn't satisfy Cooper. Cooper requires him to turn out and find a dry twig; and if he can't do it, go and borrow one. In fact, the Leather Stocking Series ought to have been called the Broken Twig Series.

I am sorry there is not room to put in a few dozen instances of the delicate art of the forest, as practised by Natty Bumppo and some of the other Cooperian experts. Perhaps we may venture two or three samples. Cooper was a sailor — a naval officer; yet he gravely tells us how a vessel, driving towards a lee shore in a gale, is steered for a particular spot by her skipper because he knows of an *undertow* there which will hold her back against the gale and save her. For just pure woodcraft, or sailorcraft, or whatever it is, isn't that neat? For several years Cooper was daily in the society of artillery, and he ought to have noticed that when a cannon-ball strikes the ground it either buries itself or skips a hundred feet or so; skips again a hundred feet or so — and so on, till finally it gets tired and rolls. Now in one place he loses some "females" — as he always calls women — in the edge of a wood near a plain at night in a fog, on purpose to give Bumppo a chance to show off the delicate art of the forest before the reader. These mislaid people are hunting for a fort. They hear a cannon-blast, and a cannon-ball presently comes rolling into the wood and stops at their feet. To the females this suggests nothing. The case is very different with the admirable Bumppo. I wish I may never know peace again if he doesn't strike out promptly and *follow the track* of that cannon-ball across the plain through the dense fog and find the fort. Isn't it a daisy? If Cooper had any real knowledge of Nature's ways of doing things, he had a most delicate art in concealing the fact. For instance: one of his acute Indian experts, Chingachgook (pronounced Chicago, I think), has lost the trail of a person he is tracking through the forest. Apparently that trail is hopelessly lost. Neither you nor I could ever have guessed out the way to find it. It was very different with Chicago. Chicago was not stumped for long. He turned a running stream out of its course, and there, in the slush in its old

F*₊*₊

bed, were that person's moccasin-tracks. The current did not wash them away, as it would have done in all other like cases — no, even the eternal laws of Nature have to vacate when Cooper wants to put up a delicate job of woodcraft on the reader.

We must be a little wary when Brander Matthews tells us that Cooper's books " reveal an extraordinary fulness of invention." As a rule, I am quite willing to accept Brander Matthews's literary judgments and applaud his lucid and graceful phrasing of them; but that particular statement needs to be taken with a few tons of salt. Bless your heart, Cooper hadn't any more invention than a horse; and I don't mean a high-class horse, either; I mean a clothes-horse. It would be very difficult to find a really clever " situation " in Cooper's books, and still more difficult to find one of any kind which he has failed to render absurd by his handling of it. Look at the episodes of " the caves " ; and at the celebrated scuffle between Maqua and those others on the table-land a few days later; and at Hurry Harry's queer water-transit from the castle to the ark; and at Deerslayer's half-hour with his first corpse; and at the quarrel between Hurry Harry and Deerslayer later; and at — but choose for yourself; you can't go amiss.

If Cooper had been an observer his inventive faculty would have worked better; not more interestingly, but more rationally, more plausibly. Cooper's proudest creations in the way of " situations " suffer

noticeably from the absence of the observer's protecting gift. Cooper's eye was splendidly inaccurate.
Cooper seldom saw anything correctly. He saw
nearly all things as through a glass eye, darkly. Of
course a man who cannot see the commonest little
every-day matters accurately is working at a disad-
vantage when he is constructing a "situation." In
the *Deerslayer* tale Cooper has a stream which is
fifty feet wide where it flows out of a lake; it
presently narrows to twenty as it meanders along
for no given reason, and yet when a stream acts like
that it ought to be required to explain itself. Fourteen pages later the width of the brook's outlet from
the lake has suddenly shrunk thirty feet, and become "the narrowest part of the stream." This
shrinkage is not accounted for. The stream has
bends in it, a sure indication that it has alluvial
banks and cuts them; yet these bends are only
thirty and fifty feet long. If Cooper had been a
nice and punctilious observer he would have noticed
that the bends were oftener nine hundred feet long
than short of it.

Cooper made the exit of that stream fifty feet
wide, in the first place, for no particular reason; in
the second place, he narrowed it to less than twenty
to accommodate some Indians. He bends a "sapling" to the form of an arch over this narrow
passage, and conceals six Indians in its foliage.
They are "laying" for a settler's scow or ark
which is coming up the stream on its way to the

lake; it is being hauled against the stiff current by a rope whose stationary end is anchored in the lake; its rate of progress cannot be more than a mile an hour. Cooper describes the ark, but pretty obscurely. In the matter of dimensions " it was little more than a modern canal-boat." Let us guess, then, that it was about one hundred and forty feet long. It was of " greater breadth than common." Let us guess, then, that it was about sixteen feet wide. This leviathan had been prowling down bends which were but a third as long as itself, and scraping between banks where it had only two feet of space to spare on each side. We cannot too much admire this miracle. A low-roofed log dwelling occupies " two-thirds of the ark's length " — a dwelling ninety feet long and sixteen feet wide, let us say — a kind of vestibule train. The dwelling has two rooms — each forty-five feet long and sixteen feet wide, let us guess. One of them is the bedroom of the Hutter girls, Judith and Hetty; the other is the parlor in the daytime, at night it is papa's bedchamber. The ark is arriving at the stream's exit now, whose width has been reduced to less than twenty feet to accommodate the Indians — say to eighteen. There is a foot to spare on each side of the boat. Did the Indians notice that there was going to be a tight squeeze there? Did they notice that they could make money by climbing down out of that arched sapling and just stepping aboard when the ark scraped by? No, other Indians would have noticed these things, but Cooper's Indians never notice anything. Cooper thinks they are marvelous creatures for noticing, but he was almost always in error about his Indians. There was seldom a sane one among them.

The ark is one hundred and forty feet long; the dwelling is ninety feet long. The idea of the Indians is to drop softly and secretly from the arched sapling to the dwelling as the ark creeps along under it at the rate of a mile an hour, and butcher the family. It will take the ark a minute and a half to pass under. It will take the ninety foot dwelling a minute to pass under. Now, then, what did the six Indians do? It would take you thirty years to guess, and even then you would have to give it up, I believe. Therefore, I will tell you what the Indians did. Their chief, a person of quite extraordinary intellect for a Cooper Indian, warily watched the canal-boat as it squeezed along under him, and when he had got his calculations fined down to exactly the right shade, as he judged, he let go and dropped. And *missed the house!* That is actually what he did. He missed the house, and landed in the stern of the scow. It was not much of a fall, yet it knocked him silly. He lay there unconscious. If the house had been ninety-seven feet long he would have made the trip. The fault was Cooper's, not his. The error lay in the construction of the house. Cooper was no architect.

There still remained in the roost five Indians.

The boat has passed under and is now out of their reach. Let me explain what the five did — you would not be able to reason it out for yourself. No. 1 jumped for the boat, but fell in the water astern of it. Then No. 2 jumped for the boat, but fell in the water still farther astern of it. Then No. 3 jumped for the boat, and fell a good way astern of it. Then No. 4 jumped for the boat, and fell in the water *away* astern. Then even No. 5 made a jump for the boat — for he was a Cooper Indian. In the matter of intellect, the difference between a Cooper Indian and the Indian that stands in front of the cigar-shop is not spacious. The scow episode is really a sublime burst of invention; but it does not thrill, because the inaccuracy of the details throws a sort of air of fictitiousness and general improbability over it. This comes of Cooper's inadequacy as an observer.

The reader will find some examples of Cooper's high talent for inaccurate observation in the account of the shooting-match in *The Pathfinder*.

"A common wrought nail was driven lightly into the target, its head having been first touched with paint."

The color of the paint is not stated — an important omission, but Cooper deals freely in important omissions. No, after all, it was not an important omission; for this nail-head is *a hundred yards from* the marksmen, and could not be seen by them at that distance, no matter what its color might be.

How far can the best eyes see a common house-fly?
A hundred yards? It is quite impossible. Very
well; eyes that cannot see a house-fly that is a hundred yards away cannot see an ordinary nail-head at
that distance, for the size of the two objects is the
same. It takes a keen eye to see a fly or a nail-
head at fifty yards — one hundred and fifty feet.
Can the reader do it?

The nail was lightly driven, its head painted, and
game called. Then the Cooper miracles began. The
bullet of the first marksman chipped an edge of the
nail-head; the next man's bullet drove the nail a
little way into the target — and removed all the
paint. Haven't the miracles gone far enough now?
Not to suit Cooper; for the purpose of this whole
scheme is to show off his prodigy, Deerslayer-
Hawkeye - Long - Rifle-Leather-Stocking-Pathfinder-
Bumppo before the ladies.

" ' Be all ready to clench it, boys! ' cried out Pathfinder, stepping
into his friend's tracks the instant they were vacant. ' Never mind a
new nail; I can see that, though the paint is gone, and what I can see
I can hit at a hundred yards, though it were only a mosquito's eye. Be
ready to clench! '

"The rifle cracked, the bullet sped its way, and the head of the nail
was buried in the wood, covered by the piece of flattened lead."

There, you see, is a man who could hunt flies
with a rifle, and command a ducal salary in a Wild
West show to-day if we had him back with us.

The recorded feat is certainly surprising just as it
stands; but it is not surprising enough for Cooper.

Cooper adds a touch. He has made Pathfinder do this miracle with another man's rifle; and not only that, but Pathfinder did not have even the advantage of loading it himself. He had everything against him, and yet he made that impossible shot; and not only made it, but did it with absolute confidence, saying, " Be ready to clench." Now a person like that would have undertaken that same feat with a brickbat, and with Cooper to help he would have achieved it, too.

Pathfinder showed off handsomely that day before the ladies. His very first feat was a thing which no Wild West show can touch. He was standing with the group of marksmen, observing — a hundred yards from the target, mind; one Jasper raised his rifle and drove the centre of the bull's-eye. Then the Quartermaster fired. The target exhibited no result this time. There was a laugh. " It's a dead miss," said Major Lundie. Pathfinder waited an impressive moment or two; then said, in that calm, indifferent, know-it-all way of his, " No, Major, he has covered Jasper's bullet, as will be seen if any one will take the trouble to examine the target."

Wasn't it remarkable! How *could* he see that little pellet fly through the air and enter that distant bullet-hole? Yet that is what he did; for nothing is impossible to a Cooper person. Did any of those people have any deep-seated doubts about this thing? No; for that would imply sanity, and these were all Cooper people.

"The respect for Pathfinder's skill and for his *quickness and accuracy of sight*" (the italics are mine) "was so profound and general, that the instant he made this declaration the spectators began to distrust their own opinions, and a dozen rushed to the target in order to ascertain the fact. There, sure enough, it was found that the Quartermaster's bullet had gone through the hole made by Jasper's, and that, too, so accurately as to require a minute examination to be certain of the circumstance, which, however, was soon clearly established by discovering one bullet over the other in the stump against which the target was placed."

They made a " minute " examination; but never mind, how could they know that there were two bullets in that hole without digging the latest one out? for neither probe nor eyesight could prove the presence of any more than one bullet. Did they dig? No; as we shall see. It is the Pathfinder's turn now; he steps out before the ladies, takes aim, and fires.

But, alas! here is a disappointment; an incredible, an unimaginable disappointment — for the target's aspect is unchanged; there is nothing there but that same old bullet-hole!

" 'If one dared to hint at such a thing,' cried Major Duncan, 'I should say that the Pathfinder has also missed the target!' "

As nobody had missed it yet, the " also " was not necessary; but never mind about that, for the Pathfinder is going to speak.

" 'No, no, Major,' said he, confidently, 'that *would* be a risky declaration. I didn't load the piece, and can't say what was in it; but if it was lead, you will find the bullet driving down those of the Quartermaster and Jasper, else is not my name Pathfinder.'

"A shout from the target announced the truth of this assertion."

Is the miracle sufficient as it stands? Not for Cooper. The Pathfinder speaks again, as he " now slowly advances towards the stage occupied by the females " :

" 'That's not all, boys, that's not all; if you find the target touched at all, I'll own to a miss. The Quartermaster cut the wood, but you'll find no wood cut by that last messenger."

The miracle is at last complete. He knew — doubtless *saw* — at the distance of a hundred yards — that his bullet had passed into the hole *without fraying the edges*. There were now three bullets in that one hole — three bullets embedded procession-ally in the body of the stump back of the target. Everybody knew this — somehow or other — and yet nobody had dug any of them out to make sure. Cooper is not a close observer, but he is interesting. He is certainly always that, no matter what happens. And he is more interesting when he is not noticing what he is about than when he is. This is a con-siderable merit.

The conversations in the Cooper books have a curious sound in our modern ears. To believe that such talk really ever came out of people's mouths would be to believe that there was a time when time was of no value to a person who thought he had something to say; when it was the custom to spread a two-minute remark out to ten; when a man's mouth was a rolling-mill, and busied itself all day long in turning four-foot pigs of thought into thirty-foot bars of conversational railroad iron by attenuation; when subjects were seldom faithfully stuck to, but the talk wandered all around and arrived nowhere; when conversations consisted mainly of irrelevancies, with here and there a relevancy, a relevancy with an embarrassed look, as not being able to explain how it got there.

Cooper was certainly not a master in the construction of dialogue. Inaccurate observation defeated him here as it defeated him in so many other enterprises of his. He even failed to notice that the man who talks corrupt English six days in the week must and will talk it on the seventh, and can't help himself. In the *Deerslayer* story he lets Deerslayer talk the showiest kind of book-talk sometimes, and at other times the basest of base dialects. For instance, when some one asks him if he has a sweetheart, and if so, where she abides, this is his majestic answer:

" 'She's in the forest—hanging from the boughs of the trees, in a soft rain—in the dew on the open grass—the clouds that float about in the blue heavens—the birds that sing in the woods—the sweet springs where I slake my thirst—and in all the other glorious gifts that come from God's Providence!' "

And he preceded that, a little before, with this:

" 'It consarns me as all things that touches a fri'nd consarns a fri'nd.' "

And this is another of his remarks:

" 'If I was Injin born, now, I might tell of this, or carry in the scalp and boast of the expl'ite afore the whole tribe; or if my inimy had only been a bear' " — and so on.

7 E

We cannot imagine such a thing as a veteran
Scotch Commander-in-Chief comporting himself in
the field like a windy melodramatic actor, but
Cooper could. On one occasion Alice and Cora
were being chased by the French through a fog in
the neighborhood of their father's fort:

"'*Point de quartier aux coquins!*' cried an eager pursuer, who
seemed to direct the operations of the enemy.

"'Stand firm and be ready, my gallant 60ths!' suddenly exclaimed
a voice above them; 'wait to see the enemy; fire low, and sweep the
glacis.'

"'Father! father!' exclaimed a piercing cry from out the mist; 'it
is I! Alice! thy own Elsie! spare, O! save your daughters!'

"'Hold!' shouted the former speaker, in the awful tones of parental
agony, the sound reaching even to the woods, and rolling back in solemn
echo. ''Tis she! God has restored me my children! Throw open
the sally-port; to the field, 60ths, to the field! pull not a trigger, lest ye
kill my lambs! Drive off these dogs of France with your steel!'"

Cooper's word-sense was singularly dull. When
a person has a poor ear for music he will flat and
sharp right along without knowing it. He keeps
near the tune, but it is *not* the tune. When a person
has a poor ear for words, the result is a literary flatting and sharping; you perceive what he is intending to say, but you also perceive that he doesn't
say it. This is Cooper. He was not a word-
musician. His ear was satisfied with the *approxi-
mate* word. I will furnish some circumstantial
evidence in support of this charge. My instances
are gathered from half a dozen pages of the tale
called *Deerslayer*. He uses " verbal," for " oral ";
" precision," for " facility "; " phenomena," for

" marvels "; " necessary," for " predetermined ";
" unsophisticated," for " primitive "; " preparation," for " expectancy "; " rebuked," for " subdued "; " dependent on," for " resulting from ";
" fact," for " condition "; " fact," for " conjecture "; " precaution," for " caution "; " explain,"
for " determine "; " mortified," for " disappointed"; "meretricious," for "factitious"; "materially," for " considerably "; " decreasing," for
" deepening "; " increasing," for " disappearing ";
" embedded," for " enclosed "; " treacherous,"
for " hostile "; " stood," for " stooped "; " softened," for " replaced "; " rejoined," for " remarked "; " situation," for " condition "; " different," for " differing "; " insensible," for
" unsentient "; " brevity," for " celerity "; " dis-
trusted," for " suspicious "; " mental imbecility,"
for " imbecility "; " eyes," for " sight "; " coun-
teracting," for " opposing "; " funeral obsequies,"
for " obsequies."

There have been daring people in the world who
claimed that Cooper could write English, but they
are all dead now — all dead but Lounsbury. I don't
remember that Lounsbury makes the claim in so
many words, still he makes it, for he says that *Deerslayer* is a " pure work of art." Pure, in that connection, means faultless — faultless in all details —
and language is a detail. If Mr. Lounsbury had
only compared Cooper's English with the English
which he writes himself — but it is plain that he

didn't; and so it is likely that he imagines until this day that Cooper's is as clean and compact as his own. Now I feel sure, deep down in my heart, that Cooper wrote about the poorest English that exists in our language, and that the English of *Deerslayer* is the very worst that even Cooper ever wrote.

I may be mistaken, but it does seem to me that *Deerslayer* is not a work of art in any sense; it does seem to me that it is destitute of every detail that goes to the making of a work of art; in truth, it seems to me that *Deerslayer* is just simply a literary *delirium tremens*.

A work of art? It has no invention; it has no order, system, sequence, or result; it has no life-likeness, no thrill, no stir, no seeming of reality; its characters are confusedly drawn, and by their acts and words they prove that they are not the sort of people the author claims that they are; its humor is pathetic; its pathos is funny; its conversations are — oh! indescribable; its love-scenes odious; its English a crime against the language.

Counting these out, what is left is Art. I think we must all admit that.

TRAVELING WITH A REFORMER

LAST spring I went out to Chicago to see the Fair, and although I did not see it my trip was not wholly lost — there were compensations. In New York I was introduced to a major in the regular army who said he was going to the Fair, and we agreed to go together. I had to go to Boston first, but that did not interfere; he said he would go along, and put in the time. He was a handsome man, and built like a gladiator. But his ways were gentle, and his speech was soft and persuasive. He was companionable, but exceedingly reposoful. Yes, and wholly destitute of the sense of humor. He was full of interest in everything that went on around him, but his serenity was indestructible; nothing disturbed him, nothing excited him.

But before the day was done I found that deep down in him somewhere he had a passion, quiet as he was — a passion for reforming petty public abuses. He stood for citizenship — it was his hobby. His idea was that every citizen of the republic ought to consider himself an unofficial policeman, and keep unsalaried watch and ward over the laws and their execution. He thought that the only

effective way of preserving and protecting public
rights was for each citizen to do his share in pre-
venting or punishing such infringements of them as
came under his personal notice.

It was a good scheme, but I thought it would
keep a body in trouble all the time; it seemed to
me that one would be always trying to get offend-
ing little officials discharged, and perhaps getting
laughed at for all reward. But he said no, I had
the wrong idea; that there was no occasion to get
anybody discharged; that in fact you *must n't* get
anybody discharged; that that would itself be a
failure; no, one must reform the man — reform him
and make him useful where he was.

"Must one report the offender and then beg his
superior not to discharge him, but reprimand him
and keep him?"

"No, that is not the idea; you don't report him
at all, for then you risk his bread and butter. You
can act as if you are *going* to report him — when
nothing else will answer. But that's an extreme
case. That is a sort of *force*, and force is bad.
Diplomacy is the effective thing. Now if a man has
tact — if a man will exercise diplomacy — "

For two minutes we had been standing at a tele-
graph wicket, and during all this time the Major had
been trying to get the attention of one of the young
operators, but they were all busy skylarking. The
Major spoke now, and asked one of them to take
his telegram. He got for reply:

" I reckon you can wait a minute, can't you?" and the skylarking went on.

The Major said yes, he was not in a hurry. Then he wrote another telegram:

"President Western Union Tel. Co.:
" Come and dine with me this evening. I can tell you how business is conducted in one of your branches."

Presently the young fellow who had spoken so pertly a little before reached out and took the telegram, and when he read it he lost color and began to apologize and explain. He said he would lose his place if this deadly telegram was sent, and he might never get another. If he could be let off this time he would give no cause of complaint again. The compromise was accepted.

As we walked away, the Major said:

" Now, you see, that was diplomacy — and you see how it worked. It wouldn't do any good to bluster, the way people are always doing — that boy can always give you as good as you send, and you'll come out defeated and ashamed of yourself pretty nearly always. But you see he stands no chance against diplomacy. Gentle words and diplomacy — those are the tools to work with."

" Yes, I see; but everybody wouldn't have had your opportunity. It isn't everybody that is on those familiar terms with the president of the Western Union."

" Oh, you misunderstand. I don't know the president — I only use him diplomatically. It is for

G*.*.

his good and for the public good.   There's no harm
in it."

I said, with hesitation and diffidence:

" But is it ever right or noble to tell a lie?"

He took no note of the delicate self-righteousness
of the question, but answered, with undisturbed
gravity and simplicity:

" Yes, sometimes.   Lies told to injure a person,
and lies told to profit yourself are not justifiable, but
lies told to help another person, and lies told in the
public interest — oh, well, that is quite another
matter.   Anybody knows that.   But never mind
about the methods: you see the result.   That youth
is going to be useful now, and well-behaved.   He
had a good face.   He was worth saving.   Why, he
was worth saving on his mother's account if not his
own.   Of course, he has a mother — sisters, too.
Damn these people who are always forgetting that!
Do you know, I've never fought a duel in my life —
never once — and yet have been challenged, like
other people.   I could always see the other man's
unoffending women folks or his little children standing between him and me.   *They* hadn't done anything — I couldn't break *their* hearts, you know."

He corrected a good many little abuses in the
course of the day, and always without friction —
always with a fine and dainty " diplomacy " which
left no sting behind ; and he got such happiness and
such contentment out of these performances that I
was obliged to envy him his trade — and perhaps

would have adopted it if I could have managed the necessary deflections from fact as confidently with my mouth as I believe I could with a pen, behind the shelter of print, after a little practice.

Away late that night we were coming up-town in a horse-car when three boisterous roughs got aboard, and began to fling hilarious obscenities and profanities right and left among the timid passengers, some of whom were women and children. Nobody resisted or retorted; the conductor tried soothing words and moral suasion, but the roughs only called him names and laughed at him. Very soon I saw that the Major realized that this was a matter which was in his line; evidently he was turning over his stock of diplomacy in his mind and getting ready. I felt that the first diplomatic remark he made in this place would bring down a land-slide of ridicule upon him and maybe something worse; but before I could whisper to him and check him he had begun, and it was too late. He said, in a level and dispassionate tone:

"Conductor, you must put these swine out. I will help you."

I was not looking for that. In a flash the three roughs plunged at him. But none of them arrived. He delivered three such blows as one could not expect to encounter outside the prize-ring, and neither of the men had life enough left in him to get up from where he fell. The Major dragged them out and threw them off the car, and we got under way again.

I was astonished; astonished to see a lamb act
so; astonished at the strength displayed, and the
clean and comprehensive result; astonished at the
brisk and business-like style of the whole thing.
The situation had a humorous side to it, considering
how much I had been hearing about mild persuasion
and gentle diplomacy all day from this pile-driver,
and I would have liked to call his attention to that
feature and do some sarcasms about it; but when I
looked at him I saw that it would be of no use — his
placid and contented face had no ray of humor in
it; he would not have understood. When we left
the car, I said:

"That was a good stroke of diplomacy — three
good strokes of diplomacy, in fact."

"*That?* That wasn't diplomacy. You are quite
in the wrong. Diplomacy is a wholly different thing.
One cannot apply it to that sort, they would not
understand it. No, that was not diplomacy; it was
force."

"Now that you mention it, I — yes, I think perhaps you are right."

"Right? Of course I am right. It was just
force."

"I think, myself, it had the outside aspect of it.
Do you often have to reform people in that way?"

"Far from it. It hardly ever happens. Not
oftener than once in half a year, at the outside."

"Those men will get well?"

"Get well? Why, certainly they will. They are

not in any danger. I know how to hit and where to
hit. You noticed that I did not hit them under the
jaw. That would have killed them.''

I believed that. I remarked — rather wittily, as I
thought — that he had been a lamb all day, but now
had all of a sudden developed into a ram — batter-
ing ram; but with dulcet frankness and simplicity
he said no, a battering-ram was quite a different
thing and not in use now. This was maddening,
and I came near bursting out and saying he had no
more appreciation of wit than a jackass — in fact, I
had it right on my tongue, but did not say it, knowing there was no hurry and I could say it just as
well some other time over the telephone.

We started to Boston the next afternoon. The
smoking-compartment in the parlor-car was full, and
we went into the regular smoker. Across the aisle
in the front seat sat a meek, farmer-looking old man
with a sickly pallor in his face, and he was holding
the door open with his foot to get the air. Presently
a big brakeman came rushing through, and when
he got to the door he stopped, gave the farmer an
ugly scowl, then wrenched the door to with such
energy as to almost snatch the old man's boot off.
Then on he plunged about his business. Several
passengers laughed, and the old gentleman looked
pathetically shamed and grieved.

After a little the conductor passed along, and the
Major stopped him and asked him a question in his
habitually courteous way:

" Conductor, where does one report the mis-
conduct of a brakeman? Does one report to you?''

" You can report him at New Haven if you want
to. What has he been doing?''

The Major told the story. The conductor seemed
amused. He said, with just a touch of sarcasm in
his bland tones:

" As I understand you, the brakeman didn't *say*
anything.''

" No, he didn't say anything.''

" But he scowled, you say.''

" Yes.''

" And snatched the door loose in a rough way.''

" Yes.''

" That's the whole business, is it ?''

" Yes, that is the whole of it.''

The conductor smiled pleasantly, and said:

" Well, if you want to report him, all right, but I
don't quite make out what it's going to amount to.
You'll say — as I understand you — that the brakeman insulted this old gentleman. They'll ask you
what he *said*. You'll say he didn't say anything at
all. I reckon they'll say, how are you going to
make out an insult when you acknowledge yourself
that he didn't say a word.''

There was a murmur of applause at the conductor's compact reasoning, and it gave him pleasure — you could see it in his face. But the Major
was not disturbed. He said:

" There — now you have touched upon a crying

defect in the complaint-system. The railway officials — as the public think and as you also seem to
think — are not aware that there are any kind of
insults except *spoken* ones. So nobody goes to
headquarters and reports insults of manner, insults
of gesture, look, and so forth; and yet these are
sometimes harder to bear than any words. They
are bitter hard to bear because there is nothing
tangible to take hold of; and the insulter can always
say, if called before the railway officials, that he
never dreamed of intending any offence. It seems
to me that the officials ought to specially and
urgently request the public to report *unworded*
affronts and incivilities."

The conductor laughed, and said:

" Well, that *would* be trimming it pretty fine,
sure !"

" But not too fine, I think. I will report this
matter at New Haven, and I have an idea that I'll
be thanked for it."

The conductor's face lost something of its complacency; in fact, it settled to a quite sober cast as
the owner of it moved away. I said:

" You are not really going to bother with that
trifle, are you?"

" It isn't a trifle. Such things ought always to
be reported. It is a public duty, and no citizen has
a right to shirk it. But I sha'n't have to report this
case."

" Why?"

"It won't be necessary. Diplomacy will do the business. You'll see."

Presently the conductor came on his rounds again, and when he reached the Major he leaned over and said:

"That's all right. You needn't report him. He's responsible to me, and if he does it again I'll give him a talking to."

The Major's response was cordial:

"Now that is what I like! You mustn't think that I was moved by any vengeful spirit, for that wasn't the case. It was duty — just a sense of duty, that was all. My brother-in-law is one of the directors of the road, and when he learns that you are going to reason with your brakeman the very next time he brutally insults an unoffending old man it will please him, you may be sure of that."

The conductor did not look as joyous as one might have thought he would, but on the contrary looked sickly and uncomfortable. He stood around a little; then said:

"I think something ought to be done to him *now*. I'll discharge him."

"Discharge him? What good would that do? Don't you think it would be better wisdom to teach him better ways and keep him?"

"Well, there's something in that. What would you suggest?"

"He insulted the old gentleman in presence of all

these people. How would it do to have him come
and apologize in their presence?"

" I'll have him here right off. And I want to say
this: If people would do as you've done, and report such things to me instead of keeping mum and
going off and blackguarding the road, you'd see a
different state of things pretty soon. I'm much
obliged to you."

The brakeman came and apologized. After he
was gone the Major said:

" Now, you see how simple and easy that was.
The ordinary citizen would have accomplished nothing — the brother-in-law of a director can accomplish
anything he wants to."

" But are you really the brother-in-law of a
director?"

" Always. Always when the public interests require it. I have a brother-in-law on all the boards
— everywhere. It saves me a world of trouble."

" It is a good wide relationship."

" Yes. I have over three hundred of them."

" Is the relationship never doubted by a conductor?"

" I have never met with a case. It is the honest
truth — I never have."

" Why didn't you let him go ahead and discharge
the brakeman, in spite of your favorite policy? You
know he deserved it."

The Major answered with something which really
had a sort of distant resemblance to impatience:

"If you would stop and think a moment you wouldn't ask such a question as that. Is a brake-man a dog, that nothing but dog's methods will do for him? He is a man, and has a man's fight for life. And he always has a sister, or a mother, or wife and children to support. Always — there are no exceptions. When you take his living away from him you take theirs away too — and what have they done to you? Nothing. And where is the profit in discharging an uncourteous brakeman and hiring another just like him? It's unwisdom. Don't you see that the rational thing to do is to *reform* the brakeman and keep him? Of course it is."

Then he quoted with admiration the conduct of a certain division superintendent of the Consolidated road, in a case where a switchman of two years' experience was negligent once and threw a train off the track and killed several people. Citizens came in a passion to urge the man's dismissal, but the superintendent said:

"No, you are wrong. He has learned his lesson, he will throw no more trains off the track. He is twice as valuable as he was before. I shall keep him."

We had only one more adventure on the trip. Between Hartford and Springfield the train-boy came shouting in with an armful of literature and dropped a sample into a slumbering gentleman's lap, and the man woke up with a start. He was very angry, and he and a couple of friends discussed the outrage

with much heat.   They sent for the parlor-car conductor and described the matter, and were determined to have the boy expelled from his situation.
The three complainants were wealthy Holyoke merchants, and it was evident that the conductor stood
in some awe of them.   He tried to pacify them,
and explained that the boy was not under his
authority, but under that of one of the news companies; but he accomplished nothing.

Then the Major volunteered some testimony for
the defence.   He said:

" I saw it all.   You gentlemen have not meant to
exaggerate the circumstances, but still that is what
you have done.   The boy has done nothing more
than all train-boys do.   If you want to get his ways
softened down and his manners reformed, I am with
you and ready to help, but it isn't fair to get him
discharged without giving him a chance."

But they were angry, and would hear of no compromise.   They were well acquainted with the president of the Boston & Albany, they said, and would
put everything aside next day and go up to Boston
and fix that boy.

The Major said he would be on hand too, and
would do what he could to save the boy.   One of
the gentlemen looked him over, and said:

" Apparently it is going to be a matter of who
can wield the most influence with the president.   Do
you know Mr. Bliss personally?"

The Major said, with composure:

8E

" Yes; he is my uncle."

The effect was satisfactory. There was an awkward silence for a minute or more; then the hedging and the half-confessions of over-haste and exaggerated resentment began, and soon everything was smooth and friendly and sociable, and it was resolved to drop the matter and leave the boy's bread-and-butter unmolested.

It turned out as I had expected: the president of the road was not the Major's uncle at all — except by adoption, and for this day and train only.

We got into no episodes on the return journey. Probably it was because we took a night train and slept all the way.

We left New York Saturday night by the Pennsylvania road. After breakfast the next morning we went into the parlor-car, but found it a dull place and dreary. There were but few people in it and nothing going on. Then we went into the little smoking-compartment of the same car and found three gentlemen in there. Two of them were grumbling over one of the rules of the road — a rule which forbade card-playing on the trains on Sunday. They had started an innocent game of high-low-jack and been stopped. The Major was interested. He said to the third gentleman:

" Did you object to the game?"

" Not at all. I am a Yale professor and a religious man, but my prejudices are not extensive."

Then the Major said to the others:

" You are at perfect liberty to resume your game, gentlemen; no one here objects."

One of them declined the risk, but the other one said he would like to begin again if the Major would join him. So they spread an overcoat over their knees and the game proceeded. Pretty soon the parlor-car conductor arrived, and said brusquely:

" There, there, gentlemen, that won't do. Put up the cards— it's not allowed."

The Major was shuffling. He continued to shuffle, and said:

" By whose order is it forbidden?"

" It's my order. I forbid it."

The dealing began. The Major asked:

" Did you invent the idea?"

" What idea?"

" The idea of forbidding card-playing on Sunday."

" No — of course not."

" Who did?"

" The company."

" Then it isn't your order, after all, but the company's. Is that it?"

" Yes. But you don't stop playing; I have to require you to stop playing immediately."

" Nothing is gained by hurry, and often much is lost. Who authorized the company to issue such an order?"

" My dear sir, that is a matter of no consequence to me, and — "

"But you forget that you are not the only person concerned. It may be a matter of consequence to me. It is indeed a matter of very great importance to me. I cannot violate a legal requirement of my country without dishonoring myself; I cannot allow any man or corporation to hamper my liberties with illegal rules — a thing which railway companies are always trying to do — without dishonoring my citizenship. So I come back to that question: By whose authority has the company issued this order?"

"I don't *know*. That's *their* affair."

"Mine, too. I doubt if the company has any right to issue such a rule. This road runs through several States. Do you know what State we are in now, and what its laws are in matters of this kind?"

"Its laws do not concern me, but the company's orders do. It is my duty to stop this game, gentlemen, and it *must* be stopped."

"Possibly; but still there is no hurry. In hotels they post certain rules in the rooms, but they always quote passages from the State laws as authority for these requirements. I see nothing posted here of this sort. Please produce your authority and let us arrive at a decision, for you see yourself that you are marring the game."

"I have nothing of the kind, but I have my orders, and that is sufficient. They must be obeyed."

"Let us not jump to conclusions. It will be

better all around to examine into the matter without heat or haste, and see just where we stand before either of us makes a mistake — for the curtailing of the liberties of a citizen of the United States is a much more serious matter than you and the railroads seem to think, and it cannot be done in my person until the curtailer proves his right to do so. Now — ''

'' My dear sir, *will* you put down those cards?''

'' All in good time, perhaps. It depends. You say this order must be obeyed. *Must*. It is a strong word. You see yourself how strong it is. A wise company would not arm you with so drastic an order as this, of *course*, without appointing a penalty for its infringement. Otherwise it runs the risk of being a dead letter and a thing to laugh at. What is the appointed penalty for an infringement of this law?''

'' Penalty? I never heard of any.''

'' Unquestionably you must be mistaken. Your company orders you to come here and rudely break up an innocent amusement, and furnishes you no way to enforce the order? Don't you see that that is nonsense? What do you *do* when people refuse to obey this order? Do you take the cards away from them?''

'' No.''

'' Do you put the offender off at the next station?''

'' Well, no — of course we couldn't if he had a ticket.''

8*.*.

"Do you have him up before a court?"

The conductor was silent and apparently troubled. The Major started a new deal, and said:

"You see that you are helpless, and that the company has placed you in a foolish position. You are furnished with an arrogant order, and you deliver it in a blustering way, and when you come to look into the matter you find you haven't any way of enforcing obedience."

The conductor said, with chill dignity:

"Gentlemen, you have heard the order, and my duty is ended. As to obeying it or not, you will do as you think fit." And he turned to leave.

"But wait. The matter is not yet finished. I think you are mistaken about your duty being ended; but if it really is, I myself have a duty to perform yet."

"How do you mean?"

"Are you going to report my disobedience at headquarters in Pittsburg?"

"No. What good would that do?"

"You must report me, or I will report you."

"Report me for what?"

"For disobeying the company's orders in not stopping this game. As a citizen it is my duty to help the railway companies keep their servants to their work."

"Are you in earnest?"

"Yes, I am in earnest. I have nothing against you as a man, but I have this against you as an officer — that you have not carried out that order, and if you do not report me I must report you. And I will."

The conductor looked puzzled, and was thoughtful a moment; then he burst out with:

" I seem to be getting *myself* into a scrape! It's all a muddle; I can't make head or tail of it; it's never happened before; they always knocked under and never said a word, and so *I* never saw how ridiculous that stupid order with no penalty is. *I* don't want to report anybody, and I don't want to *be* reported — why, it might do me no end of harm! Now *do* go on with the game — play the whole day if you want to — and don't let's have any more trouble about it!"

" No, I only sat down here to establish this gentleman's rights — he can have his place now. But before you go won't you tell me what you think the company made this rule for? Can you imagine an excuse for it? I mean a rational one — an excuse that is not on its face silly, and the invention of an idiot?"

" Why, surely I can. The reason it was made is plain enough. It is to save the feelings of the other passengers — the religious ones among them, I mean. They would not like it, to have the Sabbath desecrated by card-playing on the train."

" I just thought as much. They are willing to desecrate it themselves by traveling on Sunday, but they are not willing that other people — "

H*₊*₊

" By gracious, you've hit it! I never thought of that before. The fact is, it *is* a silly rule when you come to look into it."

At this point the train-conductor arrived, and was going to shut down the game in a very high-handed fashion, but the parlor-car conductor stopped him and took him aside to explain. Nothing more was heard of the matter.

I was ill in bed eleven days in Chicago and got no glimpse of the Fair, for I was obliged to return east as soon as I was able to travel. The Major secured and paid for a state-room in a sleeper the day before we left, so that I could have plenty of room and be comfortable; but when we arrived at the station a mistake had been made and our car had not been put on. The conductor had reserved a section for us — it was the best he could do, he said. But the Major said we were not in a hurry, and would wait for the car to be put on. The conductor responded, with pleasant irony:

" It may be that *you* are not in a hurry, just as you say, but we *are*. Come, get aboard, gentlemen, get aboard — don't keep us waiting."

But the Major would not get aboard himself nor allow me to do it. He wanted his car, and said he must have it. This made the hurried and perspiring conductor impatient, and he said:

" It's the best we can *do* — we can't do impossibilities. You will take the section or go without. A mistake has been made and can't be rectified at this late hour. It's a thing that happens now and then, and there is nothing for it but to put up with it and make the best of it. Other people do."

" Ah, that is just it, you see. If they had stuck to their rights and enforced them you wouldn't be trying to trample mine under foot in this bland way now. I haven't any disposition to give you unnecessary trouble, but it is my duty to protect the next man from this kind of imposition. So I must have my car. Otherwise I will wait in Chicago and sue the company for violating its contract."

" Sue the company? — for a thing like that!"

" Certainly."

" Do you really mean that?"

" Indeed, I do."

The conductor looked the Major over wonderingly, and then said:

" It beats me — it's bran-new — I've never struck the mate to it before. But I swear I think you'd do it. Look here, I'll send for the station-master."

When the station-master came he was a good deal annoyed — at the Major, not at the person who had made the mistake. He was rather brusque, and took the same position which the conductor had taken in the beginning; but he failed to move the soft-spoken artilleryman, who still insisted that he must have his car. However, it was plain that there was only one strong side in this case, and that that side was the Major's. The station-master banished his annoyed manner, and became pleasant and even half-apologetic.   This made a good opening for a compromise, and the Major made a concession. He said he would give up the engaged state-room, but he must have *a* state-room.   After a deal of ransacking, one was found whose owner was persuadable; he exchanged it for our section, and we got away at last.   The conductor called on us in the evening, and was kind and courteous and obliging, and we had a long talk and got to be good friends. He said he wished the public would make trouble oftener — it would have a good effect.   He said that the railroads could not be expected to do their whole duty by the traveler unless the traveler would take some interest in the matter himself.

I hoped that we were done reforming for the trip now, but it was not so.   In the hotel-car, in the morning, the Major called for broiled chicken.   The waiter said:

" It's not in the bill of fare, sir; we do not serve anything but what is in the bill."

" That gentleman yonder is eating a broiled chicken."

" Yes, but that is different.   He is one of the superintendents of the road."

" Then all the more must I have broiled chicken. I do not like these discriminations.   Please hurry — bring me a broiled chicken."

The waiter brought the steward, who explained in a low and polite voice that the thing was impossible — it was against the rule, and the rule was rigid.

"Very well, then, you must either apply it impartially or break it impartially. You must take that gentleman's chicken away from him or bring me one."

The steward was puzzled, and did not quite know what to do. He began an incoherent argument, but the conductor came along just then, and asked what the difficulty was. The steward explained that here was a gentleman who was insisting on having a chicken when it was dead against the rule and not in the bill. The conductor said:

"Stick by your rules — you haven't any option. Wait a moment — is this the gentleman?" Then he laughed and said: "Never mind your rules — it's my advice, and sound; give him anything he wants — don't get him started on his rights. Give him whatever he asks for; and if you haven't got it, stop the train and get it."

The Major ate the chicken, but said he did it from a sense of duty and to establish a principle, for he did not like chicken.

I missed the Fair, it is true, but I picked up some diplomatic tricks which I and the reader may find handy and useful as we go along.

PRIVATE HISTORY OF THE "JUMPING FROG" STORY

FIVE or six years ago a lady from Finland asked me to tell her a story in our negro dialect, so that she could get an idea of what that variety of speech was like. I told her one of Hopkinson Smith's negro stories, and gave her a copy of *Harper's Monthly* containing it. She translated it for a Swedish newspaper, but by an oversight named me as the author of it instead of Smith. I was very sorry for that, because I got a good lashing in the Swedish press, which would have fallen to his share but for that mistake; for it was shown that Boccaccio had told that very story, in his curt and meagre fashion, five hundred years before Smith took hold of it and made a good and tellable thing out of it.

I have always been sorry for Smith. But my own turn has come now. A few weeks ago Professor Van Dyke, of Princeton, asked this question:

" Do you know how old your Jumping Frog story is?"

And I answered:

"Yes — forty-five years. The thing happened in Calaveras County in the spring of 1849."

"No; it happened earlier — a couple of thousand years earlier; it is a Greek story."

I was astonished — and hurt. I said:

"I am willing to be a literary thief if it has been so ordained; I am even willing to be caught robbing the ancient dead alongside of Hopkinson Smith, for he is my friend and a good fellow, and I think would be as honest as any one if he could do it without occasioning remark; but I am not willing to ante-date his crimes by fifteen hundred years. I must ask you to knock off part of that."

But the professor was not chaffing; he was in earnest, and could not abate a century. He named the Greek author, and offered to get the book and send it to me and the college text-book containing the English translation also. I thought I would like the translation best, because Greek makes me tired. January 30th he sent me the English version, and I will presently insert it in this article. It is my Jumping Frog tale in every essential. It is not strung out as I have strung it out, but it is all there.

To me this is very curious and interesting. Curious for several reasons. For instance:

I heard the story told by a man who was not telling it to his hearers as a thing new to them, but as a thing which *they had witnessed and would remember*. He was a dull person, and ignorant; he had no gift as a story-teller, and no invention; in his mouth this episode was merely history — history and statistics; and the gravest sort of history, too; he was entirely serious, for he was dealing with what to him were austere facts, and they interested him solely because they *were* facts; he was drawing on his memory, not his mind; he saw no humor in his tale, neither did his listeners; neither he nor they ever smiled or laughed; in my time I have not attended a more solemn conference. To him and to his fellow gold-miners there were just two things in the story that were worth considering. One was the smartness of the stranger in taking in its hero, Jim Smiley, with a loaded frog; and the other was the stranger's deep knowledge of a frog's nature — for he knew (as the narrator asserted and the listeners conceded) that a frog *likes shot* and is always ready to eat it. Those men discussed those two points, and those only. They were hearty in their admiration of them, and none of the party was aware that a first-rate story had been told in a first-rate way, and that it was brimful of a quality whose presence they never suspected — humor.

Now, then, the interesting question is, *did* the frog episode happen in Angel's Camp in the spring of '49, as told in my hearing that day in the fall of 1865? I am perfectly sure that it did. I am also sure that its duplicate happened in Bœotia a couple of thousand years ago. I think it must be a case of history actually repeating itself, and not a case of a good story floating down the ages and surviving because too good to be allowed to perish.

I would now like to have the reader examine the Greek story and the story told by the dull and solemn Californian, and observe how exactly alike they are in essentials.

[*Translation.*]

THE ATHENIAN AND THE FROG.*

An Athenian once fell in with a Bœotian who was sitting by the roadside looking at a frog.   Seeing the other approach, the Bœotian said his was a remarkable frog, and asked if he would agree to start a contest of frogs, on condition that he whose frog jumped farthest should receive a large sum of money.   The Athenian replied that he would if the other would fetch him a frog, for the lake was near.   To this he agreed, and when he was gone the Athenian took the frog, and, opening its mouth, poured some stones into its stomach, so that it did not indeed seem larger than before, but could not jump.   The Bœotian soon returned with the other frog, and the contest began.   The second frog first was pinched, and jumped moderately; then they pinched the Bœotian frog. And he gathered himself for a leap, and used the utmost effort, but he could not move his body the least.   So the Athenian departed with the money.   When he was gone the Bœotian, wondering what was the matter with the frog, lifted him up and examined him.   And being turned upside down, he opened his mouth and vomited out the stones.

And here is the way it happened in California:

FROM "THE CELEBRATED JUMPING FROG OF CALAVERAS COUNTY."

Well, thish-yer Smiley had rat-tarriers, and chicken cocks, and tomcats, and all them kind of things, till you couldn't rest, and you couldn't fetch nothing for him to bet on but he'd match you.   He ketched a frog one day, and took him home, and said he cal'lated to educate him; and so he never done nothing for three months but set in his back yard

---

* Sidgwick, *Greek Prose Composition*, page 116.

and learn that frog to jump. And you bet you he *did* learn him, too. He'd give him a little punch behind, and the next minute you'd see that frog whirling in the air like a doughnut — see him turn one summer-set, or maybe a couple if he got a good start, and come down flat-footed and all right, like a cat. He got him up so in the matter of ketching flies, and kep' him in practice so constant, that he'd nail a fly every time as fur as he could see him. Smiley said all a frog wanted was educa-tion, and he could do 'most anything — and I believe him. Why, I've seen him set Dan'l Webster down here on this floor — Dan'l Webster was the name of the frog — and sing out "Flies, Dan'l, flies!" and quicker'n you could wink he'd spring straight up and snake a fly off'n the counter there, and flop down on the floor ag'in as solid as a gob of mud, and fall to scratching the side of his head with his hind foot as indifferent as if he hadn't no idea he'd been doin' any more'n any frog might do. You never see a frog so modest and straightfor'ard as he was, for all he was so gifted. And when it come to fair and square jumping on a dead level, he could get over more ground at one straddle than any animal of his breed you ever see. Jumping on a dead level was his strong suit, you understand; and when it came to that, Smiley would ante up money on him as long as he had a red. Smiley was monstrous proud of his frog, and well he might be, for fellers that had traveled and been everywheres all said he laid over any frog that ever *they* see.

Well, Smiley kep' the beast in a little lattice box, and he used to fetch him down-town sometimes and lay for a bet. One day a feller — a stranger in the camp, he was — come acrost him with his box, and says:

"What might it be that you've got in the box?"

And Smiley says, sorter indifferent-like, "It might be a parrot, or it might be a canary, maybe, but it ain't — it's only just a frog."

And the feller took it, and looked at it careful, and turned it round this way and that, and says, "H'm — so 'tis. Well, what's *he* good for?"

"Well," Smiley says, easy and careless, "he's good enough for *one* thing, I should judge — he can outjump any frog in Calaveras County."

The feller took the box again and took another long, particular look, and gave it back to Smiley, and says, very deliberate, "Well," he says, "I don't see no p'ints about that frog that's any better'n any other frog."

"Maybe you don't," Smiley says. "Maybe you understand frogs

and maybe you don't understand 'em; maybe you've had experience, and maybe you ain't only a amature, as it were. Anyways, I've got *my* opinion, and I'll resk forty dollars that he can outjump any frog in Calaveras County."

And the feller studies a minute, and then says, kinder sad-like, "Well, I'm only a stranger here, and I ain't got no frog, but if I had a frog I'd bet you."

And then Smiley says: "That's all right — that's all right — if you'll hold my box a minute, I'll go and get you a frog." And so the feller took the box and put up his forty dollars along with Smiley's and set down to wait.

So he set there a good while thinking and thinking to hisself, and then he got the frog out and prized his mouth open and took a teaspoon and filled him full of quail shot — filled him pretty near up to his chin — and set him on the floor. Smiley he went to the swamp and slopped around in the mud for a long time, and finally he ketched a frog and fetched him in and give him to this feller, and says:

"Now, if you're ready, set him alongside of Dan'l, with his fore-paws just even with Dan'l's, and I'll give the word." Then he says, "One — two — three — *git!*" and him and the feller touched up the frogs from behind, and the new frog hopped off lively; but Dan'l give a heave, and hysted up his shoulders — so — like a Frenchman, but it warn't no use — he couldn't budge; he was planted as solid as a church, and he couldn't no more stir than if he was anchored out. Smiley was a good deal surprised, and he was disgusted, too, but he didn't have no idea what the matter was, of course.

The feller took the money and started away; and when he was going out at the door he sorter jerked his thumb over his shoulder — so — at Dan'l, and says again, very deliberate: "Well," he says, "*I* don't see no p'ints about that frog that's any better'n any other frog."

Smiley he stood scratching his head and looking down at Dan'l a long time, and at last he says, "I do wonder what in the nation that frog throw'd off for — I wonder if there ain't something the matter with him — he 'pears to look mighty baggy, somehow." And he ketched Dan'l by the nap of the neck, and hefted him, and says, "Why, blame my cats if he don't weigh five pound!" and turned him upside down, and he belched out a double handful of shot. And then he see how it was, and he was the maddest man — he set the frog down and took out after that feller, but he never ketched him.

The resemblances are deliciously exact. There you have the wily Bœotian and the wily Jim Smiley waiting — two thousand years apart — and waiting, each equipped with his frog and "laying" for the stranger. A contest is proposed — for money. The Athenian would take a chance " if the other would fetch him a frog"; the Yankee says: " I'm only a stranger here, and I ain't got no frog; but if I had a frog I'd bet you." The wily Bœotian and the wily Californian, with that vast gulf of two thousand years between, retire eagerly and go frogging in the marsh; the Athenian and the Yankee remain behind and work a base advantage, the one with pebbles, the other with shot. Presently the contest began. In the one case " they pinched the Bœotian frog "; in the other, " him and the feller touched up the frogs from behind." The Bœotian frog " gathered himself for a leap " (you can just *see* him!), " but could not move his body in the least ": the Californian frog " give a heave, but it warn't no use — he couldn't budge." In both the ancient and the modern cases the strangers departed with the money. The Bœotian and the Californian wonder what is the matter with their frogs; they lift them and examine; they turn them upside down and out spills the informing ballast.

Yes, the resemblances are curiously exact. I used to tell the story of the Jumping Frog in San Francisco, and presently Artemus Ward came along and wanted it to help fill out a little book which he was about to publish; so I wrote it out and sent it to his publisher, Carleton; but Carleton thought the book had enough matter in it, so he gave the story to Henry Clapp as a present, and Clapp put it in his *Saturday Press*, and it killed that paper with a suddenness that was beyond praise. At least the paper died with that issue, and none but envious people have ever tried to rob me of the honor and credit of killing it. The "Jumping Frog" was the first piece of writing of mine that spread itself through the newspapers and brought me into public notice. Consequently, the *Saturday Press* was a cocoon and I the worm in it; also, I was the gay-colored literary moth which its death set free. This simile has been used before.

Early in '66 the "Jumping Frog" was issued in book form, with other sketches of mine. A year or two later Madame Blanc translated it into French and published it in the *Revue des Deux Mondes*, but the result was not what should have been expected, for the *Revue* struggled along and pulled through, and is alive yet. I think the fault must have been in the translation. I ought to have translated it myself. I think so because I examined into the matter and finally retranslated the sketch from the French back into English, to see what the trouble was; that is, to see just what sort of a focus the French people got upon it. Then the mystery was explained. In French the story is too confused, and chaotic, and unreposeful, and ungrammatical, and insane; consequently it could only cause grief and sickness — it could not kill. A glance at my re-translation will show the reader that this must be true.

[*My Re-translation.*]

THE FROG JUMPING OF THE COUNTY OF CALAVERAS.

Eh bien! this Smiley nourished some terriers à rats, and some cocks of combat, and some cats, and all sort of things; and with his rage of betting one no had more of repose. He trapped one day a frog and him imported with him (et l'emporta chez lui) saying that he pretended to make his education. You me believe if you will, but during three months he not has nothing done but to him apprehend to jump (apprendre à sauter) in a court retired of her mansion (de sa maison). And I you respond that he have succeeded. He him gives a small blow by behind, and the instant after you shall see the frog turn in the air like a grease-biscuit, make one summersault, sometimes two, when she was well started, and re-fall upon his feet like a cat. He him had accomplished in the art of to gobble the flies (gober des mouches), and him there exercised continually — so well that a fly at the most far that she appeared was a fly lost. Smiley had custom to say that all which lacked to a frog it was the education, but with the education she could do nearly all — and I him believe. Tenez, I him have seen pose Daniel Webster there upon this plank — Daniel Webster was the name of the frog — and to him sing, " Some flies, Daniel, some flies! " — in a flash of the eye Daniel had bounded and seized a fly here upon the counter, then jumped anew at the earth, where he rested truly to himself scratch the head with his behind-foot, as if he no had not the least idea of his superiority. Never you not have seen frog as modest, as natural, sweet as she was. And when he himself agitated to jump purely and simply upon plain earth, she does more ground in one jump than any beast of his species than you can know.

To jump plain — this was his strong. When he himself agitated for that Smiley multiplied the bets upon her as long as there to him remained a red. It must to know, Smiley was monstrously proud of his frog, and he of it was right, for some men who were traveled, who had all seen, said that they to him would be injurious to him compare to another frog. Smiley guarded Daniel in a little box latticed which he carried bytimes to the village for some bet.

One day an individual stranger at the camp him arrested with his box and him said:

"What is this that you have then shut up there within?"

Smiley said, with an air indifferent:

"That could be a paroquet, or a syringe (*ou un serin*), but this no is nothing of such, it not is but a frog."

The individual it took, it regarded with care, it turned from one side and from the other, then he said:

"*Tiens!* in effect!—At what is she good?"

"My God!" respond Smiley, always with an air disengaged, "she is good for one thing, to my notice (*à mon avis*), she can batter in jumping (*elle peut batter en sautant*) all frogs of the county of Calaveras."

The individual re-took the box, it examined of new longly, and it rendered to Smiley in saying with an air deliberate:

"*Eh bien!* I no saw not that that frog had nothing of better than each frog." (*Je ne vois pas que cette grenouille ait rien de mieux qu'aucune grenouille.*) [If that isn't grammar gone to seed, then I count myself no judge.—M. T.]

"Possible that you not it saw not," said Smiley, "possible that you —you comprehend frogs; possible that you not you there comprehend nothing; possible that you had of the experience, and possible that you not be but an amateur. Of all manner (*De toute manière*) I bet forty dollars that she batter in jumping no matter which frog of the county of Calaveras."

The individual reflected a second, and said like sad:

"I not am but a stranger here, I no have not a frog; but if I of it had one, I would embrace the bet."

"Strong, well!" respond Smiley; "nothing of more facility. If you will hold my box a minute, I go you to search a frog (*j'irai vous chercher*)."

Behold, then, the individual, who guards the box, who puts his forty dollars upon those of Smiley, and who attends (*et qui attend*). He attended enough longtimes, reflecting all solely. And figure you that he takes Daniel, him opens the mouth by force and with a teaspoon him fills with shot of the hunt, even him fills just to the chin, then he him puts by the earth. Smiley during these times was at slopping in a swamp. Finally he trapped (*attrape*) a frog, him carried to that individual, and said:

"Now if you be ready, put him all against Daniel, with their before-

9*.*.*

feet upon the same line, and I give the signal" — then he added: "One, two, three — advance!"

Him and the individual touched their frogs by behind, and the frog new put to jump smartly, but Daniel himself lifted ponderously, exalted the shoulders thus, like a Frenchman — to what good? he could not budge, he is planted solid like a church, he not advance no more than if one him had put at the anchor.

Smiley was surprised and disgusted, but he not himself doubted not of the turn being intended (*mais il ne se doutait pas du tour bien entendu*). The individual empocketed the silver, himself with it went, and of it himself in going is that he no gives not a jerk of thumb over the shoulder — like that — at the poor Daniel, in saying with his air deliberate — (*L'individu empoche l'argent s'en va et en s'en allant est ce qu'il ne donne pas un coup de pouce par-dessus l'épaule, comme, ça, au pauvre Daniel, en disant de son air délibéré.*)

"Eh bien! *I no see not that that frog has nothing of better than another.*"

Smiley himself scratched longtimes the head, the eyes fixed upon Daniel, until that which at last he said:

"I me demand how the devil it makes itself that this beast has refused. Is it that she had something? One would believe that she is stuffed."

He grasped Daniel by the skin of the neck, him lifted and said:

"The wolf me bite if he no weigh not five pounds."

He him reversed and the unhappy belched two handfuls of shot (*et le malheureux*, etc.). — When Smiley recognized how it was, he was like mad. He deposited his frog by the earth and ran after that individual, but he not him caught never.

It may be that there are people who can translate better than I can, but I am not acquainted with them.

So ends the private and public history of the Jumping Frog of Calaveras County, an incident which has this unique feature about it — that it is both old and new, a "chestnut" and not a "chestnut"; for it was original when it happened two thousand years ago, and was again original when it happened in California in our own time.

MENTAL TELEGRAPHY AGAIN

I HAVE three or four curious incidents to tell about. They seem to come under the head of what I named "Mental Telegraphy" in a paper written seventeen years ago, and published long afterwards.*

Several years ago I made a campaign on the platform with Mr. George W. Cable. In Montreal we were honored with a reception. It began at two in the afternoon in a long drawing-room in the Windsor Hotel. Mr. Cable and I stood at one end of this room, and the ladies and gentlemen entered it at the other end, crossed it at that end, then came up the long left-hand side, shook hands with us, said a word or two, and passed on, in the usual way. My sight is of the telescopic sort, and I presently recognized a familiar face among the throng of strangers drifting in at the distant door, and I said to myself, with surprise and high gratification, "That is Mrs. R.; I had forgotten that she was a Canadian." She had been a great friend of mine in Carson City, Nevada, in the early days. I had not seen her or

---

* The paper entitled "Mental Telegraphy," which originally appeared in *Harper's Magazine* for December, 1893, is included in the volume entitled *The American Claimant and Other Stories and Sketches.*

I*₊*₊   (131)

heard of her for twenty years; I had not been thinking about her; there was nothing to suggest her to me, nothing to bring her to my mind; in fact, to me she had long ago ceased to exist, and had disappeared from my consciousness. But I knew her instantly; and I saw her so clearly that I was able to note some of the particulars of her dress, and did note them, and they remained in my mind. I was impatient for her to come. In the midst of the hand-shakings I snatched glimpses of her and noted her progress with the slow-moving file across the end of the room; then I saw her start up the side, and this gave me a full front view of her face. I saw her last when she was within twenty-five feet of me. For an hour I kept thinking she must still be in the room somewhere and would come at last, but I was disappointed.

When I arrived in the lecture-hall that evening some one said: "Come into the waiting-room; there's a friend of yours there who wants to see you. You'll not be introduced — you are to do the recognizing without help if you can."

I said to myself: "It is Mrs. R.; I shan't have any trouble."

There were perhaps ten ladies present, all seated. In the midst of them was Mrs. R., as I had expected. She was dressed exactly as she was when I had seen her in the afternoon. I went forward and shook hands with her and called her by name, and said:

"I knew you the moment you appeared at the reception this afternoon."

She looked surprised, and said: "But I was not at the reception. I have just arrived from Quebec, and have not been in town an hour."

It was my turn to be surprised now. I said: "I can't help it. I give you my word of honor that it is as I say. I saw you at the reception, and you were dressed precisely as you are now. When they told me a moment ago that I should find a friend in this room, your image rose before me, dress and all, just as I had seen you at the reception."

Those are the facts. She was not at the reception at all, or anywhere near it; but I saw her there nevertheless, and most clearly and unmistakably. To that I could make oath. How is one to explain this? I was not thinking of her at the time; had not thought of her for years. But she had been thinking of me, no doubt; did her thoughts flit through leagues of air to me, and bring with it that clear and pleasant vision of herself? I think so. That was and remains my sole experience in the matter of apparitions — I mean apparitions that come when one is (ostensibly) awake. I could have been asleep for a moment; the apparition could have been the creature of a dream. Still, that is nothing to the point; the feature of interest is the happening of the thing just at that time, instead of at an earlier or later time, which is argument that its origin lay in thought-transference.

My next incident will be set aside by most persons
as being merely a "coincidence," I suppose. Years
ago I used to think sometimes of making a lecturing
trip through the antipodes and the borders of the
Orient, but always gave up the idea, partly because
of the great length of the journey and partly because
my wife could not well manage to go with me.
Towards the end of last January that idea, after an
interval of years, came suddenly into my head again
— forcefully, too, and without any apparent reason.
Whence came it? What suggested it? I will touch
upon that presently.

I was at that time where I am now — in Paris. I
wrote at once to Henry M. Stanley (London), and
asked him some questions about his Australian lecture tour, and inquired who had conducted him and
what were the terms. After a day or two his answer
came. It began:

"The lecture agent for Australia and New Zealand is *par excellence*
Mr. R. S. Smythe, of Melbourne."

He added his itinerary, terms, sea expenses, and
some other matters, and advised me to write Mr.
Smythe, which I did — February 3d. I began my
letter by saying in substance that while he did not
know me personally we had a mutual friend in
Stanley, and that would answer for an introduction.
Then I proposed my trip, and asked if he would give
me the same terms which he had given Stanley.

I mailed my letter to Mr. Smythe February 6th,
and three days later I got a letter from the selfsame

Smythe, dated Melbourne, December 17th. I would
as soon have expected to get a letter from the late
George Washington. The letter began somewhat
as mine to him had begun — with a self-introduction :

"DEAR MR. CLEMENS, — It is so long since Archibald Forbes and
I spent that pleasant afternoon in your comfortable house at Hartford
that you have probably quite forgotten the occasion."

In the course of his letter this occurs :

" I am willing to give you " [here he named the terms which he had
given Stanley] " for an antipodean tour to last, say, three months."

Here was the single essential detail of my letter
answered three days after I had mailed my inquiry.
I might have saved myself the trouble and the postage
— and a few years ago I would have done that very
thing, for I would have argued that my sudden and
strong impulse to write and ask some questions of a
stranger on the under side of the globe meant that
the impulse came from that stranger, and that he
would answer my questions of his own motion if I
would let him alone.

Mr. Smythe's letter probably passed under my
nose on its way to lose three weeks traveling to
America and back, and gave me a whiff of its con-
tents as it went along.   Letters often act like that.
Instead of the *thought* coming to you in an instant
from Australia, the (apparently) unsentient letter
imparts it to you as it glides invisibly past your
elbow in the mail-bag.

Next incident.   In the following month — March
— I was in America.   I spent a Sunday at Irvington-

on-the-Hudson with Mr. John Brisben Walker, of the *Cosmopolitan* magazine. We came into New York next morning, and went to the Century Club for luncheon. He said some praiseful things about the character of the club and the orderly serenity and pleasantness of its quarters, and asked if I had never tried to acquire membership in it. I said I had not, and that New York clubs were a continuous expense to the country members without being of frequent use or benefit to them.

"And now I've got an idea!" said I. "There's the Lotos — the first New York club I was ever a member of — my very earliest love in that line. I have been a member of it for considerably more than twenty years, yet have seldom had a chance to look in and see the boys. They turn gray and grow old while I am not watching. And *my dues go on*. I am going to Hartford this afternoon for a day or two, but as soon as I get back I will go to John Elderkin very privately and say: 'Remember the veteran and confer distinction upon him, for the sake of old times. Make me an honorary member and abolish the tax. If you haven't any such thing as honorary membership, all the better — create it for my honor and glory.' That would be a great thing; I will go to John Elderkin as soon as I get back from Hartford."

I took the last express that afternoon, first telegraphing Mr. F. G. Whitmore to come and see me next day. When he came he asked:

" Did you get a letter from Mr. John Elderkin, secretary of the Lotos Club, before you left New York?"

" No."

" Then it just missed you. If I had known you were coming I would have kept it. It is beautiful, and will make you proud. The Board of Directors, by unanimous vote, have made you a life member, and *squelched those dues;* and, you are to be on hand and receive your distinction on the night of the 30th, which is the twenty-fifth anniversary of the founding of the club, and it will not surprise me if they have some great times there."

What put the honorary membership in my head that day in the Century Club? for I had never thought of it before. I don't know what brought the thought to me at *that* particular time instead of earlier, but I am well satisfied that it originated with the Board of Directors, and had been on its way to my brain through the air ever since the moment that saw their vote recorded.

Another incident. I was in Hartford two or three days as a guest of the Rev. Joseph H. Twichell. I have held the rank of Honorary Uncle to his children for a quarter of a century, and I went out with him in the trolley-car to visit one of my nieces, who is at Miss Porter's famous school in Farmington. The distance is eight or nine miles. On the way, talking, I illustrated something with an anecdote. This is the anecdote:

Two years and a half ago I and the family arrived at Milan on our way to Rome, and stopped at the Continental. After dinner I went below and took a seat in the stone-paved court, where the customary lemon-trees stand in the customary tubs, and said to myself, " Now *this* is comfort, comfort and repose, and nobody to disturb it; I do not know anybody in Milan."

Then a young gentleman stepped up and shook hands, which damaged my theory. He said, in substance:

" You won't remember me, Mr. Clemens, but I remember you very well. I was a cadet at West Point when you and Rev. Joseph H. Twichell came there some years ago and talked to us on a Hundredth Night. I am a lieutenant in the regular army now, and my name is H. I am in Europe, all alone, for a modest little tour; my regiment is in Arizona."

We became friendly and sociable, and in the course of the talk he told me of an adventure which had befallen him — about to this effect:

" I was at Bellagio, stopping at the big hotel there, and ten days ago I lost my letter of credit. I did not know what in the world to do. I was a stranger; I knew no one in Europe; I hadn't a penny in my pocket; I couldn't even send a telegram to London to get my lost letter replaced; my hotel bill was a week old, and the presentation of it imminent — so imminent that it could happen at

any moment now.   I was so frightened that my wits
seemed to leave me.   I tramped and tramped, back
and forth, like a crazy person.   If anybody ap-
proached me I hurried away, for no matter what a
person looked like, I took him for the head waiter
with the bill.

" I was at last in such a desperate state that I was
ready to do any wild thing that promised even the
shadow of help, and so this is the insane thing that
I did.   I saw a family lunching at a small table on
the veranda, and recognized their nationality —
Americans — father, mother, and several young
daughters — young, tastefully dressed, and pretty
— the rule with our people.   I went straight there
in my civilian costume, named my name, said I was
a lieutenant in the army, and told my story and
asked for help.

" What do you suppose the gentleman did?   But
you would not guess in twenty years.   He took
out a handful of gold coin and told me to help
myself — freely.   That is what he did."

The next morning the lieutenant told me his
new letter of credit had arrived in the night, so we
strolled to Cook's to draw money to pay back the
benefactor with.   We got it, and then went strolling
through the great arcade.   Presently he said, " Yonder they are; come and be introduced."   I was
introduced to the parents and the young ladies;
then we separated, and I never saw him or them any
m —

" Here we are at Farmington," said Twichell, interrupting.

We left the trolley-car and tramped through the mud a hundred yards or so to the school, talking about the time we and Warner walked out there years ago, and the pleasant time we had.

We had a visit with my niece in the parlor, then started for the trolley again. Outside the house we encountered a double rank of twenty or thirty of Miss Porter's young ladies arriving from a walk, and we stood aside, ostensibly to let them have room to file past, but really to look at them. Presently one of them stepped out of the rank and said:

" You don't know me, Mr. Twichell, but I know your daughter, and that gives me the privilege of shaking hands with you."

Then she put out her hand to me, and said:

" And I wish to shake hands with you too, Mr. Clemens. You don't remember me, but you were introduced to me in the arcade in Milan two years and a half ago by Lieutenant H."

What had put that story into my head after all that stretch of time? Was it just the proximity of that young girl, or was it merely an odd accident?

WHAT PAUL BOURGET THINKS OF US

HE reports the American joke correctly. In Boston they ask, How much does he know? in New York, How much is he worth? in Philadelphia, Who were his parents? And when an alien observer turns his telescope upon us — advertisedly in our own special interest — a natural apprehension moves us to ask, What is the diameter of his reflector?

I take a great interest in M. Bourget's chapters, for I know by the newspapers that there are several Americans who are expecting to get a whole education out of them; several who foresaw, and also foretold, that our long night was over, and a light almost divine about to break upon the land.

"His utterances concerning us are bound to be weighty and well timed."

"He gives us an object-lesson which should be thoughtfully and profitably studied."

These well-considered and important verdicts were of a nature to restore public confidence, which had been disquieted by questionings as to whether so young a teacher would be qualified to take so large a class as 70,000,000, distributed over so extensive a schoolhouse as America, and pull it through without assistance.

I was even disquieted myself, although I am of a cold, calm temperament, and not easily disturbed. I feared for my country. And I was not wholly tranquilized by the verdicts rendered as above. It seemed to me that there was still room for doubt. In fact, in looking the ground over I became more disturbed than I was before. Many worrying questions came up in my mind. Two were prominent. Where had the teacher gotten his equipment? What was his method?

He had gotten his equipment in France.

Then as to his method! I saw by his own intimations that he was an Observer, and had a System — that used by naturalists and other scientists. The naturalist collects many bugs and reptiles and butterflies and studies their ways a long time patiently. By this means he is presently able to group these creatures into families and subdivisions of families by nice shadings of differences observable in their characters. Then he labels all those shaded bugs and things with nicely descriptive group names, and is now happy, for his great work is completed, and as a result he intimately knows every bug and shade of a bug there, inside and out. It may be true, but a person who was not a naturalist would feel safer about it if he had the opinion of the bug. I think it is a pleasant System, but subject to error.

The Observer of Peoples has to be a Classifier, a

Grouper, a Deducer, a Generalizer, a Psychologizer; and, first and last, a Thinker. He has to be all these, and when he is at home, observing his own folk, he is often able to prove competency. But history has shown that when he is abroad observing unfamiliar peoples the chances are heavily against him. He is then a naturalist observing a bug, with no more than a naturalist's chance of being able to tell the bug anything new about itself, and no more than a naturalist's chance of being able to teach it any new ways which it will prefer to its own.

To return to that first question. M. Bourget, as teacher, would simply be France teaching America. It seemed to me that the outlook was dark — almost Egyptian, in fact. What would the new teacher, representing France, teach us? Railroading? No. France knows nothing valuable about railroading. Steamshipping? No. France has no superiorities over us in that matter. Steamboating? No. French steamboating is still of Fulton's date — 1809. Postal service? No. France is a back number there. Telegraphy? No, we taught her that ourselves. Journalism? No. Magazining? No, that is our own specialty. Government? No; Liberty, Equality, Fraternity, Nobility, Democracy, Adultery — the system is too variegated for our climate. Religion? No, not variegated enough for our climate. Morals? No, we cannot rob the poor to enrich ourselves. Novel-writing? No. M. Bour-

get and the others know only one plan, and when
that is expurgated there is nothing left of the book.

I wish I could think what he is going to teach us.
Can it be Deportment? But he experimented in that
at Newport and failed to give satisfaction, except to
a few. Those few are pleased. They are enjoying
their joy as well as they can. They confess their
happiness to the interviewer. They feel pretty
striped, but they remember with reverent recognition that they had sugar between the cuts. True,
sugar with sand in it, but sugar. And true, they
had some trouble to tell which was sugar and which
was sand, because the sugar itself looked just like the
sand, and also had a gravelly taste; still, they knew
that the sugar was there, and would have been very
good sugar indeed if it had been screened. Yes,
they are pleased; not noisily so, but pleased; invaded, or streaked, as one may say, with little re-
current shivers of joy — subdued joy, so to speak,
not the overdone kind. And they commune together, these, and massage each other with comfort-
ing sayings, in a sweet spirit of resignation and
thankfulness, mixing these elements in the same
proportions as the sugar and the sand, as a memo-
rial, and saying, the one to the other, and to the
interviewer: " It was severe — yes, it was bitterly
severe; but oh, how true it was; and it will do us
so much good!"

If it isn't Deportment, what is left? It was at
this point that I seemed to get on the right track at

last. M. Bourget would teach us to know ourselves;
that was it: he would reveal us to ourselves. That
would be an education. He would explain us to
ourselves. Then we should understand ourselves;
and after that be able to go on more intelligently.

It seemed a doubtful scheme. He could explain
us to *him*self — that would be easy. That would
be the same as the naturalist explaining the bug to
himself. But to explain the bug to the bug — that
is quite a different matter. The bug may not know
himself perfectly, but he knows himself better than
the naturalist can know him, at any rate.

A foreigner can photograph the exteriors of a
nation, but I think that that is as far as he can get.
I think that no foreigner can report its interior — its
soul, its life, its speech, its thought. I think that a
knowledge of these things is acquirable in only one
way; not two or four or six—*absorption ;* years and
years of unconscious absorption; years and years
of intercourse with the life concerned; of living it,
indeed; sharing personally in its shames and prides,
its joys and griefs, its loves and hates, its prosperities and reverses, its shows and shabbinesses,
its deep patriotisms, its whirlwinds of political passion, its adorations — of flag, and heroic dead, and
the glory of the national name. Observation? Of
what real value is it? One learns peoples through
the heart, not the eyes or the intellect.

There is only one expert who is qualified to examine the souls and the life of a people and make a

10*₊*₊

valuable report — the native novelist. This expert is
so rare that the most populous country can never
have fifteen conspicuously and confessedly competent
ones in stock at one time. This native specialist is
not qualified to begin work until he has been absorb-
ing during twenty-five years. How much of his
competency is derived from conscious "observation"? The amount is so slight that it counts for
next to nothing in the equipment. Almost the
whole capital of the novelist is the slow accumula-
tion of *un*conscious observation — absorption. The
native expert's intentional observation of manners,
speech, character, and ways of life can have value,
for the native knows what they mean without having
to cipher out the meaning. But I should be astonished to see a foreigner get at the right meanings,
catch the elusive shades of these subtle things.
Even the native novelist becomes a foreigner, with a
foreigner's limitations, when he steps from the State
whose life is familiar to him into a State whose life
he has not lived. Bret Harte got his California and
his Californians by unconscious absorption, and put
both of them into his tales alive. But when he
came from the Pacific to the Atlantic and tried to
do Newport life from study — conscious observation — his failure was absolutely monumental.
Newport is a disastrous place for the unacclimated
observer, evidently.

To return to novel-building. Does the native
novelist try to generalize the nation? No, he lays

plainly before you the ways and speech and life of a few people grouped in a certain place — his own place — and that is one book. In time he and his brethren will report to you the life and the people of the whole nation — the life of a group in a New England village; in a New York village; in a Texan village; in an Oregon village; in villages in fifty States and Territories; then the farm-life in fifty States and Territories; a hundred patches of life and groups of people in a dozen widely separated cities. And the Indians will be attended to; and the cowboys; and the gold and silver miners; and the negroes; and the Idiots and Congressmen; and the Irish, the Germans, the Italians, the Swedes, the French, the Chinamen, the Greasers; and the Catholics, the Methodists, the Presbyterians, the Congregationalists, the Baptists, the Spiritualists, the Mormons, the Shakers, the Quakers, the Jews, the Campbellites, the infidels, the Christian Scientists, the Mind-Curists, the Faith-Curists, the train-robbers, the White Caps, the Moonshiners. And when a thousand able novels have been written, *there* you have the soul of the people, the life of the people, the speech of the people; and not anywhere else can these be had. And the shadings of character, manners, feelings, ambitions, will be infinite.

" *The nature of a people* is always of a similar shade in its vices and its virtues, in its frivolities and in its labor. *It is this physiognomy which it is necessary to discover*, and every document is good, from the

J*₊*₊

hall of a casino to the church, from the foibles of a fashionable woman to the suggestions of a revolutionary leader. I am therefore quite sure that this *American soul*, the principal interest and the great object of my voyage, appears behind the records of Newport for those who choose to see it." — *M. Paul Bourget.*

[The italics are mine.] It is a large contract which he has undertaken. "Records" is a pretty poor word there, but I think the use of it is due to hasty translation. In the original the word is *fastes*. I think M. Bourget meant to suggest that he expected to find the great "American soul" secreted behind the *ostentations* of Newport; and that he was going to get it out and examine it, and generalize it, and psychologize it, and make it reveal to him its hidden vast mystery: "the nature of the people" of the United States of America. We have been accused of being a nation addicted to inventing wild schemes. I trust that we shall be allowed to retire to second place now.

There isn't a single human characteristic that can be safely labeled "American." There isn't a single human ambition, or religious trend, or drift of thought, or peculiarity of education, or code of principles, or breed of folly, or style of conversation, or preference for a particular subject for discussion, or form of legs or trunk or head or face or expression or complexion, or gait, or dress, or manners, or disposition, or any other human detail, inside or outside, that can rationally be generalized as "American."

Whenever you have found what seems to be an

" American " peculiarity, you have only to cross a frontier or two, or go down or up in the social scale, and you perceive that it has disappeared.   And you can cross the Atlantic and find it again.   There may be a Newport religious drift, or sporting drift, or conversational style or complexion, or cut of face, but there are entire empires in America, north, south, east, and west, where you could not find your duplicates.   It is the same with everything else which one might propose to call " American." M. Bourget thinks he has found the American Coquette.   If he had really found her he would also have found, I am sure, that she was not new, that she exists in other lands in the same forms, and with the same frivolous heart and the same ways and impulses.   I think this because I have seen our coquette; I have seen her in life; better still, I have seen her in our novels, and seen her twin in foreign novels.   I wish M. Bourget had seen ours.   He thought he saw her.   And so he applied his System to her.   She was a Species.   So he gathered a number of samples of what seemed to be her, and put them under his glass, and divided them into groups which he calls " types," and labeled them in his usual scientific way with " formulas " — brief sharp descriptive flashes that make a person blink, sometimes, they are so sudden and vivid.   As a rule they are pretty far-fetched, but that is not an important matter; they surprise, they compel admiration, and I notice by some of the comments

which his efforts have called forth that they deceive
the unwary.   Here are a few of the coquette variants
which he has grouped and labeled:

THE COLLECTOR.

THE EQUILIBREE.

THE PROFESSIONAL BEAUTY.

THE BLUFFER.

THE GIRL-BOY.

If he had stopped with describing these characters
we should have been obliged to believe that they
exist; that they exist, and that he has seen them and
spoken with them.   But he did not stop there; he
went further and furnished to us light-throwing
samples of their behavior, and also light-throwing
samples of their speeches.   He entered those things
in his note-book without suspicion, he takes them
out and delivers them to the world with a candor
and simplicity which show that he believed them
genuine.   They throw altogether too much light.
They reveal to the native the origin of his find.   I
suppose he knows how he came to make that novel
and captivating discovery, by this time.   If he
does not, any American can tell him — any American to whom he will show his anecdotes.   It was
"put up" on him, as we say.   It was a jest — to
be plain, it was a series of frauds.   To my mind it
was a poor sort of jest, witless and contemptible.
The players of it have their reward, such as it is;
they have exhibited the fact that whatever they may
be they are not ladies.   M. Bourget did not discover

a type of coquette; he merely discovered a type of practical joker. One may say *the* type of practical joker, for these people are exactly alike all over the world. Their equipment is always the same: a vulgar mind, a puerile wit, a cruel disposition as a rule, and always the spirit of treachery.

In his Chapter IV. M. Bourget has two or three columns gravely devoted to the collating and examining and psychologizing of these sorry little frauds. One is not moved to laugh. There is nothing funny in the situation; it is only pathetic. The stranger gave those people his confidence, and they dishonorably treated him in return.

But one must be allowed to suspect that M. Bourget was a little to blame himself. Even a practical joker has some little judgment. He has to exercise some degree of sagacity in selecting his prey if he would save himself from getting into trouble. In my time I have seldom seen such daring things marketed at any price as these conscienceless folk have worked off at par on this confiding observer. It compels the conviction that there was something about him that bred in those speculators a quite unusual sense of safety, and encouraged them to strain their powers in his behalf. They seem to have satisfied themselves that all he wanted was "significant" facts, and that he was not accustomed to examine the source whence they proceeded. It is plain that there was a sort of conspiracy against him almost from the start — a conspiracy to freight him up with all the strange extravagances those people's decayed brains could invent.

The lengths to which they went are next to incredible. They told him things which surely would have excited any one else's suspicion, but they did not excite his. Consider this:

" There is not in all the United States an entirely nude statue."

If an angel should come down and say such a thing about heaven, a reasonably cautious observer would take that angel's number and inquire a little further before he added it to his catch. What does the present observer do? Adds it. Adds it at once. Adds it, and labels it with this innocent comment:

"This small fact is strangely significant."

It does seem to me that this kind of observing is defective.

Here is another curiosity which some liberal person made him a present of. I should think it ought to have disturbed the deep slumber of his suspicion a little, but it didn't. It was a note from a fog-horn for strenuousness, it seems to me, but the doomed voyager did not catch it. If he had but caught it, it would have saved him from several disasters:

"If the American knows that you are traveling to take notes, he is interested in it, and at the same time rejoices in it, as in a tribute."

Again, this is defective observation. It is human to like to be praised; one can even notice it in the

French.   But it is not human to like to be ridiculed,
even when it comes in the form of a " tribute."   I
think a little psychologizing ought to have come in
there.   Something like this: A dog does not like to
be ridiculed, a redskin does not like to be ridiculed,
a negro does not like to be ridiculed, a Chinaman
does not like to be ridiculed; let us deduce from
these significant facts this formula : the American's
grade being higher than these, and the chain of
argument stretching unbroken all the way up to him,
there is room for suspicion that the person who said
the American likes to be ridiculed, and regards it as
a tribute, is not a capable observer.

I feel persuaded that in the matter of psychologizing, a professional is too apt to yield to the fascinations of the loftier regions of that great art, to the
neglect of its lowlier walks.   Every now and then,
at half-hour intervals, M. Bourget collects a hatful
of airy inaccuracies and dissolves them in a panful
of assorted abstractions, and runs the charge into
a mould and turns you out a compact principle
which will explain an American girl, or an American woman, or why new people yearn for old
things, or any other impossible riddle which a person wants answered.

It seems to be conceded that there are a few
human peculiarities that can be generalized and
located here and there in the world and named by
the name of the nation where they are found.   I
wonder what they are.   Perhaps one of them is

temperament. One speaks of French vivacity and
German gravity and English stubbornness. There
is no American temperament. The nearest that one
can come at it is to say there are two — the composed Northern and the impetuous Southern; and
both are found in other countries. Morals? Purity
of women may fairly be called universal with us,
but that is the case in some other countries. We
have no monopoly of it; it cannot be named American. I think that there is but a single specialty with
us, only one thing that can be called by the wide
name "American." That is the national devotion
to ice-water. All Germans drink beer, but the
British nation drinks beer, too; so neither of those
peoples is *the* beer-drinking nation. I suppose we
do stand alone in having a drink that nobody likes
but ourselves. When we have been a month in
Europe we lose our craving for it, and we finally
tell the hotel folk that they needn't provide it any
more. Yet we hardly touch our native shore again,
winter or summer, before we are eager for it. The
reasons for this state of things have not been
psychologized yet. I drop the hint and say no
more.

It is my belief that there are some "national"
traits and things scattered about the world that are
mere superstitions, frauds that have lived so long
that they have the solid look of facts. One of them
is the dogma that the French are the only chaste
people in the world. Ever since I arrived in France

this last time I have been accumulating doubts about that; and before I leave this sunny land again I will gather in a few random statistics and psychologize the plausibilities out of it. If people are to come over to America and find fault with our girls and our women, and psychologize every little thing they do, and try to teach them how to behave, and how to cultivate themselves up to where one cannot tell them from the French model, I intend to find out whether those missionaries are qualified or not. A nation ought always to examine into this detail before engaging the teacher for good. This last one has let fall a remark which renewed those doubts of mine when I read it:

"In our high Parisian existence, for instance, we find applied to arts and luxury, and to debauchery, all the powers and all the weaknesses of the French soul."

You see, it amounts to a trade with the French soul; a profession; a science; the serious business of life, so to speak, in our high Parisian existence. I do not quite like the look of it. I question if it can be taught with profit in our country, except, of course, to those pathetic, neglected minds that are waiting there so yearningly for the education which M. Bourget is going to furnish them from the serene summits of our high Parisian life.

I spoke a moment ago of the existence of some superstitions that have been parading the world as facts this long time. For instance, consider the Dollar. The world seems to think that the love of money is " American "; and that the mad desire to get suddenly rich is " American." I believe that both of these things are merely and broadly human, not American monopolies at all. The love of money is natural to all nations, for money is a good and strong friend. I think that this love has existed everywhere, ever since the Bible called it the root of all evil.

I think that the reason why we Americans seem to be so addicted to trying to get rich suddenly is merely because the *opportunity* to make promising efforts in that direction has offered itself to us with a frequency out of all proportion to the European experience. For eighty years this opportunity has been offering itself in one new town or region after another straight westward, step by step, all the way from the Atlantic coast to the Pacific. When a mechanic could buy ten town lots on tolerably long credit for ten months' savings out of his wages, and reasonably expect to sell them in a couple of years for ten times what he gave for them, it was human for him to try the venture, and he did it no matter what his nationality was. He would have done it in Europe or China if he had had the same chance.

In the flush times in the silver regions a cook or any other humble worker stood a very good chance to get rich out of a trifle of money risked in a stock deal; and that person promptly took that risk, no matter what his or her nationality might be. I was there, and saw it.

But these opportunities have not been plenty in our Southern States; so there you have a prodigious region where the rush for sudden wealth is almost an unknown thing — and has been, from the beginning.

Europe has offered few opportunities for poor Tom, Dick, and Harry; but when she has offered one, there has been no noticeable difference between European eagerness and American. England saw this in the wild days of the Railroad King; France saw it in 1720 — time of Law and the Mississippi Bubble. I am sure I have never seen in the gold and silver mines any madness, fury, frenzy to get suddenly rich which was even remotely comparable to that which raged in France in the Bubble day. If I had a cyclopædia here I could turn to that memorable case, and satisfy nearly anybody that the hunger for the sudden dollar is no more " American " than it is French. And if I could furnish an American opportunity to staid Germany, I think I could wake her up like a house afire.

But I must return to the Generalizations, Psychologizings, Deductions. When M. Bourget is exploiting these arts, it is then that he is peculiarly and particularly himself. His ways are wholly original when he encounters a trait or a custom which is new to him. Another person would merely examine the find, verify it, estimate its value, and let it go; but that is not sufficient for M. Bourget: he always wants to know *why* that thing exists, he wants to know how it came to happen; and he will not let go

11E

of it until he has found out.   And in every instance
he will find that reason where no one but himself
would have thought of looking for it.   He does not
seem to care for a reason that is not picturesquely
located; one might almost say picturesquely and
impossibly located.

He found out that in America men do not try to
hunt down young married women.   At once, as
usual, he wanted to know *why*.   Any one could
have told him.   He could have divined it by the
lights thrown by the novels of the country.   But
no, he preferred to find out for himself.   He has a
trustfulness as regards men and facts which is fine
and unusual; he is not particular about the source
of a fact, he is not particular about the character
and standing of the fact itself; but when it comes to
pounding out the reason for the existence of the
fact, he will trust no one but himself.

In the present instance here was his fact: American young married women are not pursued by the
corruptor; and here was the question: What is it
that protects her?

It seems quite unlikely that that problem could
have offered difficulties to any but a trained philosopher.   Nearly any person would have said to M.
Bourget: "Oh, that is very simple.   It is very
seldom in America that a marriage is made on a
commercial basis; our marriages, from the beginning, have been made for love; and where love is
there is no room for the corruptor."

Now, it is interesting to see the formidable way in which M. Bourget went at that poor, humble little thing. He moved upon it in column — three columns — and with artillery.

" Two reasons of a very different kind explain " — that fact.

And now that I have got so far, I am almost afraid to say what his two reasons are, lest I be charged with inventing them. But I will not retreat now; I will condense them and print them, giving my word that I am honest and not trying to deceive any one.

1. Young married women are protected from the approaches of the seducer in New England and vicinity by the diluted remains of a prudence created by a Puritan law of two hundred years ago, which for a while punished adultery with death.

2. And young married women of the other forty or fifty States are protected by laws which afford extraordinary facilities for divorce.

If I have not lost my mind I have accurately conveyed those two Vesuvian irruptions of philosophy. But the reader can consult Chapter IV. of *Outre-Mer*, and decide for himself. Let us examine this paralyzing Deduction or Explanation by the light of a few sane facts.

1. This universality of " protection " has existed in our country *from the beginning;* before the death penalty existed in New England, and during all the generations that have dragged by since it was annulled.

2. Extraordinary facilities for divorce are of such recent creation that any middle-aged American can remember a time when such things had not yet been thought of.

Let us suppose that the first easy divorce law went into effect forty years ago, and got noised around and fairly started in business thirty-five years ago, when we had, say, 25,000,000 of white population. Let us suppose that among 5,000,000 of them the young married women were " protected " by the surviving shudder of that ancient Puritan scare — what is M. Bourget going to do about those who lived among the 20,000,000?   They were clean in their morals, they were pure, yet there was no easy divorce law to protect them.

Awhile ago I said that M. Bourget's method of truth-seeking — hunting for it in out-of-the-way places — was new; but that was an error. I remember that when Leverrier discovered the Milky Way, he and the other astronomers began to theorize about it in substantially the same fashion which M. Bourget employs in his reasonings about American social facts and their origin. Leverrier advanced the hypothesis that the Milky Way was caused by gaseous protoplasmic emanations from the field of Waterloo, which, ascending to an altitude determinable by their own specific gravity, became luminous through the development and exposure — by the natural processes of animal decay — of the phosphorus contained in them.

This theory was warmly complimented by Ptolemy, who, however, after much thought and research, decided that he could not accept it as final. His own theory was that the Milky Way was an emigration of lightning bugs; and he supported and reinforced this theorem by the well-known fact that the locusts do like that in Egypt.

Giordano Bruno also was outspoken in his praises of Leverrier's important contribution to astronomical science, and was at first inclined to regard it as conclusive; but later, conceiving it to be erroneous, he pronounced against it, and advanced the hypothesis that the Milky Way was a detachment or corps of stars which became arrested and held in *suspenso suspensorum* by refraction of gravitation while on the march to join their several constellations; a proposition for which he was afterwards burned at the stake in Jacksonville, Illinois.

These were all brilliant and picturesque theories, and each was received with enthusiasm by the scientific world; but when a New England farmer, who was not a thinker, but only a plain sort of person who tried to account for large facts in simple ways, came out with the opinion that the Milky Way was just common, ordinary stars, and was put where it was because God "wanted to hev it so," the admirable idea fell perfectly flat.

As a literary artist, M. Bourget is as fresh and striking as he is as a scientific one. He says, " Above all, I do not believe much in anecdotes."

11*_**

Why? "In history they are all false"—a sufficiently broad statement—"in literature all libelous"—also a sufficiently sweeping statement, coming from a critic who notes that we are a people who are peculiarly extravagant in our language—"and when it is a matter of social life, almost all biased." It seems to amount to stultification, almost. He has built two or three breeds of American coquettes out of anecdotes—mainly "biased" ones, I suppose; and, as they occur "in literature," furnished by his pen, they must be "all libelous." Or did he mean not *in* literature or anecdotes *about* literature or literary people? I am not able to answer that. Perhaps the original would be clearer, but I have only the translation of this installment by me. I think the remark had an intention; also that this intention was booked for the trip; but that either in the hurry of the remark's departure it got left, or in the confusion of changing cars at the translator's frontier it got side-tracked.

"But on the other hand I believe in statistics; and those on divorces appear to me to be most conclusive." And he sets himself the task of explaining—in a couple of columns—the process by which Easy-Divorce conceived, invented, originated, developed, and perfected an empire-embracing condition of sexual purity in the States. *In 40 years*. No, he doesn't state the interval. With all his passion for statistics he forgot to ask how long it took to produce this gigantic miracle.

I have followed his pleasant but devious trail through those columns, but I was not able to get hold of his argument and find out what it was. I was not even able to find out where it left off. It seemed to gradually dissolve and flow off into other matters. I followed it with interest, for I was anxious to learn how easy-divorce eradicated adultery in America, but I was disappointed; I have no idea yet how it did it. I only know it didn't. But that is not valuable; I knew it before.

Well, humor is the great thing, the saving thing, after all. The minute it crops up, all our hardnesses yield, all our irritations and resentments flit away, and a sunny spirit takes their place. And so, when M. Bourget said that bright thing about our grandfathers, I broke all up. I remember exploding its American countermine once, under that grand hero, Napoleon. He was only First Consul then, and I was Consul-General — for the United States, of course; but we were very intimate, notwithstanding the difference in rank, for I waived that. One day something offered the opening, and he said:

" Well, General, I suppose life can never get entirely dull to an American, because whenever he can't strike up any other way to put in his time he can always get away with a few years trying to find out who his grandfather was!"

I fairly shouted, for I had never heard it sound better; and then I was back at him as quick as a flash:

K*.*.*

"Right, your Excellency! But I reckon a Frenchman's got *his* little stand-by for a dull time, too; because when all other interests fail he can turn in and see if he can't find out who his father was!"

Well, you should have heard him just whoop, and cackle, and carry on! He reached up and hit me one on the shoulder, and says:

"Land, but it's good! It's im-mensely good! I'George, I never heard it said so good in my life before! Say it again."

So I said it again, and he said his again, and I said mine again, and then he did, and then I did, and then he did, and we kept on doing it, and doing it, and I *never* had such a good time, and he said the same. In my opinion there isn't anything that is as killing as one of those dear old ripe pensioners if you know how to snatch it out in a kind of a fresh sort of original way.

But I wish M. Bourget had read more of our novels before he came. It is the only way to thoroughly understand a people. When I found I was coming to Paris, I read *La Terre*.

A LITTLE NOTE TO M. PAUL BOURGET

[The preceding squib was assailed in the *North American Review* in an article entitled "Mark Twain and Paul Bourget," by Max O'Rell. The following little note is a Rejoinder to that article. It is possible that the position assumed here — that M. Bourget dictated the O'Rell article himself — is untenable.]

YOU have every right, my dear M. Bourget, to retort upon me by dictation, if you prefer that method to writing at me with your pen; but if I may say it without hurt — and certainly I mean no offence — I believe you would have acquitted yourself better with the pen. With the pen you are at home; it is your natural weapon; you use it with grace, eloquence, charm, persuasiveness, when men are to be convinced, and with formidable effect when they have earned a castigation. But I am sure I see signs in the above article that you are either unaccustomed to dictating or are out of practice. If you will re-read it you will notice, yourself, that it lacks definiteness; that it lacks purpose; that it lacks coherence; that it lacks a subject to talk about; that it is loose and wabbly; that it wanders around; that it loses itself early and does not find itself any more. There are some other defects, as you will notice, but I think I have named the main ones.   I feel sure that they are all due to your lack of practice in dictating.

Inasmuch as you had not signed it I had the impression at first that you had not dictated it.   But only for a moment.   Certain quite simple and definite facts reminded me that the article *had* to come from you, for the reason that it could not come from any one else without a specific invitation from you or from me.   I mean, it could not except as an intrusion, a transgression of the law which forbids strangers to mix into a private dispute between friends, unasked.

Those simple and definite facts were these : I had published an article in this magazine, with you for my subject; just you yourself; I stuck strictly to that one subject, and did not interlard any other. No one, of course, could call me to account but you alone, or your authorized representative.   I asked some questions — asked them of myself.   I answered them myself.   My article was thirteen pages long, and all devoted to you ; devoted to you, and divided up in this way : one page of guesses as to what subjects you would instruct us in, as teacher ; one page of doubts as to the effectiveness of your method of examining us and our ways ; two or three pages of criticism of your method, and of certain results which it furnished you ; two or three pages of attempts to show the justness of these same criticisms ; half a dozen pages made up of slight fault-findings with certain minor details of your literary workmanship, of extracts from your *Outre-Mer* and comments upon them; then I closed with an anecdote. I repeat — for certain reasons — that *I closed with an anecdote*.

When I was asked by this magazine if I wished to " answer " a " reply " to that article of mine, I said " yes," and waited in Paris for the proof-sheets of the " reply " to come. I already knew, by the cablegram, that the " reply " would not be signed by you, but upon reflection I knew it would be dictated by you, because no volunteer would feel himself at liberty to assume your championship in a private dispute, unasked, in view of the fact that you are quite well able to take care of your matters of that sort yourself and are not in need of any one's help. No, a volunteer could not make such a venture. It would be too immodest. Also too gratuitously generous. And a shade too self-sufficient. No, he could not venture it. It would look too much like anxiety to get in at a feast where no plate had been provided for him. In fact he could not get in at all, except by the back way, and with a false key; that is to say, a pretext — a pretext invented for the occasion by putting into my mouth words which I did not use, and by wresting sayings of mine from their plain and true meaning. Would he resort to methods like those to get in? No; there are no people of that kind. So then I knew for a certainty that you dictated the

Reply yourself.   I knew you did it to save yourself manual labor.

And you had the right, as I have already said; and I am content — perfectly content. Yet it would have been little trouble to you, and a great kindness to me, if you had written your Reply all out with your own capable hand.

Because then it would have replied — and that is really what a Reply is for. Broadly speaking, its function is to refute — as you will easily concede. That leaves something for the other person to take hold of : he has a chance to reply to the Reply, he has a chance to refute the refutation. This would have happened if you had written it out instead of dictating. Dictating is nearly sure to unconcentrate the dictator's mind, when he is out of practice, confuse him, and betray him into using one set of literary rules when he ought to use a quite different set. Often it betrays him into employing the RULES FOR CONVERSATION BETWEEN A SHOUTER AND A DEAF PERSON — as in the present case — when he ought to employ the RULES FOR CONDUCTING DISCUSSION WITH A FAULT-FINDER. The great foundation-rule and basic principle of discussion with a fault-finder is relevancy and concentration upon the subject; whereas the great foundation-rule and basic principle governing conversation between a shouter and a deaf person is irrelevancy and persistent desertion of the topic in hand. If I may be allowed to illustrate by quoting example IV., section 7, from chapter ix. of " Revised Rules for Conducting Conversation between a Shouter and a Deaf Person," it will assist us in getting a clear idea of the difference between the two sets of rules:

Shouter. Did you say his name is WETHERBY?

Deaf Person. Change? Yes, I think it will. Though if it should clear off I —

Shouter. It's his NAME I want — his NAME.

Deaf Person. Maybe so, maybe so; but it will only be a shower, I think.

Shouter. No, no, *no!* — you have quite misunderSTOOD me. If —

Deaf Person. Ah! GOOD morning; I am sorry you must go. But call again, and let me continue to be of assistance to you in every way I can.

You see it is a perfect kodak of the article you have dictated. It is really curious and interesting when you come to compare it with yours; in detail, with my former article to which it is a Reply in your hand. I talk twelve pages about your American instruction projects, and your doubtful scientific system, and your painstaking classification of non-existent things, and your diligence and zeal and sincerity, and your disloyal attitude towards anecdotes, and your undue reverence for unsafe statistics and for facts that lack a pedigree; and you turn around and come back at me with eight pages of weather.

I do not see how a person can act so. It is good of you to repeat, with change of language, in the bulk of your rejoinder, so much of my own article, and adopt my sentiments, and make them over, and put new buttons on; and I like the compliment, and am frank to say so; but *agreeing* with a person cripples controversy and ought not to be allowed. It is weather; and of almost the worst sort. It pleases me greatly to hear you discourse with such approval and expansiveness upon my text:

" A foreigner can photograph the exteriors of a nation, but I think that is as far as he can get. I think that no foreigner can report its interior;"* which is a quite clear way of saying that a foreigner's report is only valuable when it restricts itself to *impressions*. It pleases me to have you follow my lead in that glowing way, but it leaves me nothing to combat. You should give me something to deny and refute; I would do as much for you.

It pleases me to have you playfully warn the public against taking one of your books seriously.† Because I used to do that cunning thing myself in earlier days. I did it in a prefatory note to a book of mine called *Tom Sawyer*.

---

* And you say: "A man of average intelligence, who has passed six months among a people, cannot express opinions that are worth jotting down, but he can form impressions that are worth repeating. For my part, I think that foreigners' impressions are more interesting than native opinions. After all, such impressions merely mean 'how the country *struck* the foreigner.' "

† When I published *Jonathan and his Continent*, I wrote in a preface addressed to Jonathan: " If ever you should insist in seeing in this little volume a serious study of your country and of your countrymen, I warn you that your world-wide fame for humor will be exploded."

NOTICE.

Persons attempting to find a motive in this narrative will be prosecuted; persons attempting to find a moral in it will be banished; persons attempting to find a plot in it will be shot.

BY ORDER OF THE AUTHOR
PER G. G., CHIEF OF ORDNANCE.

The kernel is the same in both prefaces, you see — the public must not take us too seriously. If we remove that kernel we remove the life-principle, and the preface is a corpse. Yes, it pleases me to have you use that idea, for it is a high compliment. But is leaves me nothing to combat; and that is damage to me.

Am I seeming to say that your Reply is not a reply at all, M. Bourget? If so, I must modify that; it is too sweeping. For you have furnished a general answer to my inquiry as to what France — through you — can teach us.* It is a good answer.

---

* "What could France teach America?" exclaims Mark Twain. France can teach America all the higher pursuits of life, and there is more artistic feeling and refinement in a street of French workingmen than in many avenues inhabited by American millionaires. She can teach her, not perhaps how to work, but how to rest, how to live, how to be happy. She can teach her that the aim of life is not money-making, but that money-making is only a means to obtain an end. She can teach her that wives are not expensive toys, but useful partners, friends, and confidants, who should always keep men under their wholesome influence by their diplomacy, their tact, their common-sense, without bumptiousness. These qualities, added to the highest standard of morality (not angular and morose, but cheerful morality), are conceded to Frenchwomen by whoever knows something of French life outside of the Paris boulevards, and Mark Twain's ill-natured sneer cannot even so much as stain them.

I might tell Mark Twain that in France a man who was seen tipsy in

It relates to manners, customs, and morals — three things concerning which we can never have exhaustive and determinate statistics, and so the verdicts delivered upon them must always lack conclusiveness and be subject to revision; but you have stated the truth, possibly, as nearly as any one could do it, in the circumstances.   But why did you choose a detail of my question which could be answered only with vague hearsay evidence, and go right by one which could have been answered with deadly facts? — facts in everybody's reach, facts which none can dispute.   I asked what France could teach us about government.   I laid myself pretty wide open, there; and I thought I was handsomely generous, too, when I did it.   France can teach us how to levy village and city taxes which distribute the burden with a nearer approach to perfect fairness than is the case in any other land; and she can teach us the wisest and surest system of collecting them that exists.   She can teach us how to elect a President in a sane way; and also how to do it without throwing the country into earthquakes and convulsions that cripple and embarrass business, stir up party hatred in the hearts of men, and make

his club would immediately see his name canceled from membership.   A man who had settled his fortune on his wife to avoid meeting his creditors would be refused admission into any decent society.   Many a Frenchman has blown his brains out rather than declare himself a bankrupt.   Now would Mark Twain remark to this: "An American is not such a fool: when a creditor stands in his way he closes his doors, and reopens them the following day.   When he has been a bankrupt three times he can retire from business?"

peaceful people wish the term extended to thirty years. France can teach us — but enough of that part of the question. And what else can France teach us? She can teach us all the fine arts — and does. She throws open her hospitable art academies, and says to us, " Come " — and we come, troops and troops of our young and gifted; and she sets over us the ablest masters in the world and bearing the greatest names; and she teaches us all that we are capable of learning, and persuades us and encourages us with prizes and honors, much as if we were somehow children of her own; and when this noble education is finished and we are ready to carry it home and spread its gracious ministries abroad over our nation, and we come with homage and gratitude and ask France for the bill — *there is nothing to pay*. And in return for this imperial generosity, what does America do? She charges a duty on French works of art!

I wish I had your end of this dispute; I should have something worth talking about. If you would only furnish me something to argue, something to refute — but you persistently won't. You leave good chances unutilized and spend your strength in proving and establishing unimportant things. For instance, you have proven and established these eight facts here following — a good score as to number, but not worth while:

Mark Twain is —

1. " Insulting."

12E

2. (Sarcastically speaking) " This refined humor-ist."

3. Prefers the manure-pile to the violets.

4. Has uttered " an ill-natured sneer."

5. Is " nasty."

6. Needs a " lesson in politeness and good man-ners."

7. Has published a " nasty article."

8. Has made remarks " unworthy of a gentle-man."*   These are all true, but really they are not valuable; no one cares much for such finds.   In our American magazines we recognize this and sup-press them.   We avoid naming them.   American writers never allow themselves to name them.   It would look as if they were in a temper, and we hold that exhibitions of temper in public are not good form — except in the very young and inexperienced. And even if we had the disposition to name them,

---

* " It is more funny than his " (Mark Twain's) " anecdote, and would have been less insulting."

A quoted remark of mine " is a gross insult to a nation friendly to America."

" He has read *La Terre*, this refined humorist."

" When Mark Twain visits a garden . . . he goes in the far-away corner where the soil is prepared."

" Mark Twain's ill-natured sneer cannot so much as stain them " (the Frenchwomen).

" When he " (Mark Twain) " takes his revenge he is unkind, un-fair, bitter, nasty."

" But not even your nasty article on my country, Mark," etc.

" Mark might certainly have derived from it " (M. Bourget's book) " a lesson in politeness and good manners."

A quoted remark of mine is " unworthy of a gentleman."

in order to fill up a gap when we were short of ideas and arguments, our magazines would not allow us to do it, because they think that such words sully their pages. This present magazine is particularly strenuous about it. Its note to me announcing the forwarding of your proof-sheets to France closed thus — for your protection:

"*It is needless to ask you to avoid anything that he might consider as personal.*"

It was well enough, as a measure of precaution, but really it was not needed. You can trust me implicitly, M. Bourget; I shall never call you any names in print which I should be ashamed to call you with your unoffending and dearest ones present.

Indeed, we are reserved, and particular in America to a degree which you would consider exaggerated. For instance, we should not write notes like that one of yours to a lady for a small fault — or a large one.* We should not think it kind. No matter

---

* When M. Paul Bourget indulges in a little chaffing at the expense of the Americans, "who can always get away with a few years' trying to find out who their grandfathers were," he merely makes an allusion to an American foible; but, forsooth, what a kind man, what a humorist Mark Twain is when he retorts by calling France a nation of bastards! How the Americans of culture and refinement will admire him for thus speaking in their name!

Snobbery. . . . I could give Mark Twain an example of the American specimen. It is a piquant story. I never published it because I feared my readers might think that I was giving them a typical illustration of American character instead of a rare exception.

I was once booked by my manager to give a *causerie* in the drawing-room of a New York millionaire. I accepted with reluctance. I do

how much we might have associated with kings and
nobilities, we should not think it right to crush her
with it and make her ashamed of her lowlier walk in
life; for we have a saying, "Who humiliates my
mother includes his own."

Do I seriously imagine you to be the author of
that strange letter, M. Bourget? Indeed I do not.
I believe it to have been surreptitiously inserted by
your amanuensis when your back was turned. I
think he did it with a good motive, expecting it to

---

not like private engagements. At five o'clock on the day the *causerie*
was to be given, the lady sent to my manager to say that she would
expect me to arrive at nine o'clock and to speak for about an hour.
Then she wrote a postscript. Many women are unfortunate there.
Their minds are full of after-thoughts, and the most important part of
their letters is generally to be found after their signature. This lady's
P. S. ran thus: "I suppose he will not expect to be entertained after
the lecture."

I fairly shouted, as Mark Twain would say, and then, indulging
myself in a bit of snobbishness, I was back at her as quick as a flash —

"Dear Madam: As a literary man of some reputation, I have many
times had the pleasure of being entertained by the members of the old
aristocracy of France. I have also many times had the pleasure of
being entertained by the members of the old aristocracy of England.
If it may interest you, I can even tell you that I have several times had
the honor of being entertained by royalty; but my ambition has never
been so wild as to expect that one day I might be entertained by the
aristocracy of New York. No, I do not expect to be entertained by
you, nor do I want you to expect me to entertain you and your friends
to-night, for I decline to keep the engagement."

Now, I could fill a book on America with reminiscences of this sort,
adding a few chapters on bosses and boodlers, on New York *chronique
scandaleuse*, on the tenement houses of the large cities, on the gambling-
hells of Denver, and the dens of San Francisco, and what not! But
not even your nasty article on my country, Mark, will make me do it.

add force and piquancy to your article, but it does not reflect your nature, and I know it will grieve you when you see it. I also think he interlarded many other things which you will disapprove of when you see them. I am certain that all the harsh names discharged at me come from him, not you. No doubt you could have proved me entitled to them with as little trouble as it has cost him to do it, but it would have been your disposition to hunt game of a higher quality.

Why, I even doubt if it is you who furnish me all that excellent information about Balzac and those others.* All this in simple justice to you — and to me; for, to gravely accept those interlardings as yours would be to wrong your head and heart, and at the same time convict myself of being equipped

---

* " Now the style of M. Bourget and many other French writers is apparently a closed letter to Mark Twain; but let us leave that alone. Has he read Erckmann-Chatrian, Victor Hugo, Lamartine, Edmond About, Cherbuliez, Renan? Has he read Gustave Droz's *Monsieur, Madame, et Bébé,* and those books which leave for a long time a perfume about you? Has he read the novels of Alexandre Dumas, Eugène Sue, George Sand, and Balzac? Has he read Victor Hugo's *Les Misérables* and *Notre Dame de Paris?* Has he read or heard the plays of Sandeau, Augier, Dumas, and Sardou, the works of those Titans of modern literature, whose names will be household words all over the world for hundreds of years to come? He has read *La Terre* — this kind-hearted, refined humorist! When Mark Twain visits a garden does he smell the violets, the roses, the jasmine, or the honeysuckle? No, he goes in the far-away corner where the soil is prepared. Hear what he says: "I wish M. Paul Bourget had read more of our novels before he came. It is the only way to thoroughly understand a people. When I found I was coming to Paris I read *La Terre.*"

12*₊*₊

with a vacancy where my penetration ought to be lodged.

And now finally I must uncover the secret pain, the wee sore from which the Reply grew —*the anecdote which closed my recent article*— and consider how it is that this pimple has spread to these cancerous dimensions.   If any but you had dictated the Reply, M. Bourget, I would know that that anecdote was twisted around and its intention magnified some hundreds of times, in order that it might be used as a pretext to creep in the back way.   But I accuse you of nothing — nothing but error.   When you say that I '' retort by calling France a nation of bastards,'' it is an error.   And not a small one, but a large one.   I made no such remark, nor anything resembling it.   Moreover, the magazine would not have allowed me to use so gross a word as that.

You told an anecdote.   A funny one—I admit that.   It hit a foible of our American aristocracy, and it stung me — I admit that; it stung me sharply.   It was like this: You found some ancient portraits of French kings in the gallery of one of our aristocracy, and you said:

'' He has the Grand Monarch, but *where is the portrait of his grandfather?*''   That is, the American aristocrat's grandfather.

Now that hits only a few of us, I grant — just the upper crust only — but it hits exceedingly hard.

I wondered if there was any way of getting back at you.   In one of your chapters I found this chance:

" In our high Parisian existence, for instance, we find applied to arts and luxury, and to debauchery, all the powers and all the weaknesses of the French soul."

You see? Your " higher Parisian " class — not everybody, not the nation, but only the *top crust* of the nation — *applies to debauchery all the powers of its soul.*

I argued to myself that that energy must produce results. So I built an anecdote out of your remark. In it I make Napoleon Bonaparte say to me — but see for yourself the anecdote (ingeniously clipped and curtailed) in paragraph eleven of your Reply.*

---

* So, I repeat, Mark Twain does not like M. Paul Bourget's book. So long as he makes light fun of the great French writer he is at home, he is pleasant, he is the American humorist we know. When he takes his revenge (and where is the reason for taking a revenge?) he is unkind, unfair, bitter, nasty.

For example:

See his answer to a Frenchman who jokingly remarks to him:

" I suppose life can never get entirely dull to an American, because whenever he can't strike up any other way to put in his time, he can always get away with a few years trying to find out who his grandfather was."

Hear the answer:

" I reckon a Frenchman's got *his* little standby for a dull time, too; because when all other interests fail, he can turn in and see if he can't find out who his father was."

The first remark is a good-humored bit of chaffing on American snobbery. I may be utterly destitute of humor, but I call the second remark a gratuitous charge of immorality hurled at the French women — a remark unworthy of a man who has the ear of the public, unworthy of a gentleman, a gross insult to a nation friendly to America, a nation that helped Mark Twain's ancestors in their struggle for liberty, a nation

L*₊*₊

Now, then, your anecdote about the grandfathers hurt me. Why? Because it had a *point*. It wouldn't have hurt me if it hadn't had point. You wouldn't have wasted space on it if it hadn't had point.

My anecdote has hurt you. Why? Because it had point, I suppose. It wouldn't have hurt you if it hadn't had point. I judged from your remark about the diligence and industry of the high Parisian upper crust that it would have *some* point, but really I had no idea what a gold-mine I had struck. I never suspected that the point was going to stick into the entire nation; but of course you know your nation better than I do, and if you think it punctures them all, I have to yield to your judgment. But you are to blame, your own self. Your remark misled me. I supposed the industry was confined to that little unnumerous upper layer.

Well, now that the unfortunate thing has been done, let us do what we can to undo it. There must be a way, M. Bourget, and I am willing to do anything that will help; for I am as sorry as you can be yourself.

I will tell you what I think will be the very thing.

---

where to-day it is enough to say that you are American to see every door open wide to you.

If Mark Twain was hard up in search of a French "chestnut," I might have told him the following little anecdote. It is more funny than his, and would have been less insulting: Two little street boys are abusing each other. "Ah, hold your tongue," says one, "you ain't got no father."

"Ain't got no father!" replies the other; "I've got more fathers than you."

We will *swap anecdotes*. I will take your anecdote and you take mine. I will say to the dukes and counts and princes of the ancient nobility of France: " Ha, ha! You must have a pretty hard time trying to find out who your grandfathers were?"

They will merely smile indifferently and not feel hurt, because they can trace their lineage back through centuries.

And you will hurl mine at every individual in the American nation, saying:

" And *you* must have a pretty hard time trying to find out who your *fathers* were." They will merely smile indifferently, and not feel hurt, because they haven't any difficulty in finding their fathers.

Do you get the idea? The whole harm in the anecdotes is in the *point*, you see; and when we swap them around that way, they *haven't* any.

That settles it perfectly and beautifully, and I am glad I thought of it. I am very glad indeed, M. Bourget; for it was just that little wee thing that caused the whole difficulty and made you dictate the Reply, and your amanuensis call me all those hard names which the magazines dislike so. And I did it all in fun, too, trying to cap your funny anecdote with another one — on the give-and-take principle, you know — which is American. *I* didn't know that with the French it was all give and no take, and you didn't tell me. But now that I have made everything comfortable again, and fixed both anecdotes so they can never have any point any more, I know you will forgive me.

THE INVALID'S STORY

I SEEM sixty and married, but these effects are due to my condition and sufferings, for I am a bachelor, and only forty-one. It will be hard for you to believe that I, who am now but a shadow, was a hale, hearty man two short years ago,— a man of iron, a very athlete! — yet such is the simple truth. But stranger still than this fact is the way in which I lost my health. I lost it through helping to take care of a box of guns on a two-hundred-mile railway journey one winter's night. It is the actual truth, and I will tell you about it.

I belong in Cleveland, Ohio. One winter's night, two years ago, I reached home just after dark, in a driving snow-storm, and the first thing I heard when I entered the house was that my dearest boyhood friend and schoolmate, John B. Hackett, had died the day before, and that his last utterance had been a desire that I would take his remains home to his poor old father and mother in Wisconsin. I was greatly shocked and grieved, but there was no time to waste in emotions; I must start at once. I took the card, marked "Deacon Levi Hackett, Bethlehem, Wisconsin," and hurried off through the whistling storm to the railway station. Arrived there I found the long white-pine box which had been described to me; I fastened the card to it with some tacks, saw it put safely aboard the express car, and then ran into the eating-room to provide myself with a sandwich and some cigars. When I returned, presently, there was my coffin-box *back again*, apparently, and a young fellow examining around it, with a card in his hands, and some tacks and a hammer! I was astonished and puzzled. He began to nail on his card, and I rushed out to the express car, in a good deal of a state of mind, to ask for an explanation. But no — there was my box, all right, in the express car; it hadn't been disturbed. [The fact is that without my suspecting it a pro-digious mistake had been made. I was carrying off a box of *guns* which that young fellow had come to the station to ship to a rifle company in Peoria, Illinois, and *he* had got my corpse!] Just then the conductor sung out "All aboard," and I jumped into the express car and got a comfortable seat on a bale of buckets. The expressman was there, hard at work, — a plain man of fifty, with a simple, honest, good-natured face, and a breezy, practical heartiness in his general style. As the train moved off a stranger skipped into the car and set a package of peculiarly mature and capable Limburger cheese on one end of my coffin-box — I mean my box of guns. That is to say, I know *now* that it was Limburger cheese, but at that time I never had heard of the article in my life, and of course was wholly ignorant of its character. Well, we sped through the wild night, the bitter storm raged on, a cheerless misery stole over me, my heart went down, down, down! The old expressman made a brisk remark or two about the tempest and the arctic weather, slammed his sliding doors to, and bolted them, closed his window down tight, and then went bustling around, here and there and yonder, setting things to rights, and all the time contentedly humming "Sweet By and By," in a low tone, and flatting a good deal. Presently I began to detect a most evil and searching odor stealing about on the frozen air. This depressed my spirits still more, because of course I attributed it to my poor departed friend. There was something infinitely saddening about his calling himself to my remembrance in this dumb pathetic way, so it was hard to keep the tears back. Moreover, it distressed me on account of the old expressman, who, I was afraid, might notice it. However, he went humming tranquilly on, and gave no sign; and for this I was grateful. Grateful, yes, but still uneasy; and soon I began to feel more and more uneasy every minute, for every minute that went by that odor thickened up the more, and got to be more and more gamey and hard to stand. Presently, having got things arranged to his satisfaction, the expressman got some wood and made up a tremendous fire in his stove.

This distressed me more than I can tell, for I could not but feel that it was a mistake. I was sure that the effect would be deleterious upon my poor departed friend. Thompson — the expressman's name was Thompson, as I found out in the course of the night — now went poking around his car, stopping up whatever stray cracks he could find, remarking that it didn't make any difference what kind of a night it was outside, he calculated to make *us* comfortable, anyway. I said nothing, but I believed he was not choosing the right way. Meantime he was humming to himself just as before; and meantime, too, the stove was getting hotter and hotter, and the place closer and closer. I felt myself growing pale and qualmish, but grieved in silence and said nothing. Soon I noticed that the " Sweet By and By " was gradually fading out; next it ceased altogether, and there was an ominous stillness. After a few moments Thompson said,—

" Pfew! I reckon it ain't no cinnamon 't I've loaded up thish-yer stove with!"

He gasped once or twice, then moved toward the cof—gun-box, stood over that Limburger cheese part of a moment, then came back and sat down near me, looking a good deal impressed. After a contemplative pause, he said, indicating the box with a gesture,—

" Friend of yourn ?"

" Yes," I said with a sigh.

" He's pretty ripe, *ain't* he!"

Nothing further was said for perhaps a couple of minutes, each being busy with his own thoughts; then Thompson said, in a low, awed voice,—

" Sometimes it's uncertain whether they're really gone or not,— *seem* gone, you know — body warm, joints limber — and so, although you *think* they're gone, you don't really know. I've had cases in my car. It's perfectly awful, becuz *you* don't know what minute they'll rise up and look at you!" Then, after a pause, and slightly lifting his elbow toward the box,—"But *he* ain't in no trance! No, sir, I go bail for *him!*"

We sat some time, in meditative silence, listening to the wind and the roar of the train; then Thompson said, with a good deal of feeling,—

" Well-a-well, we've all got to go, they ain't no getting around it. Man that is born of woman is of few days and far between, as Scriptur' says. Yes, you look at it any way you want to, it's awful solemn and cur'us: they ain't *nobody* can get around it; *all's* got to go — just *everybody*, as you may say. One day you're hearty and strong" — here he scrambled to his feet and broke a pane and stretched his nose out at it a moment or two, then sat down again while I struggled up and thrust my nose out at the same place, and this we kept on doing every now and then —" and next day he's cut down like the grass, and the places which knowed him then knows him no more forever, as Scriptur' says. Yes'ndeedy, it's awful solemn and cur'us; but we've all got to

go, one time or another; they ain't no getting
around it."

There was another long pause; then,—

" What did he die of?"

I said I didn't know.

" How long has he ben dead?"

It seemed judicious to enlarge the facts to fit the
probabilities; so I said,—

" Two or three days."

But it did no good; for Thompson received it
with an injured look which plainly said, "Two or
three *years*, you mean." Then he went right along,
placidly ignoring my statement, and gave his views
at considerable length upon the unwisdom of putting
off burials too long. Then he lounged off toward
the box, stood a moment, then came back on a sharp
trot and visited the broken pane, observing,—

" 'Twould 'a' ben a dum sight better, all around,
if they'd started him along last summer."

Thompson sat down and buried his face in his red
silk handkerchief, and began to slowly sway and
rock his body like one who is doing his best to
endure the almost unendurable. By this time the
fragrance — if you may call it fragrance — was just
about suffocating, as near as you can come at it.
Thompson's face was turning gray; I knew mine
hadn't any color left in it. By and by Thompson
rested his forehead in his left hand, with his elbow
on his knee, and sort of waved his red handkerchief
towards the box with his other hand, and said,—

"I've carried a many a one of 'em,— some of 'em considerable overdue, too,— but, lordy, he just lays over 'em all! — and does it *easy*. Cap., they was heliotrope to *him!*"

This recognition of my poor friend gratified me, in spite of the sad circumstances, because it had so much the sound of a compliment.

Pretty soon it was plain that something had got to be done. I suggested cigars. Thompson thought it was a good idea. He said,—

"Likely it'll modify him some."

We puffed gingerly along for a while, and tried hard to imagine that things were improved. But it wasn't any use. Before very long, and without any consultation, both cigars were quietly dropped from our nerveless fingers at the same moment. Thompson said, with a sigh,—

"No, Cap., it don't modify him worth a cent. Fact is, it makes him worse, becuz it appears to stir up his ambition. What do you reckon we better do, now?"

I was not able to suggest anything; indeed, I had to be swallowing and swallowing, all the time, and did not like to trust myself to speak. Thompson fell to maundering, in a desultory and low-spirited way, about the miserable experiences of this night; and he got to referring to my poor friend by various titles,— sometimes military ones, sometimes civil ones; and I noticed that as fast as my poor friend's effectiveness grew, Thompson promoted him ac-

cordingly,— gave him a bigger title. Finally he
said,—

"I've got an idea. Suppos'n we buckle down to
it and give the Colonel a bit of a shove towards
t'other end of the car? — about ten foot, say. He
wouldn't have so much influence, then, don't you
reckon?"

I said it was a good scheme. So we took in
a good fresh breath at the broken pane, calculat-
ing to hold it till we got through; then we went
there and bent over that deadly cheese and took a
grip on the box. Thompson nodded "All ready,"
and then we threw ourselves forward with all our
might; but Thompson slipped, and slumped down
with his nose on the cheese, and his breath got
loose. He gagged and gasped, and floundered up
and made a break for the door, pawing the air
and saying hoarsely, "Don't hender me! — gimme
the road! I'm a-dying; gimme the road!" Out
on the cold platform I sat down and held his head
a while, and he revived. Presently he said,—

"Do you reckon we started the Gen'rul any?"
I said no; we hadn't budged him.

"Well, then, *that* idea's up the flume. We got
to think up something else. He's suited wher' he
is, I reckon; and if that's the way he feels about it,
and has made up his mind that he don't wish to be
disturbed, you bet he's a-going to have his own way
in the business. Yes, better leave him right wher'
he is, long as he wants it so; becuz he holds all the

13E

trumps, don't you know, and so it stands to reason that the man that lays out to alter his plans for him is going to get left."

But we couldn't stay out there in that mad storm; we should have frozen to death. So we went in again and shut the door, and began to suffer once more and take turns at the break in the window. By and by, as we were starting away from a station where we had stopped a moment Thompson pranced in cheerily, and exclaimed,—

"We're all right, now! I reckon we've got the Commodore this time. I judge I've got the stuff here that'll take the tuck out of him."

It was carbolic acid. He had a carboy of it. He sprinkled it all around everywhere; in fact he drenched everything with it, rifle-box, cheese and all. Then we sat down, feeling pretty hopeful. But it wasn't for long. You see the two perfumes began to mix, and then — well, pretty soon we made a break for the door; and out there Thompson swabbed his face with his bandanna and said in a kind of disheartened way,—

"It ain't no use. We can't buck agin *him*. He just utilizes everything we put up to modify him with, and gives it his own flavor and plays it back on us. Why, Cap., don't you know, it's as much as a hundred times worse in there now than it was when he first got a-going. I never *did* see one of 'em warm up to his work so, and take such a dumnation interest in it. No, sir, I never did, as long as I've

THESE GAVE IT A BETTER HOLD

ben on the road; and I've carried a many a one of
'em, as I was telling you.''

We went in again after we were frozen pretty
stiff; but my, we couldn't *stay* in, now.   So
we just waltzed back and forth, freezing, and
thawing, and stifling, by turns.   In about an hour
we stopped at another station; and as we left it
Thompson came in with a bag, and said,—

" Cap., I'm a-going to chance him once more,—
just this once; and if we don't fetch him this time,
the thing for us to do, is to just throw up the sponge
and withdraw from the canvass.   That's the way *I*
put it up.''

He had brought a lot of chicken feathers, and
dried apples, and leaf tobacco, and rags, and old
shoes, and sulphur, and asafœtida, and one thing or
another; and he piled them on a breadth of sheet
iron in the middle of the floor, and set fire to them.

When they got well started, I couldn't see, myself,
how even the corpse could stand it.   All that went
before was just simply poetry to that smell,—but
mind you, the original smell stood up out of it just
as sublime as ever,—fact is, these other smells just
seemed to give it a better hold; and my, how rich it
was !   I didn't make these reflections there — there
wasn't time — made them on the platform.   And
breaking for the platform, Thompson got suffocated
and fell; and before I got him dragged out, which I
did by the collar, I was mighty near gone myself.
When we revived, Thompson said dejectedly,—

"We got to stay out here, Cap.   We got to do it. They ain't no other way.   The Governor wants to travel alone, and he's fixed so he can outvote us."

And presently he added,—

"And don't you know, we're *pisoned*.   It's *our* last trip, you can make up your mind to it.   Typhoid fever is what's going to come of this.   I feel it a-coming right now.   Yes, sir, we're elected, just as sure as you're born."

We were taken from the platform an hour later, frozen and insensible, at the next station, and I went straight off into a virulent fever, and never knew anything again for three weeks.   I found out, then, that I had spent that awful night with a harmless box of rifles and a lot of innocent cheese; but the news was too late to save *me;* imagination had done its work, and my health was permanently shattered; neither Bermuda nor any other land can ever bring it back to me.   This is my last trip; I am on my way home to die.

THE CAPTAIN'S STORY

THERE was a good deal of pleasant gossip about old Captain " Hurricane " Jones, of the Pacific Ocean,— peace to his ashes! Two or three of us present had known him; I, particularly well, for I had made four sea-voyages with him. He was a very remarkable man. He was born on a ship; he picked up what little education he had among his shipmates; he began life in the forecastle, and climbed grade by grade to the captaincy. More than fifty years of his sixty-five were spent at sea. He had sailed all oceans, seen all lands, and borrowed a tint from all climates. When a man has been fifty years at sea, he necessarily knows nothing of men, nothing of the world but its surface, nothing of the world's thought, nothing of the world's learning but its A B C, and that blurred and distorted by the unfocused lenses of an untrained mind. Such a man is only a gray and bearded child. That is what old Hurricane Jones was,— simply an innocent, lovable old infant. When his spirit was in repose he was as sweet and gentle as a girl; when his wrath was up he was a hurricane

13*.*.   (193)

that made his nickname seem tamely descriptive. He was formidable in a fight, for he was of powerful build and dauntless courage. He was frescoed from head to heel with pictures and mottoes tattooed in red and blue India ink. I was with him one voyage when he got his last vacant space tattooed; this vacant space was around his left ankle. During three days he stumped about the ship with his ankle bare and swollen, and this legend gleaming red and angry out from a clouding of India ink: " Virtue is its own R'd." (There was a lack of room.) He was deeply and sincerely pious, and swore like a fish-woman. He considered swearing blameless, because sailors would not understand an order unilluminated by it. He was a profound Biblical scholar, — that is, he thought he was. He believed everything in the Bible, but he had his own methods of arriving at his beliefs. He was of the " advanced " school of thinkers, and applied natural laws to the interpretation of all miracles, somewhat on the plan of the people who make the six days of creation six geological epochs, and so forth. Without being aware of it, he was a rather severe satire on modern scientific religionists. Such a man as I have been describing is rabidly fond of disquisition and argument; one knows that without being told it.

One trip the captain had a clergyman on board, but did not know he was a clergyman, since the passenger list did not betray the fact. He took a great liking to this Rev. Mr. Peters, and talked with him a great deal: told him yarns, gave him toothsome scraps of personal history, and wove a glittering streak of profanity through his garrulous fabric that was refreshing to a spirit weary of the dull neutralities of undecorated speech. One day the captain said, " Peters, do you ever read the Bible?"

" Well — yes."

" I judge it ain't often, by the way you say it. Now, you tackle it in dead earnest once, and you'll find it'll pay. Don't you get discouraged, but hang right on. First, you won't understand it; but by and by things will begin to clear up, and then you wouldn't lay it down to eat."

" Yes, I have heard that said."

" And it's so, too. There ain't a book that begins with it. It lays over 'em all, Peters. There's some pretty tough things in it,— there ain't any getting around that,— but you stick to them and think them out, and when once you get on the inside everything's plain as day."

" The miracles, too, captain?"

" Yes, sir! the miracles, too. Every one of them. Now, there's that business with the prophets of Baal; like enough that stumped you?"

" Well, I don't know but —"

" Own up, now; it stumped you. Well, I don't wonder. You hadn't had any experience in raveling such things out, and naturally it was too many for you. Would you like to have me explain that thing

M*.*.

to you, and show you how to get at the meat of these matters?''

" Indeed, I would, captain, if you don't mind.''

Then the captain proceeded as follows: " I'll do it with pleasure. First, you see, I read and read, and thought and thought, till I got to understand what sort of people they were in the old Bible times, and then after that it was clear and easy. Now, this was the way I put it up, concerning Isaac* and the prophets of Baal. There was some mighty sharp men amongst the public characters of that old ancient day, and Isaac was one of them. Isaac had his failings,— plenty of them, too; it ain't for me to apologize for Isaac; he played on the prophets of Baal, and like enough he was justifiable, considering the odds that was against him. No, all I say is, 't wa'n't any miracle, and that I'll show you so's't you can see it yourself.

" Well, times had been getting rougher and rougher for prophets,— that is, prophets of Isaac's denomination. There were four hundred and fifty prophets of Baal in the community, and only one Presbyterian; that is, if Isaac *was* a Presbyterian, which I reckon he was, but it don't say. Naturally, the prophets of Baal took all the trade. Isaac was pretty low-spirited, I reckon, but he was a good deal of a man, and no doubt he went a-prophesying around, letting on to be doing a land-office busi-

---

* This is the captain's own mistake.

ness, but 't wa'n't any use; he couldn't run any opposition to amount to anything. By and by things got desperate with him; he sets his head to work and thinks it all out, and then what does he do? Why, he begins to throw out hints that the other parties are this and that and t'other,— nothing very definite, may be, but just kind of undermining their reputation in a quiet way. This made talk, of course, and finally got to the king. The king asked Isaac what he meant by his talk. Says Isaac, ' Oh, nothing particular; only, can they pray down fire from heaven on an altar? It ain't much, maybe, your majesty, only can they *do* it? That's the idea.' So the king was a good deal disturbed, and he went to the prophets of Baal, and they said, pretty airy, that if he had an altar ready, *they* were ready; and they intimated he better get it insured, too.

" So next morning all the children of Israel and their parents and the other people gathered themselves together. Well, here was that great crowd of prophets of Baal packed together on one side, and Isaac walking up and down all alone on the other, putting up his job. When time was called, Isaac let on to be comfortable and indifferent; told the other team to take the first innings. So they went at it, the whole four hundred and fifty, praying around the altar, very hopeful, and doing their level best. They prayed an hour,— two hours,— three hours,— and so on, plumb till noon. It wa'n't any use; they hadn't took a trick. Of course they felt kind of ashamed before all those people, and well they might. Now, what would a magnanimous man do? Keep still, wouldn't he? Of course. What did Isaac do? He graveled the prophets of Baal every way he could think of. Says he, 'You don't speak up loud enough; your god's asleep, like enough, or maybe he's taking a walk; you want to holler, you know,' — or words to that effect; I don't recollect the exact language. Mind, I don't apologize for Isaac; he had his faults.

"Well, the prophets of Baal prayed along the best they knew how all the afternoon, and never raised a spark. At last, about sundown, they were all tuckered out, and they owned up and quit.

"What does Isaac do, now? He steps up and says to some friends of his, there, 'Pour four barrels of water on the altar!' Everybody was astonished; for the other side had prayed at it dry, you know, and got whitewashed. They poured it on. Says he, 'Heave on four more barrels.' Then he says, 'Heave on four more.' Twelve barrels, you see, altogether. The water ran all over the altar, and all down the sides, and filled up a trench around it that would hold a couple of hogsheads, — 'measures,' it says; I reckon it means about a hogshead. Some of the people were going to put on their things and go, for they allowed he was crazy. They didn't know Isaac. Isaac knelt down and began to pray: he strung along, and strung along, about the heathen in distant lands, and about the sister churches, and about the state and the country at large, and about those that's in authority in the government, and all the usual programme, you know, till everybody had got tired and gone to thinking about something else, and then, all of a sudden, when nobody was noticing, he outs with a match and rakes it on the under side of his leg, and pff! up the whole thing blazes like a house afire! Twelve barrels of *water*? *Petroleum*, sir, PETROLEUM! that's what it was!"

"Petroleum, captain?"

"Yes, sir; the country was full of it. Isaac knew all about that. You read the Bible. Don't you worry about the tough places. They ain't tough when you come to think them out and throw light on them. There ain't a thing in the Bible but what is true; all you want is to go prayerfully to work and cipher out how 't was done."

STIRRING TIMES IN AUSTRIA

I. THE GOVERNMENT IN THE FRYING-PAN

HERE in Vienna in these closing days of 1897 one's blood gets no chance to stagnate. The atmosphere is brimful of political electricity. All conversation is political; every man is a battery, with brushes overworn, and gives out blue sparks when you set him going on the common topic. Everybody has an opinion, and lets you have it frank and hot, and out of this multitude of counsel you get merely confusion and despair. For no one really understands this political situation, or can tell you what is going to be the outcome of it.

Things have happened here recently which would set any country but Austria on fire from end to end, and upset the government to a certainty; but no one feels confident that such results will follow here. Here, apparently, one must wait and see what will happen, then he will know, and not before; guessing is idle; guessing cannot help the matter. This is

what the wise tell you; they all say it; they say it
every day, and it is the sole detail upon which they
all agree.

There is some approach to agreement upon another point: that there will be no revolution. Men
say: "Look at our history — revolutions have not
been in our line; and look at our political map
— its construction is unfavorable to an organized
uprising, and without unity what could a revolt
accomplish? It is *dis*union which has held our
empire together for centuries, and what it has
done in the past it may continue to do now and
in the future."

The most intelligible sketch I have encountered
of this unintelligible arrangement of things was contributed to the *Travelers Record* by Mr. Forrest
Morgan, of Hartford, three years ago. He says:

The Austro-Hungarian Monarchy is the patchwork quilt, the Mid-
way Plaisance, the national chain-gang of Europe; a state that is not a
nation but a collection of nations, some with national memories and
aspirations and others without, some occupying distinct provinces almost
purely their own, and others mixed with alien races, but each with a
different language, and each mostly holding the others foreigners as
much as if the link of a common government did not exist. Only one of
its races even now comprises so much as *one-fourth* of the whole, and
not another so much as *one-sixth ;* and each has remained for ages as
unchanged in isolation, however mingled together in locality, as glob-
ules of oil in water. There is nothing else in the modern world that is
nearly like it, though there have been plenty in past ages; it seems un-
real and impossible even though we know it is true; it violates all our
feeling as to what a country should be in order to have a right to exist;
and it seems as though it was too ramshackle to go on holding together
any length of time. Yet it has survived, much in its present shape, two

centuries of storms that have swept perfectly unified countries from existence and others that have brought it to the verge of ruin, has survived formidable European coalitions to dismember it, and has steadily gained force after each; forever changing in its exact make-up, losing in the West but gaining in the East, the changes leave the structure as firm as ever, like the dropping off and adding on of logs in a raft, its mechanical union of pieces showing all the vitality of genuine national life.

That seems to confirm and justify the prevalent Austrian faith that in this confusion of unrelated and irreconcilable elements, this condition of incurable disunion, there is strength — for the government. Nearly every day some one explains to me that a revolution would not succeed here. "It couldn't, you know. Broadly speaking, all the nations in the empire hate the government — but they all hate each other, too, and with devoted and enthusiastic bitterness; no two of them can combine; the nation that rises must rise alone; then the others would joyfully join the government against her, and she would have just a fly's chance against a combination of spiders. This government is entirely independent. It can go its own road, and do as it pleases; it has nothing to fear. In countries like England and America, where there is one tongue and the public interests are common, the government must take account of public opinion; but in Austria-Hungary there are nineteen public opinions — one for each state. No — two or three for each state, since there are two or three nationalities in each. A government cannot satisfy all these public opinions; it can only go through the motions of trying. This government does that. It

goes through the motions, and they do not succeed;
but that does not worry the government much."

The next man will give you some further information. " The government has a policy — a wise one
— and sticks steadily to it.   This policy is — *tranquillity:* keep this hive of excitable nations as quiet
as possible; encourage them to amuse themselves
with things less inflammatory than politics.   To this
end it furnishes them an abundance of Catholic priests
to teach them to be docile and obedient, and to be
diligent in acquiring ignorance about things here
below, and knowledge about the kingdom of heaven,
to whose historic delights they are going to add the
charm of their society by-and-by; and further — to
this same end — it cools off the newspapers every
morning at five o'clock, whenever warm events are
happening."   There is a censor of the press, and
apparently he is always on duty and hard at work.
A copy of each morning paper is brought to him at
five o'clock.   His official wagons wait at the doors
of the newspaper offices and scud to him with the
first copies that come from the press.   His company
of assistants read every line in these papers, and mark
everything which seems to have a dangerous look;
then he passes final judgment upon these markings.
Two things conspire to give to the results a capricious
and unbalanced look: his assistants have diversified
notions as to what is dangerous and what isn't; he
can't get time to examine their criticisms in much
detail; and so sometimes the very same matter which

is suppressed in one paper fails to be damned in another one, and gets published in full feather and unmodified. Then the paper in which it was suppressed blandly copies the forbidden matter into its evening edition — provokingly giving credit and detailing all the circumstances in courteous and inoffensive language — and of course the censor cannot say a word.

Sometimes the censor sucks all the blood out of a newspaper and leaves it colorless and inane; sometimes he leaves it undisturbed, and lets it talk out its opinions with a frankness and vigor hardly to be surpassed, I think, in the journals of any country. Apparently the censor sometimes revises his verdicts upon second thought, for several times lately he has suppressed journals after their issue and partial distribution. The distributed copies are then sent for by the censor and destroyed. I have two of these, but at the time they were sent for I could not remember what I had done with them.

If the censor did his work before the morning edition was printed, he would be less of an inconvenience than he is; but of course the papers cannot wait many minutes after five o'clock to get his verdict; they might as well go out of business as do that; so they print, and take the chances. Then, if they get caught by a suppression, they must strike out the condemned matter and print the edition over again. That delays the issue several hours, and is expensive besides. The government gets the suppressed edition for nothing. If it bought it, that would be joyful, and would give great satisfaction. Also, the edition would be larger. Some of the papers do not replace the condemned paragraphs with other matter; they merely snatch them out and leave blanks behind — mourning blanks, marked " *Confiscated.*"

The government discourages the dissemination of newspaper information in other ways. For instance, it does not allow newspapers to be sold on the streets; therefore the newsboy is unknown in Vienna. And there is a stamp duty of nearly a cent upon each copy of a newspaper's issue. Every American paper that reaches me has a stamp upon it, which has been pasted there in the post-office or downstairs in the hotel office; but no matter who put it there, I have to pay for it, and that is the main thing. Sometimes friends send me so many papers that it takes all I can earn that week to keep this government going.

I must take passing notice of another point in the government's measures for maintaining tranquillity. Everybody says it does not like to see any individual attain to commanding influence in the country, since such a man can become a disturber and an inconvenience. "We have as much talent as the other nations," says the citizen, resignedly, and without bitterness, " but for the sake of the general good of the country we are discouraged from making it overconspicuous; and not only discouraged, but tactfully and skillfully prevented from doing it, if we show

14E

too much persistence. Consequently we have no renowned men; in centuries we have seldom produced one — that is, seldom allowed one to produce himself. We can say to-day what no other nation of first importance in the family of Christian civilizations can say: that there exists no Austrian who has made an enduring name for himself which is familiar all around the globe.''

Another helper toward tranquillity is the army. It is as pervasive as the atmosphere. It is everywhere. All the mentioned creators, promoters, and preservers of the public tranquillity do their several shares in the quieting work. They make a restful and comfortable serenity and reposefulness. This is disturbed sometimes for a little while: a mob assembles to protest against something; it gets noisy — noisier — still noisier — finally *too* noisy; then the persuasive soldiery come charging down upon it, and in a few minutes all is quiet again, and there is no mob.

There is a Constitution and there is a Parliament. The House draws its membership of 425 deputies from the nineteen or twenty states heretofore mentioned. These men represent peoples who speak eleven languages. That means eleven distinct varieties of jealousies, hostilities, and warring interests. This could be expected to furnish forth a parliament of a pretty inharmonious sort, and make legislation difficult at times — and it does that. The parliament is split up into many parties — the Clericals, the Progressists, the German Nationalists, the Young Czechs, the Social Democrats, the Christian Socialists, and some others — and it is difficult to get up working combinations among them. They prefer to fight apart sometimes.

The recent troubles have grown out of Count Badeni's necessities. He could not carry on his government without a majority vote in the House at his back, and in order to secure it he had to make a trade of some sort. He made it with the Czechs — the Bohemians. The terms were not easy for him: he must pass a bill making the Czech tongue the official language in Bohemia in place of the German. This created a storm. All the Germans in Austria were incensed. In numbers they form but a fourth part of the empire's population, but they urge that the country's public business should be conducted in one common tongue, and that tongue a world language — which German is.

However, Badeni secured his majority. The German element in parliament was apparently become helpless. The Czech deputies were exultant.

Then the music began. Badeni's voyage, instead of being smooth, was disappointingly rough from the start. The government must get the *Ausgleich* through. It must not fail. Badeni's majority was ready to carry it through; but the minority was determined to obstruct it and delay it until the obnoxious Czech-language measure should be shelved.

The *Ausgleich* is an Adjustment, Arrangement, Settlement, which holds Austria and Hungary together. It dates from 1867, and has to be renewed every ten years. It establishes the share which Hungary must pay toward the expenses of the imperial government. Hungary is a kingdom (the Emperor of Austria is its King), and has its own parliament and governmental machinery. But it has no foreign office, and it has no army — at least its army is a part of the imperial army, is paid out of the imperial treasury, and is under the control of the imperial war office.

The ten-year rearrangement was due a year, ago, but failed to connect. At least completely. A year's compromise was arranged. A new arrangement must be effected before the last day of this year. Otherwise the two countries become separate entities. The Emperor would still be King of Hungary — that is, King of an independent foreign country. There would be Hungarian custom-houses on the Austrian frontier, and there would be a Hungarian army and a Hungarian foreign office. Both countries would be weakened by this, both would suffer damage.

The Opposition in the House, although in the minority, had a good weapon to fight with in the pending *Ausgleich*. If it could delay the *Ausgleich* a few weeks, the government would doubtless have to withdraw the hated language bill or lose Hungary.

The Opposition began its fight. Its arms were
the Rules of the House. It was soon manifest that
by applying these Rules ingeniously it could make
the majority helpless, and keep it so as long as it
pleased. It could shut off business every now and
then with a motion to adjourn. It could require the
ayes and noes on the motion, and use up thirty
minutes on that detail. It could call for the reading
and verification of the minutes of the preceding
meeting, and use up half a day in that way. It could
require that several of its members be entered upon
the list of permitted speakers previously to the opening of a sitting; and as there is no time limit, further delays could thus be accomplished.

These were all lawful weapons, and the men of
the Opposition (technically called the Left) were
within their rights in using them. They used them
to such dire purpose that all parliamentary business
was paralyzed. The Right (the government side)
could accomplish nothing. Then it had a saving
idea. This idea was a curious one. It was to
have the President and the Vice-Presidents of the
parliament trample the Rules under foot upon occasion !

This, for a profoundly embittered minority con-
structed out of fire and gun-cotton ! It was time
for idle strangers to go and ask leave to look
down out of a gallery and see what would be the
result of it.

14*.*.*

II. A MEMORABLE SITTING

And now took place that memorable sitting of the
House which broke two records.   It lasted the best
part of two days and a night, surpassing by half an
hour the longest sitting known to the world's previous
parliamentary history, and breaking the long-speech
record with Dr. Lecher's twelve-hour effort, the
longest flow of unbroken talk that ever came out of
one mouth since the world began.

At 8:45, on the evening of the 28th of October,
when the House had been sitting a few minutes short
of ten hours, Dr. Lecher was granted the floor.   It
was a good place for theatrical effects.   I think that
no other Senate House is so shapely as this one,
or so richly and showily decorated.   Its plan is that
of an opera-house.   Up toward the straight side of
it — the stage side — rise a couple of terraces of
desks for the ministry, and the official clerks or
secretaries — terraces thirty feet long, and each sup-
porting about half a dozen desks with spaces between
them.   Above these is the President's terrace, against
the wall.   Along it are distributed the proper accom-
modations for the presiding officer and his assistants.
The wall is of richly colored marble highly polished,
its paneled sweep relieved by fluted columns and
pilasters of distinguished grace and dignity, which
glow softly and frostily in the electric light.   Around
the spacious half-circle of the floor bends the great
two-storied curve of the boxes, its frontage elaborately
ornamented and sumptuously gilded.   On the floor

of the House the 425 desks radiate fanwise from the
President's tribune.

The galleries are crowded on this particular evening,
for word has gone about that the *Ausgleich* is before
the House; that the President, Ritter von Abraham-
owicz, has been throttling the Rules; that the
Opposition are in an inflammable state in consequence, and that the night session is likely to be
of an exciting sort.

The gallery guests are fashionably dressed, and
the finery of the women makes a bright and pretty
show under the strong electric light. But down on
the floor there is no costumery.

The deputies are dressed in day clothes; some of
the clothes neat and trim, others not; there may be
three members in evening dress, but not more.
There are several Catholic priests in their long black
gowns, and with crucifixes hanging from their necks.
No member wears his hat. One may see by these
details that the aspects are not those of an evening
sitting of an English House of Commons, but rather
those of a sitting of our House of Representatives.

In his high place sits the President, Abrahamowicz,
object of the Opposition's limitless hatred. He is
sunk back in the depths of his arm-chair, and has his
chin down. He brings the ends of his spread fingers
together in front of his breast, and reflectively taps
them together, with the air of one who would like to
begin business, but must wait, and be as patient as
he can. It makes you think of Richelieu. Now

N*.*.*

and then he swings his head up to the left or to the right and answers something which some one has bent down to say to him. Then he taps his fingers again. He looks tired, and maybe a trifle harassed. He is a gray-haired, long, slender man, with a colorless long face, which, in repose, suggests a deathmask; but when not in repose is tossed and rippled by a turbulent smile which washes this way and that, and is not easy to keep up with — a pious smile, a holy smile, a saintly smile, a deprecating smile, a beseeching and supplicating smile; and when it is at work the large mouth opens and the flexible lips crumple, and unfold, and crumple again, and move around in a genial and persuasive and angelic way, and expose large glimpses of the teeth; and that interrupts the sacredness of the smile and gives it momentarily a mixed worldly and political and satanic cast. It is a most interesting face to watch. And then the long hands and the body — they furnish great and frequent help to the face in the business of adding to the force of the statesman's words.

To change the tense. At the time of which I have just been speaking the crowds in the galleries were gazing at the stage and the pit with rapt interest and expectancy. One half of the great fan of desks was in effect empty, vacant; in the other half several hundred members were bunched and jammed together as solidly as the bristles in a brush; and they also were waiting and expecting. Presently the Chair delivered this utterance:

" Dr. Lecher has the floor.''

Then burst out such another wild and frantic and deafening clamor as has not been heard on this planet since the last time the Comanches surprised a white settlement at midnight.   Yells from the Left, counter-yells from the Right, explosions of yells from all sides at once, and all the air sawed and pawed and clawed and cloven by a writhing confusion of gesturing arms and hands.   Out of the midst of this thunder and turmoil and tempest rose Dr. Lecher, serene and collected, and the providential length of him enabled his head to show out above it.   He began his twelve-hour speech.   At any rate, his lips could be seen to move, and that was evidence.   On high sat the President imploring order, with his long hands put together as in prayer, and his lips visibly but not hearably speaking.   At intervals he grasped his bell and swung it up and down with vigor, adding its keen clamor to the storm weltering there below.

Dr. Lecher went on with his pantomime speech, contented, untroubled.   Here and there and now and then powerful voices burst above the din, and de-livered an ejaculation that was heard.   Then the din ceased for a moment or two, and gave opportunity to hear what the Chair might answer ; then the noise broke out again.   Apparently the President was being charged with all sorts of illegal exercises of power in the interest of the Right (the government side) : among these, with arbitrarily closing an Order of Business before it was finished ; with an unfair dis-

tribution of the right to the floor; with refusal of
the floor, upon quibble and protest, to members entitled to it; with stopping a speaker's speech upon
quibble and protest; and with other transgressions
of the Rules of the House. One of the interrupters
who made himself heard was a young fellow of slight
build and neat dress, who stood a little apart from
the solid crowd and leaned negligently, with folded
arms and feet crossed, against a desk. Trim and
handsome; strong face and thin features; black hair
roughed up; parsimonious mustache; resonant great
voice, of good tone and pitch. It is Wolf, capable
and hospitable with sword and pistol; fighter of the
recent duel with Count Badeni, the head of the
government. He shot Badeni through the arm, and
then walked over in the politest way and inspected
his game, shook hands, expressed regret, and all
that. Out of him came early this thundering peal,
audible above the storm:

"I demand the floor. I wish to offer a motion."

In the sudden lull which followed, the President
answered, "Dr. Lecher has the floor."

Wolf. "I move the close of the sitting!"

P. "Representative Lecher has the floor."
[Stormy outburst from the Left — that is, the
Opposition.]

Wolf. "I demand the floor for the introduction
of a formal motion. [Pause.] Mr. President, are
you going to grant it, or not? [Crash of approval

from the Left.]   I will keep on demanding the floor
till I get it.''

P. " I call Representative Wolf to order. Dr.
Lecher has the floor.''

Wolf. " Mr. President, are you going to observe
the Rules of this House?'' [Tempest of applause
and confused ejaculations from the Left — a boom
and roar which long endured, and stopped all business for the time being.]

Dr. von Pessler. " By the Rules motions are in
order, and the Chair *must* put them to vote.''

For answer the President (who is a Pole — I make
this remark in passing) began to jangle his bell with
energy at the moment that that wild pandemonium
of voices burst out again.

Wolf (hearable above the storm). " Mr. President, I demand the floor. We intend to find out,
here and now, which is the hardest, *a Pole's skull or
a German's !* ''

This brought out a perfect cyclone of satisfaction
from the Left. In the midst of it some one again
moved an adjournment. The President blandly
answered that Dr. Lecher had the floor. Which was
true; and he was speaking, too, calmly, earnestly,
and argumentatively; and the official stenographers
had left their places and were at his elbows taking
down his words, he leaning and orating into their ears
— a most curious and interesting scene.

Dr. von Pessler (to the Chair). " Do not drive
us to extremities !''

The tempest burst out again; yells of approval
from the Left, catcalls, an ironical laughter from
the Right. At this point a new and most effective
noisemaker was pressed into service. Each desk has
an extension, consisting of a removable board
eighteen inches long, six wide, and a half-inch thick.
A member pulled one of these out and began to
belabor the top of his desk with it. Instantly other
members followed suit, and perhaps you can imagine
the result. Of all conceivable rackets it is the most
ear-splitting, intolerable, and altogether fiendish.

The persecuted President leaned back in his chair,
closed his eyes, clasped his hands in his lap, and a
look of pathetic resignation crept over his long face.
It is the way a country schoolmaster used to look in
days long past when he had refused his school a
holiday and it had risen against him in ill-mannered
riot and violence and insurrection. Twice a motion
to adjourn had been offered — a motion always in
order in other Houses, and doubtless so in this one
also. The President had refused to put these motions.
By consequence, he was not in a pleasant place now,
and was having a right hard time. Votes upon
motions, whether carried or defeated, could make
endless delay, and postpone the *Ausgleich* to next
century.

In the midst of these sorrowful circumstances and
this hurricane of yells and screams and satanic clatter
of desk-boards, Representative Dr. Kronawetter un-
feelingly reminds the Chair that a motion has been

offered, and adds: "Say yes, or no! What do you sit there for, and give no answer?"

P. "After I have given a speaker the floor, I cannot give it to another. After Dr. Lecher is through, I will put your motion." [Storm of indignation from the Left.]

Wolf (to the Chair). "Thunder and lightning! look at the Rule governing the case!"

Kronawetter. "I move the close of the sitting! And I demand the ayes and noes!"

Dr. Lecher. "Mr. President, have I the floor?"

P. "You have the floor."

Wolf (to the Chair, in a stentorian voice which cleaves its way through the storm). "It is by such brutalities as these that you drive us to extremities! Are you waiting till some one shall throw into your face the word that shall describe what you are bringing about?* [Tempest of insulted fury from the Right.] *Is that what you are waiting for, old Grayhead?*" [Long-continued clatter of desk-boards from the Left, with shouts of "The vote! the vote!" An ironical shout from the Right, "Wolf is boss!"]

Wolf keeps on demanding the floor for his motion. At length —

P. "I call Representative Wolf to order! Your conduct is unheard-of, sir! You forget that you are in a parliament; you must remember where you are, sir." [Applause from the Right. Dr. Lecher is still

---

* That is, *revolution.*

peacefully speaking, the stenographers listening at
his lips.]

Wolf (banging on his desk with his desk-board).
" I demand the floor for my motion! I won't stand
this trampling of the Rules under foot — no, not if
I die for it! I will never yield! You have got to stop
me by force.   Have I the floor?"

P. " Representative Wolf, what kind of behavior
is this? I call you to order again.   You should have
some regard for your dignity."

Dr. Lecher speaks on.   Wolf turns upon him with
an offensive innuendo.

Dr. Lecher. " Mr. Wolf, I beg you to refrain
from that sort of suggestions."   [Storm of hand-
clapping from the Right.]

This was applause from the enemy, for Lecher
himself, like Wolf, was an Obstructionist.

Wolf growls to Lecher: " You can scribble that
applause in your album!"

P. " Once more I call Representative Wolf to
order! Do not forget that you are a Representative,
sir!"

Wolf (slam-banging with his desk-board). " I
will force this matter!   Are you going to grant me
the floor, or not?"

And still the sergeant-at-arms did not appear.   It
was because there wasn't any.   It is a curious thing,
but the Chair has no effectual means of compelling
order.

After some more interruptions:

Wolf (banging with his board).   " I demand the floor.   I will not yield!"

P. " I have no recourse against Representative Wolf.   In the presence of behavior like this it is to be regretted that such is the case."   [A shout from the Right, " Throw him out!"]

It is true, he had no effective recourse.   He had an official called an " Ordner," whose help he could invoke in desperate cases, but apparently the Ordner is only a persuader, not a compeller.   Apparently he is a sergeant-at-arms who is not loaded; a good enough gun to look at, but not valuable for business.

For another twenty or thirty minutes Wolf went on banging with his board and demanding his rights; then at last the weary President threatened to summon the dread order-maker.   But both his manner and his words were reluctant.   Evidently it grieved him to have to resort to this dire extremity.   He said to Wolf, " If this goes on, I shall feel obliged to summon the Ordner, and beg him to restore order in the House."

Wolf. " I'd like to see you do it!   Suppose you fetch in a few policemen, too!   [Great tumult.] Are you going to put my motion to adjourn, or not?"

Dr. Lecher continues his speech.   Wolf accompanies him with his board-clatter.

The President despatches the Ordner, Dr. Lang (himself a deputy), on his order-restoring mission. Wolf, with his board uplifted for defence, confronts the Ordner with a remark which Boss Tweed might have translated into " Now let's see what you are going to do about it!" [Noise and tumult all over the House.]

Wolf stands upon his rights, and says he will maintain them till he is killed in his tracks. Then he resumes his banging, the President jangles his bell and begs for order, and the rest of the House augments the racket the best it can.

Wolf. " I require an adjournment, because I find myself personally threatened. [Laughter from the Right.] Not that I fear for myself; I am only anxious about what will happen to the man who touches me."

The Ordner. " I am not going to fight with you."

Nothing came of the efforts of the angel of peace, and he presently melted out of the scene and disappeared. Wolf went on with his noise and with his demands that he be granted the floor, resting his board at intervals to discharge criticisms and epithets at the Chair. Once he reminded the Chairman of his violated promise to grant him (Wolf) the floor, and said, " Whence I came, we call promise-breakers rascals!" And he advised the Chairman to take his conscience to bed with him and use it as a pillow. Another time he said that the Chair was making itself ridiculous before all Europe. In fact, some of Wolf's language was almost unparliamentary. By-and-by he struck the idea of beating out a *tune* with his board. Later he decided to stop asking for the floor, and to confer it upon himself.   And so he and Dr. Lecher now spoke at the same time, and mingled their speeches with the other noises, and nobody heard either of them.   Wolf rested himself now and then from speech-making by reading, in his clarion voice, from a pamphlet.

I will explain that Dr. Lecher was not making a twelve-hour speech for pastime, but for an important purpose.   It was the government's intention to push the *Ausgleich* through its preliminary stages in this one sitting (for which it was the Order of the Day), and then by vote refer it to a select committee. It was the Majority's scheme — as charged by the Opposition — to drown debate upon the bill by pure noise — drown it out and stop it.   The debate being thus ended, the vote upon the reference would follow — with victory for the government.   But into the government's calculations had not entered the possibility of a single-barreled speech which should occupy the entire time-limit of the sitting, and also get itself delivered in spite of all the noise.   Goliah was not expecting David.   But David was there; and during twelve hours he tranquilly pulled statistical, historical, and argumentative pebbles out of his scrip and slung them at the giant; and when he was done he was victor, and the day was saved.

In the English House an obstructionist has held the floor with Bible-readings and other outside matters; but Dr. Lecher could not have that restful and recuperative privilege — he must confine himself

15E

strictly to the subject before the House.   More than once, when the President could not hear him because of the general tumult, he sent persons to listen and report as to whether the orator was speaking to the subject or not.

The subject was a peculiarly difficult one, and it would have troubled any other deputy to stick to it three hours without exhausting his ammunition, because it required a vast and intimate knowledge — detailed and particularized knowledge — of the commercial, railroading, financial, and international banking relations existing between two great sovereignties, Hungary and the Empire.   But Dr. Lecher is President of the Board of Trade of his city of Brünn, and was master of the situation.   His speech was not formally prepared.   He had a few notes jotted down for his guidance; he had his facts in his head; his heart was in his work; and for twelve hours he stood there, undisturbed by the clamor around him, and with grace and ease and confidence poured out the riches of his mind, in closely reasoned arguments, clothed in eloquent and faultless phrasing.

He is a young man of thirty-seven.   He is tall and well-proportioned, and has cultivated and fortified his muscle by mountain-climbing.   If he were a little handsomer he would sufficiently reproduce for me the Chauncey Depew of the great New England dinner nights of some years ago; he has Depew's charm of manner and graces of language and delivery.

There was but one way for Dr. Lecher to hold the floor — he must stay on his legs. If he should sit down to rest a moment, the floor would be taken from him by the enemy in the Chair. When he had been talking three or four hours he himself proposed an adjournment, in order that he might get some rest from his wearing labors; but he limited his motion with the condition that if it was lost he should be allowed to continue his speech, and if it carried he should have the floor at the next sitting. Wolf was now appeased, and withdrew his own thousand-times offered motion, and Dr. Lecher's was voted upon — and lost. So he went on speaking.

By one o'clock in the morning, excitement and noise-making had tired out nearly everybody but the orator. Gradually the seats of the Right underwent depopulation; the occupants had slipped out to the refreshment-rooms to eat and drink, or to the corridors to chat. Some one remarked that there was no longer a quorum present, and moved a call of the House. The Chair (Vice-President Dr. Kramarz) refused to put it to vote. There was a small dispute over the legality of this ruling, but the Chair held its ground.

The Left remained on the battle-field to support their champion. He went steadily on with his speech; and always it was strong, virile, felicitous, and to the point. He was earning applause, and this enabled his party to turn that fact to account. Now and then they applauded him a couple of minutes on a stretch.

and during that time he could stop speaking and rest his voice without having the floor taken from him.

At a quarter to two a member of the Left demanded that Dr. Lecher be allowed a recess for rest, and said that the Chairman was " heartless." Dr. Lecher himself asked for ten minutes. The Chair allowed him five. Before the time had run out Dr. Lecher was on his feet again.

Wolf burst out again with a motion to adjourn. Refused by the Chair. Wolf said the whole parliament wasn't worth a pinch of powder. The Chair retorted that that was true in a case where a single member was able to make all parliamentary business impossible. Dr. Lecher continued his speech.

The members of the Majority went out by detachments from time to time and took naps upon sofas in the reception-rooms; and also refreshed themselves with food and drink — in quantities nearly unbelievable — but the Minority staid loyally by their champion. Some distinguished deputies of the Majority staid by him, too, compelled thereto by admiration of his great performance. When a man has been speaking eight hours, is it conceivable that he can still be interesting, still fascinating? When Dr. Lecher had been speaking eight hours he was still compactly surrounded by friends who would not leave him and by foes (of all parties)who *could* not; and all hung enchanted and wondering upon his words, and all testified their admiration with constant

and cordial outbursts of applause.   Surely this was
a triumph without precedent in history.

During the twelve-hour effort friends brought to
the orator three glasses of wine, four cups of coffee,
and one glass of beer — a most stingy re-enforce-
ment of his wasting tissues, but the hostile Chair
would permit no addition to it.   But no matter, the
Chair could not beat that man.   He was a garrison
holding a fort, and was not to be starved out.

When he had been speaking eight hours his pulse
was 72; when he had spoken twelve, it was 100.

He finished his long speech in these terms, as
nearly as a permissibly free translation can convey
them:

"I will now hasten to close my examination of
the subject.   I conceive that we of the Left have
made it clear to the honorable gentlemen of the other
side of the House that we are stirred by no in-
temperate enthusiasm for this measure in its present
shape. . . .

"What we require, and shall fight for with all
lawful weapons, is a formal, comprehensive, and
definitive solution and settlement of these vexed
matters.   We desire the restoration of the earlier
condition of things; the cancellation of all this in-
capable government's pernicious trades with Hungary; and then — release from the sorry burden of
the Badeni ministry!

"I voice the hope — I know not if it will be fulfilled — I voice the deep and sincere and patriotic

15*⁎*⁎

hope that the committee into whose hands this bill
will eventually be committed will take its stand upon
high ground, and will return the *Ausgleich-Pro-
visorium* to this House in a form which shall make
it the protector and promoter alike of the great
interests involved and of the honor of our father-
land.'' After a pause, turning toward the government benches: '' But in any case, gentlemen of the
Majority, make sure of this: henceforth, as before,
you will find us at our post. The Germans of Austria
will neither surrender nor die!''

Then burst a storm of applause which rose and
fell, rose and fell, burst out again and again and
again, explosion after explosion, hurricane after
hurricane, with no apparent promise of ever coming
to an end; and meantime the whole Left was surging
and weltering about the champion, all bent upon
wringing his hand and congratulating him and glori-
fying him.

Finally he got away, and went home and ate five
loaves and twelve baskets of fishes, read the morning
papers, slept three hours, took a short drive, then
returned to the House and sat out the rest of the
thirty-three-hour session.

To merely *stand up* in one spot twelve hours on
a stretch is a feat which very few men could achieve;
to add to the task the utterance of a hundred thousand
words would be beyond the possibilities of the most
of those few; to superimpose the requirement that
the words should be put into the form of a compact,

coherent, and symmetrical oration would probably rule out the rest of the few, bar Dr. Lecher.

III. CURIOUS PARLIAMENTARY ETIQUETTE

In consequence of Dr. Lecher's twelve-hour speech and the other obstructions furnished by the Minority, the famous thirty-three-hour sitting of the House accomplished nothing. The government side had made a supreme effort, assisting itself with all the helps at hand, both lawful and unlawful, yet had failed to get the *Ausgleich* into the hands of a committee. This was a severe defeat. The Right was mortified, the Left jubilant.

Parliament was adjourned for a week — to let the members cool off, perhaps — a sacrifice of precious time, for but two months remained in which to carry the all-important *Ausgleich* to a consummation.

If I have reported the behavior of the House intelligibly, the reader has been surprised at it, and has wondered whence these law-makers come and what they are made of; and he has probably supposed that the conduct exhibited at the Long Sitting was far out of the common, and due to special excitement and irritation. As to the make-up of the House, it is this: the deputies come from all the walks of life and from all the grades of society. There are princes, counts, barons, priests, peasants, mechanics, laborers, lawyers, judges, physicians, professors, merchants, bankers, shopkeepers. They are religious men, they are earnest, sincere, devoted, and they hate the Jews. The title of Doctor is so common in the House that one may almost say that the deputy who does not bear it is by that reason conspicuous. I am assured that it is not a self-granted title, and not an honorary one, but an *earned* one; that in Austria it is very seldom conferred as a mere compliment; that in Austria the degrees of Doctor of Music, Doctor of Philosophy, and so on, are not conferred by the seats of learning; and so, when an Austrian is called Doctor it means that he is either a lawyer or a physician, and that he is not a self-educated man, but is college-bred, and has been diplomaed for merit.

That answers the question of the constitution of the House.   Now as to the House's curious manners. The manners exhibited by this convention of Doctors were not at that time being tried as a wholly new experiment. I will go back to a previous sitting in order to show that the deputies had already had some practice.

There had been an incident. The dignity of the House had been wounded by improprieties indulged in in its presence by a couple of the members. This matter was placed in the hands of a committee to determine where the guilt lay, and the degree of it, and also to suggest the punishment. The chairman of the committee brought in his report. By this it appeared that, in the course of a speech, Deputy Schrammel said that religion had no proper place in the public schools — it was a private matter.

Whereupon Deputy Gregorig shouted, " How about free love !"

To this, Deputy Iro flung out this retort: " Soda-water at the Wimberger !"

This appeared to deeply offend Deputy Gregorig, who shouted back at Iro, " You cowardly blather-skite, say that again !"

The committee had sat three hours. Gregorig had apologized; Iro had explained. Iro explained that he didn't say anything about soda-water at the Wimberger. He explained in writing, and was very explicit: " I declare *upon my word of honor* that I did not say the words attributed to me."

Unhappily for his word of honor it was proved by the official stenographers and by the testimony of several deputies that he *did* say them.

The committee did not officially know why the apparently inconsequential reference to soda-water at the Wimberger should move Deputy Gregorig to call the utterer of it a cowardly blatherskite; still, after proper deliberation, it was of the opinion that the House ought to formally censure the whole busi-ness. This verdict seems to have been regarded as sharply severe. I think so because Deputy Dr. Lueger, Bürgermeister of Vienna, felt it a duty to soften the blow to his friend Gregorig by showing that the soda-water remark was not so innocuous as it might look; that indeed Gregorig's tough retort was justifiable — and he proceeded to explain why. He read a number of scandalous post-cards which

he intimated had proceeded from Iro, as indicated
by the handwriting, though they were anonymous.
Some of them were posted to Gregorig at his place
of business, and could have been read by all his
subordinates; the others were posted *to Gregorig's
wife*. Lueger did not say — but everybody knew
— that the cards referred to a matter of town gossip
which made Mr. Gregorig a chief actor in a tavern
scene where siphon squirting played a prominent and
humorous part, and wherein women had a share.

There were several of the cards; more than several,
in fact; no fewer than five were sent in one day.
Dr. Lueger read some of them, and described others.
Some of them had pictures on them; one a picture
of a hog with a monstrous snout, and beside it
a squirting soda-siphon; below it some sarcastic
doggerel.

Gregorig deals in shirts, cravats, etc. One of the
cards bore these words: " Much respected Deputy
and collar-sewer — or *stealer*."

Another: " Hurrah for the Christian-Social work
among the women-assemblages! Hurrah for the
soda-squirter!" Comment by Dr. Lueger: " I
cannot venture to read the rest of that one, nor
the signature, either."

Another: "Would you mind telling me if . . ."

Comment by Dr. Lueger: "The rest of it is
not properly readable."

To Deputy Gregorig's wife: " Much respected
Madam Gregorig, — The undersigned desires **an**

invitation to the next soda-squirt." Comment by Dr. Lueger: "Neither the rest of the card nor the signature can I venture to read to the House, so vulgar are they."

The purpose of this card — to expose Gregorig to his family — was repeated in others of these anonymous missives.

The House, by vote, censured the two improper deputies.

This may have had a modifying effect upon the phraseology of the membership for awhile, and upon its general exuberance also, but it was not for long. As has been seen, it had become lively once more on the night of the Long Sitting. At the next sitting after the long one there was certainly no lack of liveliness. The President was persistently ignoring the Rules of the House in the interest of the government side, and the Minority were in an unappeasable fury about it. The ceaseless din and uproar, the shouting and stamping and desk-banging, were deafening, but through it all burst voices now and then that made themselves heard. Some of the remarks were of a very candid sort, and I believe that if they had been uttered in our House of Representatives they would have attracted attention. I will insert some samples here. Not in their order, but selected on their merits:

Dr. Mayreder (to the President). "You have lied! You conceded the floor to me; make it good, or you have lied!"

Mr. Glöckner (to the President). "Leave! Get out!"

Wolf (indicating the President). "There sits a man to whom a certain title belongs!"

Unto Wolf, who is continuously reading, in a powerful voice, from a newspaper, arrive these personal remarks from the Majority: "Oh, shut your mouth!" "Put him out!" "Out with him!" Wolf stops reading a moment to shout at Dr. Lueger, who has the floor, but cannot get a hearing, "Please, Betrayer of the People, begin!"

Dr. Lueger. "Meine Herren —" ["Oho!" and groans.]

Wolf. "*That's* the holy light of the Christian Socialists!"

Mr. Kletzenbauer (Christian Socialist). "Dam — nation! are you ever going to quiet down?"

Wolf discharges a galling remark at Mr. Wohlmeyer.

Wohlmeyer (responding). "You Jew, you!"

There is a moment's lull, and Dr. Lueger begins his speech. Graceful, handsome man, with winning manners and attractive bearing, a bright and easy speaker, and is said to know how to trim his political sails to catch any favoring wind that blows. He manages to say a few words, then the tempest overwhelms him again.

Wolf stops reading his paper a moment to say a drastic thing about Lueger and his Christian-Social pieties, which sets the C. S.'s in a sort of frenzy.

Mr. Vielohlawek. "You leave the Christian Socialists alone, you word-of-honor-breaker! Obstruct all you want to, but you leave *them* alone! You've no business in this House; you belong in a gin-mill!"

Mr. Prochazka. "In a lunatic-asylum, you mean!"

Vielohlawek. "It's a pity that such a man should be leader of the Germans; he disgraces the German name!"

Dr. Scheicher. "It's a shame that the like of him should insult us."

Strohbach (to Wolf). "Contemptible cub — we will bounce thee out of this!" [It is inferable that the "thee" is not intended to indicate affection this time, but to re-enforce and emphasize Mr. Strohbach's scorn.]

Dr. Scheicher. "His insults are of no consequence. He wants his ears boxed."

Dr. Lueger (to Wolf). "You'd better worry a trifle over your Iro's word of honor. You are behaving like a street arab."

Dr. Scheicher. "It's infamous!"

Dr. Lueger. "And *these* shameless creatures are the leaders of the German People's Party!"

Meantime Wolf goes whooping along with his newspaper-readings in great contentment.

Dr. Pattai. "Shut up! Shut up! Shut *up!* You haven't the floor!"

Strohbach. "The miserable cub!"

Dr. Lueger (to Wolf, raising his voice strenuously above the storm). "You are a wholly honorless street brat!" [A voice, "Fire the rapscallion out!" But Wolf's soul goes marching noisily on, just the same.]

Schönerer (vast and muscular, and endowed with the most powerful voice in the Reichsrath; comes ploughing down through the standing crowds, red, and choking with anger; halts before Deputy Wohlmeyer, grabs a rule and smashes it with a blow upon a desk, threatens Wohlmeyer's face with his fist, and bellows out some personalities, and a promise). "Only you wait — we'll teach you!" [A whirlwind of offensive retorts assails him from the band of meek and humble Christian Socialists compacted around their leader, that distinguished religious expert, Dr. Lueger, Bürgermeister of Vienna. Our breath comes in excited gasps now, and we are full of hope. We imagine that we are back fifty years ago in the Arkansas Legislature, and we think we know what is going to happen, and are glad we came, and glad we are up in the gallery, out of the way, where we can see the whole thing and yet not have to supply any of the material for the inquest. However, as it turns out, our confidence is abused, our hopes are misplaced.]

Dr. Pattai (wildly excited). "You quiet down, or we shall turn ourselves loose! There will be a cuffing of ears!"

Prochazka (in a fury). "No — *not* ear-boxing, but genuine *blows!*"

Vielohlawek. "I would rather take my hat off to a Jew than to Wolf!"

Strohbach (to Wolf). " Jew-flunky! Here we have been fighting the Jews for ten years, and now you are helping them to power again. How much do you get for it?"

Holansky. " What he wants is a strait-jacket!"

Wolf continues his readings. It is a market report now.

Remark flung across the House to Schönerer: "*Die Grossmutter auf dem Misthaufen erzeugt worden!*"

It will be judicious not to translate that. Its flavor is pretty high, in any case, but it becomes particularly gamey when you remember that the first gallery was well stocked with ladies.

Apparently it was a great hit. It fetched thunders of joyous enthusiasm out of the Christian Socialists, and in their rapture they flung biting epithets with wasteful liberality at specially detested members of the Opposition; among others, this one at Schönerer: "*Bordell in der Krugerstrasse!*" Then they added these words, which they whooped, howled, and also even sang, in a deep-voiced chorus: " *Schmul Leeb Kohn! Schmul Leeb Kohn! Schmul Leeb Kohn!*" and made it splendidly audible above the banging of desk-boards and the rest of the roaring cyclone of fiendish noises. [A gallery witticism comes flitting

by from mouth to mouth around the great curve:
" The swan-song of Austrian representative government!" You can note its progress by the
applausive smiles and nods it gets as it skims
along.]

Kletzenbauer. " Holofernes, where is Judith?"
[Storm of laughter.]

Gregorig (the shirt-merchant). " This Wolf-
Theater is costing 6,000 florins!"

Wolf (with sweetness). " Notice him, gentlemen;
it is Mr. Gregorig." [Laughter.]

Vielohlawek (to Wolf). " You Judas!"

Schneider. " Brothel-Knight!"

Chorus of Voices. " East-German offal-tub!"

And so the war of epithets crashes along, with
never-diminishing energy, for a couple of hours.

The ladies in the gallery were learning. That was
well; for by-and-by ladies will form a part of the
membership of all the legislatures in the world; as
soon as they can prove competency they will be
admitted. At present, men only are competent to
legislate; therefore they look down upon women,
and would feel degraded if they had to have them
for colleagues in their high calling.

Wolf is yelling another market report now.

Gessman. "Shut up, infamous louse-brat!"

During a momentary lull Dr. Lueger gets a hearing
for three sentences of his speech. They demand
and require that the President shall suppress the four
noisiest members of the Opposition.

Wolf (with a that-settles-it toss of the head).
" The shifty trickster of Vienna has spoken !"

Iro belonged to Schönerer's party. The word-of-
honor incident has given it a new name. Gregorig
is a Christian Socialist, and hero of the post-cards
and the Wimberger soda-squirting incident. He
stands vast and conspicuous, and conceited and self-
satisfied, and roosterish and inconsequential, at
Lueger's elbow, and is proud and cocky to be in
such great company. He looks very well indeed;
really majestic, and aware of it. He crows out his
little empty remark, now and then, and looks as
pleased as if he had been delivered of the *Ausgleich*.
Indeed, he does look notably fine. He wears almost
the only dress vest on the floor; it exposes a continental spread of white shirt-front; his hands are
posed at ease in the lips of his trousers pockets; his
head is tilted back complacently; he is attitudinizing;
he is playing to the gallery. However, they are all
doing that. It is curious to see. Men who only
vote, and can't make speeches, and don't know how
to invent witty ejaculations, wander about the vacated
parts of the floor, and stop in a good place and strike
attitudes — attitudes suggestive of weighty thought,
mostly — and glance furtively up at the galleries to
see how it works; or a couple will come together
and shake hands in an artificial way, and laugh a gay
manufactured laugh, and do some constrained and
self-conscious attitudinizing; and *they* steal glances
at the galleries to see if they are getting notice.

16E

It is like a scene on the stage — by-play by minor actors at the back while the stars do the great work at the front. Even Count Badeni attitudinizes for a moment; strikes a reflective Napoleonic attitude of fine picturesqueness — but soon thinks better of it and desists. There are two who do not attitudinize — poor harried and insulted President Abraham-owicz, who seems wholly miserable, and can find no way to put in the dreary time but by swinging his bell and by discharging occasional remarks which nobody can hear; and a resigned and patient priest, who sits lonely in a great vacancy on Majority territory and munches an apple.

Schönerer uplifts his fog-horn of a voice and shakes the roof with an insult discharged at the Majority.

Dr. Lueger. " The Honorless Party would better keep still here !"

Gregorig (the echo, swelling out his shirt-front). " Yes, keep quiet, pimp !"

Schönerer (to Lueger). "Political mountebank !"

Prochazka (to Schönerer). " Drunken clown !"

During the final hour of the sitting many happy phrases were distributed through the proceedings. Among them were these — and they are strikingly good ones:

Blatherskite !

Blackguard !

Scoundrel !

Brothel-daddy !

This last was the contribution of Dr. Gessman, and gave great satisfaction. And deservedly. It seems to me that it was one of the most sparkling things that was said during the whole evening.

At half-past two in the morning the House adjourned. The victory was with the Opposition. No; not quite that. The effective part of it was snatched away from them by an unlawful exercise of Presidential force — another contribution toward driving the mistreated Minority out of their minds.

At other sittings of the parliament, gentlemen of the Opposition, shaking their fists toward the President, addressed him as " Polish Dog." At one sitting an angry deputy turned upon a colleague and shouted,

" — — — — —!"

You must try to imagine what it was. If I should offer it even in the original it would probably not get by the Magazine editor's blue pencil; to offer a translation would be to waste my ink, of course. This remark was frankly printed in its entirety by one of the Vienna dailies, but the others disguised the toughest half of it with stars.

If the reader will go back over this chapter and gather its array of extraordinary epithets into a bunch and examine them, he will marvel at two things: how this convention of gentlemen could consent to use such gross terms; and why the users were allowed to get out of the place alive. There is no way to understand this strange situation. If every man in the House were a professional blackguard, and had his home in a sailor boarding-house, one could still not understand it; for although that sort do use such terms, they never *take* them. These men are not professional blackguards; they are mainly gentlemen, and educated; yet they use the terms, and take them, too. They really seem to attach no consequence to them. One cannot say that they act like schoolboys; for that is only almost true, not entirely. Schoolboys blackguard each other fiercely, and by the hour, and one would think that nothing would ever come of it but noise; but that would be a mistake. Up to a certain limit the result would be noise only, but that limit overstepped, trouble would follow right away. There are certain phrases —phrases of a peculiar character— phrases of the nature of that reference to Schönerer's grandmother, for instance, which not even the most spiritless schoolboy in the English-speaking world would allow to pass unavenged. One difference between schoolboys and the law-makers of the Reichsrath seems to be that the law-makers have no limit, no danger-line. Apparently they may call each other what they please, and go home unmutilated.

Now, in fact, they did have a scuffle on two occasions, but it was not on account of names called. There has been no scuffle where *that* was the cause.

It is not to be inferred that the House lacks a sense of honor because it lacks delicacy. That would be an error. Iro was caught in a lie, and it profoundly disgraced him. The House cut him, turned its back upon him. He resigned his seat; otherwise he would have been expelled. But it was lenient with Gregorig, who had called Iro a cowardly blatherskite in debate. It merely went through the form of mildly censuring him. That did not trouble Gregorig.

The Viennese say of themselves that they are an easy-going, pleasure-loving community, making the best of life, and not taking it very seriously. Nevertheless, they are grieved about the ways of their parliament, and say quite frankly that they are ashamed. They claim that the low condition of the parliament's manners is new, not old. A gentleman who was at the head of the government twenty years ago confirms this, and says that in his time the parliament was orderly and well-behaved. An English gentleman of long residence here endorses this, and says that a low order of politicians originated the present forms of questionable speech on the stump some years ago, and imported them into the parliament.* However, some day there will be a Minister of Etiquette and a sergeant-at-arms, and then things will go better. I mean if parliament and the Constitution survive the present storm.

---

* In that gracious bygone time when a mild and good-tempered spirit was the atmosphere of our House, when the manner of our speakers was studiously formal and academic, and the storms and explosions of to-day were wholly unknown," etc.— *Translation of the opening remark of an editorial in this morning's Neue Freie Presse, December* 3.

16*₊*₊

IV. THE HISTORIC CLIMAX.

During the whole of November things went from bad to worse. The all-important *Ausgleich* remained hard aground, and could not be sparred off. Badeni's government could not withdraw the Language Ordinance and keep its majority, and the Opposition could not be placated on easier terms. One night, while the customary pandemonium was crashing and thundering along at its best, a fight broke out. It was a surging, struggling, shoulder-to-shoulder scramble. A great many blows were struck. Twice Schönerer lifted one of the heavy ministerial fauteuils—some say with one hand—and threatened members of the Majority with it, but it was wrenched away from him; a member hammered Wolf over the head with the President's bell, and another member choked him; a professor was flung down and belabored with fists and choked; he held up an open penknife as a defence against the blows; it was snatched from him and flung to a distance; it hit a peaceful Christian Socialist who wasn't doing anything, and brought blood from his hand. This was the only blood drawn. The men who got hammered and choked looked sound and well next day. The fists and the bell were not properly handled, or better results would have been apparent. I am quite sure that the fighters were not in earnest.

On Thanksgiving day the sitting was a history-making one. On that day the harried, bedeviled, and despairing government went insane. In order to free itself from the thraldom of the Opposition it committed this curiously juvenile crime : it moved an important change of the Rules of the House, forbade debate upon the motion, put it to a stand-up vote instead of ayes and noes, and then gravely claimed that it had been adopted; whereas, to even the dullest witness — if I without immodesty may pretend to that place — it was plain that nothing legitimately to be called a vote had been taken at all.

I think that Saltpeter never uttered a truer thing than when he said, " Whom the gods would destroy they first make mad."

Evidently the government's mind was tottering when this bald insult to the House was the best way it could contrive for getting out of the frying-pan.

The episode would have been funny if the matter at stake had been a trifle; but in the circumstances it was pathetic. The usual storm was raging in the House. As usual, many of the Majority and the most of the Minority were standing up — to have a better chance to exchange epithets and make other noises. Into this storm Count Falkenhayn entered, with his paper in his hand; and at once there was a rush to get near him and hear him read his motion. In a moment he was walled in by listeners. The several clauses of his motion were loudly applauded by these allies, and as loudly disapplauded — if I may invent a word — by such of the Opposition as could hear his voice. When he took his seat the President promptly put the motion — persons desiring

to vote in the affirmative, *stand up!* The House
was already standing up; had been standing for an
hour; and before a third of it had found out what
the President had been saying, he had proclaimed
the adoption of the motion! And only a few heard
that. In fact, when that House is legislating you
can't tell it from artillery-practice.

You will realize what a happy idea it was to
side-track the lawful ayes and noes and substitute
a stand-up vote by this fact: that a little later,
when a deputation of deputies waited upon the
President and asked him if he was actually willing to claim that that measure had been passed,
he answered, "Yes—and *unanimously.*" It shows
that in effect the whole house was on its feet
when that trick was sprung.

The "Lex Falkenhayn," thus strangely born,
gave the President power to suspend for three days
any deputy who should continue to be disorderly
after being called to order twice, and it also placed
at his disposal such force as might be necessary to
make the suspension effective. So the House had a
sergeant-at-arms at last, and a more formidable one,
as to power, than any other legislature in Christen-
dom had ever possessed. The Lex Falkenhayn also
gave the House itself authority to suspend members
for *thirty* days.

On these terms the *Ausgleich* could be put through
in an hour — apparently. The Opposition would
have to sit meek and quiet, and stop obstructing, or

be turned into the street, deputy after deputy, leaving the Majority an unvexed field for its work.

Certainly the thing looked well. The government was out of the frying-pan at last. It congratulated itself, and was almost girlishly happy. Its stock rose suddenly from less than nothing to a premium. It confessed to itself, with pride, that its Lex Falkenhayn was a master-stroke — a work of genius.

However, there were doubters; men who were troubled, and believed that a grave mistake had been made. It might be that the Opposition was crushed, and profitably for the country, too; but the *manner* of it — the *manner* of it! That was the serious part. It could have far-reaching results; results whose gravity might transcend all guessing. It might be the initial step toward a return to government by force, a restoration of the irresponsible methods of obsolete times.

There were no vacant seats in the galleries next day. In fact, standing-room outside the building was at a premium. There were crowds there, and a glittering array of helmeted and brass-buttoned police, on foot and on horseback, to keep them from getting too much excited. No one could guess what was going to happen, but every one felt that *some-thing* was going to happen, and hoped he might have a chance to see it, or at least get the news of it while it was fresh.

At noon the House was empty — for I do not count myself. Half an hour later the two galleries were solidly packed, the floor still empty. Another half-hour later Wolf entered and passed to his place; then other deputies began to stream in, among them many forms and faces grown familiar of late. By one o'clock the membership was present in full force. A band of Socialists stood grouped against the ministerial desks, in the shadow of the Presidential tribune. It was observable that these official strong-holds were now protected against rushes by bolted gates, and that these were in ward of servants wearing the House's livery. Also the removable desk-boards had been taken away, and nothing left for disorderly members to slat with.

There was a pervading, anxious hush — at least what stood very well for a hush in that house. It was believed by many that the Opposition was cowed, and that there would be no more obstruction, no more noise. That was an error.

Presently the President entered by the distant door to the right, followed by Vice-President Fuchs, and the two took their way down past the Polish benches toward the tribune. Instantly the customary storm of noises burst out, and rose higher and higher, and wilder and wilder, and really seemed to surpass any-thing that had gone before it in that place. The President took his seat, and begged for order, but no one could hear him. His lips moved — one could see that; he bowed his body forward appealingly, and spread his great hand eloquently over his breast — one could see that; but as concerned his uttered

words, he probably could not hear them himself.
Below him was that crowd of two dozen Socialists
glaring up at him, shaking their fists at him, roaring
imprecations and insulting epithets at him. This
went on for some time. Suddenly the Socialists
burst through the gates and stormed up through the
ministerial benches, and a man in a red cravat reached
up and snatched the documents that lay on the President's desk and flung them abroad. The next
moment he and his allies were struggling and fighting
with the half-dozen uniformed servants who were
there to protect the new gates. Meantime a detail
of Socialists had swarmed up the side steps and over-
flowed the President and the Vice, and were crowd-
ing and shouldering and shoving them out of the
place. They crowded them out, and down the steps
and across the House, past the Polish benches; and
all about them swarmed hostile Poles and Czechs,
who resisted them. One could see fists go up and
come down, with other signs and shows of a heady
fight; then the President and the Vice disappeared
through the door of entrance, and the victorious
Socialists turned and marched back, mounted the
tribune, flung the President's bell and his remaining
papers abroad, and then stood there in a compact
little crowd, eleven strong, and held the place as if it
were a fortress. Their friends on the floor were in
a frenzy of triumph, and manifested it in their
deafening way. The whole House was on its feet,
amazed and wondering.

It was an astonishing situation, and imposingly dramatic. Nobody had looked for this. The unexpected had happened. What next? But there *can* be no next; the play is over; the grand climax is reached; the possibilities are exhausted: ring down the curtain.

Not yet. That distant door opens again. And now we see what history will be talking of five centuries hence: a uniformed and helmeted battalion of bronzed and stalwart men marching in double file down the floor of the House — a free parliament profaned by an invasion of brute force

It was an odious spectacle — odious and awful. For one moment it was an unbelievable thing — a thing beyond all credibility; it must be a delusion, a dream, a nightmare. But no, it was real — pitifully real, shamefully real, hideously real. These sixty policemen had been soldiers, and they went at their work with the cold unsentimentality of their trade. They ascended the steps of the tribune, laid their hands upon the inviolable persons of the representatives of a nation, and dragged and tugged and hauled them down the steps and out at the door; then ranged themselves in stately military array in front of the ministerial *estrade*, and so stood.

It was a tremendous episode. The memory of it will outlast all the thrones that exist to-day. In the whole history of free parliaments the like of it had been seen but three times before. It takes its imposing place among the world's unforgettable things.

I think that in my lifetime I have not twice seen abiding history made before my eyes, but I know that I have seen it once.

Some of the results of this wild freak followed instantly. The Badeni government came down with a crash; there was a popular outbreak or two in Vienna; there were three or four days of furious rioting in Prague, followed by the establishing there of martial law; the Jews and Germans were harried and plundered, and their houses destroyed; in other Bohemian towns there was rioting — in some cases the Germans being the rioters, in others the Czechs — and in all cases the Jew had to roast, no matter which side he was on. We are well along in December now;* the new Minister-President has not been able to patch up a peace among the warring factions of the parliament, therefore there is no use in calling it together again for the present; public opinion believes that parliamentary government and the Constitution are actually threatened with extinction, and that the permanency of the monarchy itself is a not absolutely certain thing!

Yes, the Lex Falkenhayn was a great invention, and did what was claimed for it — it got the government out of the frying-pan.

_____

* It is the 9th.— M. T.

CONCERNING THE JEWS

SOME months ago I published a magazine article descriptive of a remarkable scene in the Imperial Parliament in Vienna. Since then I have received from Jews in America several letters of inquiry. They were difficult letters to answer, for they were not very definite. But at last I received a definite one. It is from a lawyer, and he really asks the questions which the other writers probably believed they were asking. By help of this text I will do the best I can to publicly answer this correspondent, and also the others — at the same time apologizing for having failed to reply privately. The lawyer's letter reads as follows:

I have read "Stirring Times in Austria." One point in particular is of vital import to not a few thousand people, including myself, being a point about which I have often wanted to address a question to some disinterested person. The show of military force in the Austrian Parliament, which precipitated the riots, was not introduced by any Jew. No Jew was a member of that body. No Jewish question was involved in the Ausgleich or in the language proposition. No Jew was insulting anybody. In short, no Jew was doing any mischief toward anybody whatsoever. In fact, the Jews were the only ones of the nineteen different races in Austria which did not have a party — they are absolutely non-participants. Yet in your article you say that in the rioting which followed, all classes of people were unanimous only on one thing, viz., in being against the Jews. Now will you kindly tell me why, in your judgment, the Jews have thus ever been, and are even now, in these days of supposed intelligence, the butt of baseless, vicious animosities? I dare say that for centuries there has been no more quiet, undisturbing, and well-behaving citizens, as a class, than that same Jew. It seems to me that ignorance and fanaticism cannot alone account for these horrible and unjust persecutions.

Tell me, therefore, from your vantage-point of cold view, what in your mind is the cause. Can American Jews do anything to correct it either in America or abroad? Will it ever come to an end? Will a Jew be permitted to live honestly, decently, and peaceably like the rest of mankind? What has become of the golden rule?

I will begin by saying that if I thought myself prejudiced against the Jew, I should hold it fairest to leave this subject to a person not crippled in that way. But I think I have no such prejudice. A few years ago a Jew observed to me that there was no uncourteous reference to his people in my books, and asked how it happened. It happened because the disposition was lacking. I am quite sure that (bar one) I have no race prejudices, and I think I have no color prejudices nor caste prejudices nor creed prejudices. Indeed, I know it. I can stand any society. All that I care to know is that a man is a human being — that is enough for me; he can't be any worse. I have no special regard for Satan; but I can at least claim that I have no prejudice against him. It may even be that I lean a little his way, on account of his not having a fair show. All religions issue bibles against him, and say the most injurious things about him, but we never hear *his* side. We have none but the evidence for the prosecution, and yet we have rendered the verdict. To my mind, this is irregular. It is un-English; it is un-American; it is French. Without this precedent Dreyfus could not have been condemned. Of course Satan has some kind of a case, it goes without saying. It may be a poor one, but that is nothing; that can be said about any of us. As soon as I can get at the facts I will undertake his rehabilitation myself, if I can find an unpolitic publisher. It is a thing which we ought to be willing to do for any one who is under a cloud. We may not pay him reverence, for that would be indiscreet, but we can at least respect his talents. A person who has for untold centuries maintained the imposing position of spiritual head of four-fifths of the human race, and political head of the whole of it, must be granted the possession of executive abilities of the loftiest order. In his large presence the other popes and politicians shrink to midges for the microscope. I would like to see him. I would rather see him and shake him by the tail than any other member of the European Concert. In the present paper I shall allow myself to use the word Jew as if it stood for both religion and race. It is handy; and besides, that is what the term means to the general world.

In the above letter one notes these points:

1. The Jew is a well-behaved citizen.

2. Can ignorance and fanaticism *alone* account for his unjust treatment?

3. Can Jews do anything to improve the situation?

4. The Jews have no party; they are non-participants.

5. Will the persecution ever come to an end?

6. What has become of the golden rule?

Point No. 1. — We must grant proposition No. 1, for several sufficient reasons. The Jew is not a disturber of the peace of any country. Even his enemies will concede that. He is not a loafer, he is not a sot, he is not noisy, he is not a brawler nor a rioter, he is not quarrelsome. In the statistics of crime his presence is conspicuously rare — in all countries. With murder and other crimes of violence he has but little to do: he is a stranger to the hangman. In the police court's daily long roll of "assaults" and "drunk and disorderlies" his name seldom appears. That the Jewish home is a home in the truest sense is a fact which no one will dispute. The family is knitted together by the strongest affections; its members show each other every due respect; and reverence for the elders is an inviolate law of the house. The Jew is not a burden on the charities of the state nor of the city; these could cease from their functions without affecting him. When he is well enough, he works; when he is incapacitated, his own people take care of him. And not in a poor and stingy way, but with a fine and large benevolence. His race is entitled to be called the most benevolent of all the races of men. A Jewish beggar is not impossible, perhaps; such a thing may exist, but there are few

17E

men that can say they have seen that spectacle. The
Jew has been staged in many uncomplimentary
forms, but, so far as I know, no dramatist has done
him the injustice to stage him as a beggar. Whenever a Jew has real need to beg, his people save him
from the necessity of doing it. The charitable in-
stitutions of the Jews are supported by Jewish
money, and amply. The Jews make no noise about
it; it is done quietly; they do not nag and pester
and harass us for contributions; they give us peace,
and set us an example — an example which we have
not found ourselves able to follow; for by nature we
are not free givers, and have to be patiently and
persistently hunted down in the interest of the unfortunate.

These facts are all on the credit side of the proposition that the Jew is a good and orderly citizen.
Summed up, they certify that he is quiet, peaceable,
industrious, unaddicted to high crimes and brutal
dispositions; that his family life is commendable;
that he is not a burden upon public charities; that
he is not a beggar; that in benevolence he is above
the reach of competition. These are the very
quintessentials of good citizenship. If you can add
that he is as honest as the average of his neighbors
— But I think that question is affirmatively
answered by the fact that he is a successful business
man. The basis of successful business is honesty;
a business cannot thrive where the parties to it
cannot trust each other. In the matter of numbers

the Jew counts for little in the overwhelming
population of New York; but that his honesty
counts for much is guaranteed by the fact that the
immense wholesale business of Broadway, from the
Battery to Union Square, is substantially in his
hands.

I suppose that the most picturesque example in
history of a trader's trust in his fellow-trader was
one where it was not Christian trusting Christian, but
Christian trusting Jew. That Hessian Duke who
used to sell his subjects to George III. to fight
George Washington with got rich at it; and by-and-
by, when the wars engendered by the French
Revolution made his throne too warm for him, he
was obliged to fly the country. He was in a hurry,
and had to leave his earnings behind — $9,000,000.
He had to risk the money with some one without
security. He did not select a Christian, but a Jew
— a Jew of only modest means, but of high
character; a character so high that it left him lone-
some — Rothschild of Frankfort. Thirty years later,
when Europe had become quiet and safe again, the
Duke came back from overseas, and the Jew returned the loan, with interest added.*

---

* Here is another piece of picturesque history; and it reminds us
that shabbiness and dishonesty are not the monopoly of any race or
creed, but are merely human:

"Congress passed a bill to pay $379.56 to Moses Pendergrass, of Lib-
ertyville, Missouri. The story of the reason of this liberality is pathetically interesting, and shows the sort of pickle that an honest man may
get into who undertakes to do an honest job of work for Uncle Sam.

The Jew has his other side. He has some discreditable ways, though he has not a monopoly of them, because he cannot get entirely rid of vexatious Christian competition. We have seen that he seldom transgresses the laws against crimes of violence.

In 1886 Moses Pendergrass put in a bid for the contract to carry the mail on the route from Knob Lick to Libertyville and Coffman, thirty miles a day, from July 1, 1887, for one year. He got the postmaster at Knob Lick to write the letter for him, and while Moses intended that his bid should be $400, his scribe carelessly made it $4. Moses got the contract, and did not find out about the mistake until the end of the first quarter, when he got his first pay. When he found at what rate he was working he was sorely cast down, and opened communication with the Post Office Department. The department informed him that he must either carry out his contract or throw it up, and that if he threw it up his bondsmen would have to pay the government $1,459.85 damages. So Moses carried out his contract, walked thirty miles every week-day for a year, and carried the mail, and received for his labor $4 — or, to be accurate, $6.84; for, the route being extended after his bid was accepted, the pay was proportionately increased. Now, after ten years, a bill was finally passed to pay to Moses the difference between what he earned in that unlucky year and what he received."

The *Sun*, which tells the above story, says that bills were introduced in three or four Congresses for Moses's relief, and that committees repeatedly investigated his claim.

It took six Congresses, containing in their persons the compressed virtues of 70,000,000 of people, and cautiously and carefully giving expression to those virtues in the fear of God and the next election, eleven years to find out some way to cheat a fellow-Christian out of about $13 on his honestly executed contract, and out of nearly $300 due him on its enlarged terms. And they succeeded. During the same time they paid out $1,000,000,000 in pensions — a third of it unearned and undeserved. This indicates a splendid all-around competency in theft, for it starts with farthings, and works its industries all the way up to ship-loads. It may be possible that the Jews can beat this, but the man that bets on it is taking chances.

Indeed, his dealings with courts are almost restricted
to matters connected with commerce. He has a
reputation for various small forms of cheating, and
for practicing oppressive usury, and for burning
himself out to get the insurance, and arranging for
cunning contracts which leave him an exit but lock
the other man in, and for smart evasions which find
him safe and comfortable just within the strict letter
of the law, when court and jury know very well that
he has violated the spirit of it.   He is a frequent and
faithful and capable officer in the civil service, but he
is charged with an unpatriotic disinclination to stand
by the flag as a soldier — like the Christian Quaker.

Now if you offset these discreditable features by
the creditable ones summarized in a preceding paragraph beginning with the words, "These facts are all
on the credit side," and strike a balance, what must
the verdict be?   This, I think: that, the merits and
demerits being fairly weighed and measured on both
sides, the Christian can claim no superiority over the
Jew in the matter of good citizenship.

Yet, in all countries, from the dawn of history,
the Jew has been persistently and implacably hated,
and with frequency persecuted.

Point No. 2.—"Can fanaticism *alone* account for
this?"

Years ago I used to think that it was responsible
for nearly all of it, but latterly I have come to think
that this was an error.   Indeed, it is now my conviction that it is responsible for hardly any of it.

17*⁎*

In this connection I call to mind Genesis, chapter xlvii.

We have all thoughtfully — or unthoughtfully — read the pathetic story of the years of plenty and the years of famine in Egypt, and how Joseph, with that opportunity, made a corner in broken hearts, and the crusts of the poor, and human liberty — a corner whereby he took a nation's money all away, to the last penny; took a nation's live-stock all away, to the last hoof; took a nation's land away, to the last acre; then took the nation itself, buying it for bread, man by man, woman by woman, child by child, till all were slaves; a corner which took everything, left nothing; a corner so stupendous that, by comparison with it, the most gigantic corners in subsequent history are but baby things, for it dealt in hundreds of millions of bushels, and its profits were reckonable by hundreds of millions of dollars, and it was a disaster so crushing that its effects have not wholly disappeared from Egypt to-day, more than three thousand years after the event.

Is it presumable that the eye of Egypt was upon Joseph, the foreign Jew, all this time? I think it likely. Was it friendly? We must doubt it. Was Joseph establishing a character for his race which would survive long in Egypt? And in time would his name come to be familiarly used to express that character — like Shylock's? It is hardly to be doubted. Let us remember that this was *centuries before the crucifixion.*

I wish to come down eighteen hundred years later and refer to a remark made by one of the Latin historians. I read it in a translation many years ago, and it comes back to me now with force. It was alluding to a time when people were still living who could have seen the Saviour in the flesh. Christianity was so new that the people of Rome had hardly heard of it, and had but confused notions of what it was. The substance of the remark was this: Some Christians were persecuted in Rome through error, they being " *mistaken for Jews.*"

The meaning seems plain. These pagans had nothing against Christians, but they were quite ready to persecute Jews. For some reason or other they hated a Jew before they even knew what a Christian was. May I not assume, then, that the persecution of Jews is a thing which *antedates* Christianity and was not born of Christianity? I think so. What was the origin of the feeling?

When I was a boy, in the back settlements of the Mississippi Valley, where a gracious and beautiful Sunday-school simplicity and unpracticality prevailed, the " Yankee " (citizen of the New England States) was hated with a splendid energy. But religion had nothing to do with it. In a trade, the Yankee was held to be about five times the match of the Westerner. His shrewdness, his insight, his judgment, his knowledge, his enterprise, and his formidable cleverness in applying these forces were frankly confessed, and most competently cursed.

Q*₊*₊*

In the cotton States, after the war, the simple and ignorant negroes made the crops for the white planter on shares. The Jew came down in force, set up shop on the plantation, supplied all the negro's wants on credit, and at the end of the season was proprietor of the negro's share of the present crop and of part of his share of the next one. Before long, the whites detested the Jew, and it is doubtful if the negro loved him.

The Jew is being legislated out of Russia. The reason is not concealed. The movement was instituted because the Christian peasant and villager stood no chance against his commercial abilities. He was always ready to lend money on a crop, and sell vodka and other necessaries of life on credit while the crop was growing. When settlement day came he owned the crop; and next year or year after he owned the farm, like Joseph.

In the dull and ignorant England of John's time everybody got into debt to the Jew. He gathered all lucrative enterprises into his hands; he was the king of commerce; he was ready to be helpful in all profitable ways; he even financed crusades for the rescue of the Sepulchre. To wipe out his account with the nation and restore business to its natural and incompetent channels he had to be banished the realm.

For the like reasons Spain had to banish him four hundred years ago, and Austria about a couple of centuries later.

In all the ages Christian Europe has been obliged
to curtail his activities. If he entered upon a
mechanical trade, the Christian had to retire from it.
If he set up as a doctor, he was the best one, and
he took the business. If he exploited agriculture,
the other farmers had to get at something else.
Since there was no way to successfully compete
with him in any vocation, the law had to step in
and save the Christian from the poorhouse. Trade
after trade was taken away from the Jew by statute
till practically none was left. He was forbidden to
engage in agriculture; he was forbidden to practice
law; he was forbidden to practice medicine, except
among Jews; he was forbidden the handicrafts.
Even the seats of learning and the schools of science
had to be closed against this tremendous antagonist.
Still, almost bereft of employments, he found ways
to make money, even ways to get rich. Also ways
to invest his takings well, for usury was not denied
him. In the hard conditions suggested, the Jew
without brains could not survive, and the Jew with
brains had to keep them in good training and well
sharpened up, or starve. Ages of restriction to the
one tool which the law was not able to take from
him — his brain — have made that tool singularly
competent; ages of compulsory disuse of his hands
have atrophied them, and he never uses them now.
This history has a very, very commercial look, a
most sordid and practical commercial look, the business aspect of a Chinese cheap-labor crusade.

Religious prejudices may account for one part of it, but not for the other nine.

Protestants have persecuted Catholics, but they did not take their livelihoods away from them. The Catholics have persecuted the Protestants with bloody and awful bitterness, but they never closed agriculture and the handicrafts against them. Why was that ? That has the candid look of genuine religious persecution, not a trade-union boycott in a religious disguise.

The Jews are harried and obstructed in Austria and Germany, and lately in France; but England and America give them an open field and yet survive. Scotland offers them an unembarrassed field too, but there are not many takers. There are a few Jews in Glasgow, and one in Aberdeen; but that is because they can't earn enough to get away. The Scotch pay themselves that compliment, but it is authentic.

I feel convinced that the Crucifixion has not much to do with the world's attitude toward the Jew; that the reasons for it are older than that event, as suggested by Egypt's experience and by Rome's regret for having persecuted an unknown quantity called a Christian, under the mistaken impression that she was merely persecuting a Jew. *Merely* a Jew — a skinned eel who was used to it, presumably. I am persuaded that in Russia, Austria, and Germany nine-tenths of the hostility to the Jew comes from the average Christian's inability to compete successfully with the average Jew in business — in either straight business or the questionable sort.

In Berlin, a few years ago, I read a speech which frankly urged the expulsion of the Jews from Germany; and the agitator's *reason* was as frank as his proposition. It was this: *that eighty-five per cent.* of the successful lawyers of Berlin were Jews, and that about the same percentage of the great and lucrative businesses of all sorts in Germany were in the hands of the Jewish race! Isn't it an amazing confession? It was but another way of saying that in a population of 48,000,000, of whom only 500,-000 were registered as Jews, eighty-five per cent. of the brains and honesty of the whole was lodged in the Jews. I must insist upon the honesty — it is an essential of successful business, taken by and large. Of course it does not rule out rascals entirely, even among Christians, but it is a good working rule, nevertheless. The speaker's figures may have been inexact, but *the motive of persecution* stands out as clear as day.

The man claimed that in Berlin the banks, the newspapers, the theaters, the great mercantile, shipping, mining, and manufacturing interests, the big army and city contracts, the tramways, and pretty much all other properties of high value, and *also* the small businesses — were in the hands of the Jews. He said the Jew was pushing the Christian to the wall all along the line; that it was all a Christian could do to scrape together a living; and that the Jew *must* be banished, and soon — there was no other way of saving the Christian. Here in Vienna, last autumn, an agitator said that all these disastrous details were true of Austria-Hungary also; and in fierce language he demanded the expulsion of the Jews. When politicians come out without a blush and read the baby act in this frank way, *unrebuked*, it is a very good indication that they have a market back of them, and know where to fish for votes.

You note the crucial point of the mentioned agitation; the argument is that the Christian cannot *compete* with the Jew, and that hence his very bread is in peril. To human beings this is a much more hate-inspiring thing than is any detail connected with religion. With most people, of a necessity, bread and meat take first rank, religion second. I am convinced that the persecution of the Jew is not due in any large degree to religious prejudice.

No, the Jew is a money-getter; and in getting his money he is a very serious obstruction to less capable neighbors who are on the same quest. I think that that is the trouble. In estimating worldly values the Jew is not shallow, but deep. With precocious wisdom he found out in the morning of time that some men worship rank, some worship heroes, some worship power, some worship God, and that over these ideals they dispute and cannot unite — but that they all worship money; so he made it the end and aim of his life to get it. He was at it in Egypt thirty-six centuries ago; he was at it in Rome when that Christian got persecuted by mistake for him; he has been at it ever since. The cost to him has been heavy; his success has made the whole human race his enemy — but it has paid, for it has brought him envy, and that is the only thing which men will sell both soul and body to get. He long ago observed that a millionaire commands respect, a two-millionaire homage, a multi-millionaire the deepest deeps of adoration. We all know that feeling; we have seen it express itself. We have noticed that when the average man mentions the name of a multi-millionaire he does it with that mixture in his voice of awe and reverence and lust which burns in a Frenchman's eye when it falls on another man's centime.

Point No. 4. — " The Jews have no party; they are non-participants."

Perhaps you have let the secret out and given yourself away. It seems hardly a credit to the race that it is able to say that; or to you, sir, that you can say it without remorse; more, that you should offer it as a plea against maltreatment, injustice, and oppression. Who gives the Jew the right, who gives any race the right, to sit still, in a free country, and let somebody else look after its safety? The oppressed Jew was entitled to all pity in the former times under brutal autocracies, for he was weak and friendless, and had no way to help his case. But he has ways now, and he has had them

for a century, but I do not see that he has tried to
make serious use of them. When the Revolution
set him free in France it was an act of grace — the
grace of other people; he does not appear in it as
a helper. I do not know that he helped when England set him free. Among the Twelve Sane Men of
France who have stepped forward with great Zola at
their head to fight (and win, I hope and believe*)
the battle for the most infamously misused Jew of
modern times, do you find a great or rich or
illustrious Jew helping? In the United States he
was created free in the beginning — he did not need
to help, of course. In Austria, and Germany, and
France he has a vote, but of what considerable use
is it to him? He doesn't seem to know how to
apply it to the best effect. With all his splendid
capacities and all his fat wealth he is to-day not
politically important in any country. In America,
as early as 1854, the ignorant Irish hod-carrier, who
had a spirit of his own and a way of exposing it to
the weather, made it apparent to all that he must be
politically reckoned with; yet fifteen years before
that we hardly knew what an Irishman looked like.
As an intelligent force, and numerically, he has
always been away down, but he has governed the
country just the same. It was because he was
organized. It made his vote valuable — in fact,
essential.

You will say the Jew is everywhere numerically

---

* The article was written in the summer of 1898.—ED.

feeble. That is nothing to the point — with the Irishman's history for an object-lesson. But I am coming to your numerical feebleness presently. In all parliamentary countries you could no doubt elect Jews to the legislatures — and even *one* member in such a body is sometimes a force which counts. How deeply have you concerned yourselves about this in Austria, France, and Germany? Or even in America for that matter? You remark that the Jews were not to blame for the riots in this Reichsrath here, and you add with satisfaction that there wasn't one in that body. That is not strictly correct; if it were, would it not be in order for you to explain it and apologize for it, not try to make a merit of it? But I think that the Jew was by no means in as large force there as he ought to have been, with his chances. Austria opens the suffrage to him on fairly liberal terms, and it must surely be his own fault that he is so much in the background politically.

As to your numerical weakness. I mentioned some figures awhile ago — 500,000 — as the Jewish population of Germany. I will add some more — 6,000,000 in Russia, 5,000,000 in Austria, 250,000 in the United States. I take them from memory; I read them in the Encyclopædia Britannica about ten years ago. Still, I am entirely sure of them. If those statistics are correct, my argument is not as strong as it ought to be as concerns America, but it still has strength. It is plenty strong enough as concerns Austria, for ten years ago 5,000,000 was nine per cent. of the empire's population. The Irish would govern the Kingdom of Heaven if they had a strength there like that.

I have some suspicions; I got them at second hand, but they have remained with me these ten or twelve years. When I read in the E. B. that the Jewish population of the United States was 250,000, I wrote the editor, and explained to him that I was personally acquainted with more Jews than that in my country, and that his figures were without doubt a misprint for 25,000,000. I also added that I was personally acquainted with *that* many there; but that was only to raise his confidence in me, for it was not true. His answer miscarried, and I never got it; but I went around talking about the matter, and people told me they had reason to suspect that for business reasons many Jews whose dealings were mainly with the Christians did not report themselves as Jews in the census. It looked plausible; it looks plausible yet. Look at the city of New York; and look at Boston, and Philadelphia, and New Orleans, and Chicago, and Cincinnati, and San Francisco — how your race swarms in those places! — and everywhere else in America, down to the least little village. Read the signs on the marts of commerce and on the shops: Goldstein (gold stone), Edelstein (precious stone), Blumenthal (flower-vale), Rosenthal (rose-vale), Veilchenduft (violet odor), Singvogel (song-bird), Rosenzweig (rose branch), and all the amazing list of beautiful and enviable names which Prussia and Austria glorified you with so long ago. It is another instance of Europe's coarse and cruel persecution of your race; not that it was coarse and cruel to outfit it with pretty and poetical names like those, but that it was coarse and cruel to make it *pay* for them or else take such hideous and often indecent names that to-day their owners never use them; or, if they do, only on official papers. And it was the many, not the few, who got the odious names, they being too poor to bribe the officials to grant them better ones.

Now why was the race renamed? I have been told that in Prussia it was given to using fictitious names, and often changing them, so as to beat the tax-gatherer, escape military service, and so on; and that finally the idea was hit upon of furnishing all the inmates of a house with *one and the same surname*, and then holding the house responsible right along for those inmates, and accountable for any disappearances that might occur; it made the Jews keep track of *each other*, for self-interest's sake, and saved the government the trouble.*

---

* In Austria the renaming was merely done because the Jews in some newly acquired regions had no surnames, but were mostly named Abraham and Moses, and therefore the tax-gatherer could not tell t'other from which, and was likely to lose his reason over the matter. The renaming was put into the hands of the War Department, and a charming mess the graceless young lieutenants made of it. To them a Jew was of no sort of consequence, and they labeled the race in a way to make the angels weep. As an example take these two! *Abraham Bellyache* and *Schmul Godveudammd. Culled from " Namens Studien," by Karl Emil Franzos.*

If that explanation of how the Jews of Prussia came to be renamed is correct, if it is true that they fictitiously registered themselves to gain certain advantages, it may possibly be true that in America they refrain from registering themselves as Jews to fend off the damaging prejudices of the Christian customer. I have no way of knowing whether this notion is well founded or not. There may be other and better ways of explaining why only that poor little 250,000 of our Jews got into the Encyclopædia. I may, of course, be mistaken, but I am strongly of the opinion that we have an immense Jewish population in America.

Point No. 3. — " Can Jews do anything to improve the situation?"

I think so. If I may make a suggestion without seeming to be trying to teach my grandmother how to suck eggs, I will offer it. In our days we have learned the value of combination. We apply it everywhere — in railway systems, in trusts, in trade unions, in Salvation Armies, in minor politics, in major politics, in European Concerts. Whatever our strength may be, big or little, we *organize* it. We have found out that that is the only way to get the most out of it that is in it. We know the weakness of individual sticks, and the strength of the concentrated fagot. Suppose you try a scheme like this, for instance. In England and America put every Jew on the census-book *as* a Jew (in case you have not been doing that). Get up volunteer regiments composed of Jews solely, and, when the drum beats, fall in and go to the front, so as to remove the reproach that you have few Massénas among you, and that you feed on a country but don't like to fight for it. Next, in politics, organize your strength, band together, and deliver the casting vote where you can, and where you can't, compel as good terms as possible. You huddle to yourselves already in all countries, but you huddle to no sufficient purpose, politically speaking. You do not seem to be organized, except for your charities. There you are omnipotent; there you compel your due of recognition — you do not have to beg for it. It shows what you can do when you band together for a definite purpose.

And then from America and England you can encourage your race in Austria, France, and Germany, and materially help it. It was a pathetic tale that was told by a poor Jew in Galicia a fortnight ago during the riots, after he had been raided by the Christian peasantry and despoiled of everything he had. He said his vote was of no value to him, and he wished he could be excused from casting it, for indeed casting it was a sure *damage* to him, since no matter which party he voted for, the other party would come straight and take its revenge out of him. Nine per cent. of the population of the empire, these Jews, and apparently they cannot put a plank into any candidate's platform! If you will send our Irish lads over here I think they will

organize your race and change the aspect of the
Reichsrath.

You seem to think that the Jews take no hand in
politics here, that they are "absolutely non-
participants." I am assured by men competent to
speak that this is a very large error, that the Jews
are exceedingly active in politics all over the empire, but that they scatter their work and their votes
among the numerous parties, and thus lose the advantages to be had by concentration. I think that
in America they scatter too, but you know more
about that than I do.

Speaking of concentration, Dr. Herzl has a clear
insight into the value of that. Have you heard of
his plan? He wishes to gather the Jews of the world
together in Palestine, with a government of their
own — under the suzerainty of the Sultan, I suppose. At the convention of Berne, last year, there
were delegates from everywhere, and the proposal
was received with decided favor. I am not the
Sultan, and I am not objecting; but if that concentration of the cunningest brains in the world was
going to be made in a free country (bar Scotland),
I think it would be politic to stop it. It will not be
well to let that race find out its strength. If the
horses knew theirs, we should not ride any more.

Point No. 5. — "Will the persecution of the Jews
ever come to an end?"

On the score of religion, I think it has already
come to an end. On the score of race prejudice

and trade, I have the idea that it will continue. That is, here and there in spots about the world, where a barbarous ignorance and a sort of mere animal civilization prevail; but I do not think that elsewhere the Jew need now stand in any fear of being robbed and raided. Among the high civilizations he seems to be very comfortably situated indeed, and to have more than his proportionate share of the prosperities going. It has that look in Vienna. I suppose the race prejudice cannot be removed; but he can stand that; it is no particular matter. By his make and ways he is substantially a foreigner wherever he may be, and even the angels dislike a foreigner. I am using this word foreigner in the German sense — *stranger*. Nearly all of us have an antipathy to a stranger, even of our own nationality. We pile gripsacks in a vacant seat to keep him from getting it; and a dog goes further, and does as a savage would — challenges him on the spot. The German dictionary seems to make no distinction between a stranger and a foreigner; in its view a stranger *is* a foreigner — a sound position, I think. You will always be by ways and habits and predilections substantially strangers — foreigners — wherever you are, and that will probably keep the race prejudice against you alive.

But you were the favorites of Heaven originally, and your manifold and unfair prosperities convince me that you have crowded back into that snug place again. Here is an incident that is significant. Last

18*.*.*

week in Vienna a hail-storm struck the prodigious
Central Cemetery and made wasteful destruction
there. In the Christian part of it, according to the
official figures, 621 window panes were broken; more
than 900 singing-birds were killed; five great trees
and many small ones were torn to shreds and the
shreds scattered far and wide by the wind; the orna-
mental plants and other decorations of the graves
were ruined, and more than a hundred tomb-lanterns
shattered; and it took the cemetery's whole force
of 300 laborers more than three days to clear away
the storm's wreckage. In the report occurs this
remark — and in its italics you can hear it grit its
Christian teeth: ". . . . lediglich die *israelitische*
Abtheilung des Friedhofes vom Hagelwetter *ganz-
lich verschont* worden war." Not a hailstone hit the
Jewish reservation! Such nepotism makes me tired.

Point No. 6. — " What has become of the golden
rule?"

It exists, it continues to sparkle, and is well taken
care of. It is Exhibit A in the Church's assets, and
we pull it out every Sunday and give it an airing.
But you are not permitted to try to smuggle it into
this discussion, where it is irrelevant and would not
feel at home. It is strictly religious furniture, like
an acolyte, or a contribution-plate, or any of those
things. It has never been intruded into business;
and Jewish persecution is not a religious passion, it
is a business passion.

To conclude.— If the statistics are right, the Jews

constitute but *one per cent.* of the human race.   It
suggests a nebulous dim puff of star dust lost in the
blaze of the Milky Way.   Properly the Jew ought
hardly to be heard of; but he is heard of, has
always been heard of.   He is as prominent on the
planet as any other people, and his commercial
importance is extravagantly out of proportion to the
smallness of his bulk.   His contributions to the
world's list of great names in literature, science, art,
music, finance, medicine, and abstruse learning are
also away out of proportion to the weakness of his
numbers.   He has made a marvelous fight in this
world, in all the ages; and has done it with his
hands tied behind him.   He could be vain of himself, and be excused for it.   The Egyptian, the
Babylonian, and the Persian rose, filled the planet
with sound and splendor, then faded to dream-stuff
and passed away; the Greek and the Roman
followed, and made a vast noise, and they are gone;
other peoples have sprung up and held their torch
high for a time, but it burned out, and they sit in
twilight now, or have vanished.   The Jew saw them
all, beat them all, and is now what he always was,
exhibiting no decadence, no infirmities of age, no
weakening of his parts, no slowing of his energies, no
dulling of his alert and aggressive mind.   All things
are mortal but the Jew; all other forces pass, but he
remains.   What is the secret of his immortality?

R*₊*₊

FROM THE "LONDON TIMES" OF 1904

I

Correspondence of the "London Times."

CHICAGO, April 1, 1904.

I RESUME by cable-telephone where I left off yesterday. For many hours, now, this vast city — along with the rest of the globe, of course — has talked of nothing but the extraordinary episode mentioned in my last report. In accordance with your instructions, I will now trace the romance from its beginnings down to the culmination of yesterday — or to-day; call it which you like. By an odd chance, I was a personal actor in a part of this drama myself. The opening scene plays in Vienna. Date, one o'clock in the morning, March 31, 1898. I had spent the evening at a social entertainment. About midnight I went away, in company with the military attachés of the British, Italian, and American embassies, to finish with a late smoke. This function had been appointed to take place in the house of Lieutenant Hillyer, the third attaché mentioned in the above list. When we arrived there we found several visitors in the room: young Szczepanik;* Mr. K., his financial backer; Mr. W.,

---

* Pronounced (approximately) Ze*pan*nik.

the latter's secretary; and Lieutenant Clayton of the
United States army.   War was at that time threat-
ening between Spain and our country, and Lieutenant
Clayton had been sent to Europe on military business.   I was well acquainted with young Szczepanik
and his two friends, and I knew Mr. Clayton slightly.
I had met him at West Point years before, when he
was a cadet.   It was when General Merritt was
superintendent.   He had the reputation of being an
able officer, and also of being quick-tempered and
plain-spoken.

This smoking-party had been gathered together
partly for business.   This business was to consider
the availability of the telelectroscope for military
service.   It sounds oddly enough now, but it is
nevertheless true that at that time the invention was
not taken seriously by any one except its inventor.
Even his financial supporter regarded it merely as
a curious and interesting toy.   Indeed, he was so
convinced of this that he had actually postponed its
use by the general world to the end of the dying
century by granting a two years' exclusive lease of
it to a syndicate, whose intent was to exploit it at
the Paris World's Fair.

When we entered the smoking-room we found
Lieutenant Clayton and Szczepanik engaged in a
warm talk over the telelectroscope in the German
tongue.   Clayton was saying:

"Well, you know *my* opinion of it, anyway!" and he
brought his fist down with emphasis upon the table.

"And I do not value it," retorted the young inventor, with provoking calmness of tone and manner.

Clayton turned to Mr. K., and said:

"*I* cannot see why you are wasting money on this toy. In my opinion, the day will never come when it will do a farthing's worth of real service for any human being."

"That may be; yes, that may be; still, I have put the money in it, and am content. I think, myself, that it is only a toy; but Szczepanik claims more for it, and I know him well enough to believe that he can see farther than I can — either with his telelectroscope or without it."

The soft answer did not cool Clayton down; it seemed only to irritate him the more; and he repeated and emphasized his conviction that the invention would never do any man a farthing's worth of real service. He even made it a "brass" farthing, this time. Then he laid an English farthing on the table, and added:

"Take that, Mr. K., and put it away; and if ever the telelectroscope does any man an actual service, — mind, a *real* service, — please mail it to me as a reminder, and I will take back what I have been saying. Will you?"

"I will;" and Mr. K. put the coin in his pocket.

Mr. Clayton now turned toward Szczepanik, and began with a taunt — a taunt which did not reach a finish; Szczepanik interrupted it with a hardy retort, and followed this with a blow. There was a brisk

fight for a moment or two; then the attachés
separated the men.

The scene now changes to Chicago. Time, the
autumn of 1901. As soon as the Paris contract
released the telelectroscope, it was delivered to
public use, and was soon connected with the tele-
phonic systems of the whole world. The improved
"limitless-distance" telephone was presently introduced, and the daily doings of the globe made
visible to everybody, and audibly discussable, too,
by witnesses separated by any number of leagues.

By and by Szczepanik arrived in Chicago. Clayton (now captain) was serving in that military department at the time. The two men resumed the
Viennese quarrel of 1898. On three different
occasions they quarreled, and were separated by
witnesses. Then came an interval of two months,
during which time Szczepanik was not seen by any
of his friends, and it was at first supposed that he
had gone off on a sight-seeing tour and would soon
be heard from. But no; no word came from him.
Then it was supposed that he had returned to
Europe. Still, time drifted on, and he was not
heard from. Nobody was troubled, for he was like
most inventors and other kinds of poets, and went
and came in a capricious way, and often without
notice.

Now comes the tragedy. On the 29th of
December, in a dark and unused compartment of
the cellar under Captain Clayton's house, a corpse

was discovered by one of Clayton's maid-servants. It was easily identified as Szczepanik's. The man had died by violence. Clayton was arrested, indicted, and brought to trial, charged with this murder. The evidence against him was perfect in every detail, and absolutely unassailable. Clayton admitted this himself. He said that a reasonable man could not examine this testimony with a dispassionate mind and not be convinced by it; yet the man would be in error, nevertheless. Clayton swore that he did not commit the murder, and that he had had nothing to do with it.

As your readers will remember, he was condemned to death. He had numerous and powerful friends, and they worked hard to save him, for none of them doubted the truth of his assertion. I did what little I could to help, for I had long since become a close friend of his, and thought I knew that it was not in his character to inveigle an enemy into a corner and assassinate him. During 1902 and 1903 he was several times reprieved by the governor; he was reprieved once more in the beginning of the present year, and the execution-day postponed to March 31st.

The governor's situation has been embarrassing, from the day of the condemnation, because of the fact that Clayton's wife is the governor's niece. The marriage took place in 1899, when Clayton was thirty-four and the girl twenty-three, and has been a happy one. There is one child, a little girl three

years old. Pity for the poor mother and child
kept the mouths of grumblers closed at first; but
this could not last forever,— for in America politics
has a hand in everything,— and by and by the
governor's political opponents began to call attention to his delay in allowing the law to take its
course. These hints have grown more and more
frequent of late, and more and more pronounced.
As a natural result, his own party grew nervous.
Its leaders began to visit Springfield and hold long
private conferences with him. He was now between
two fires. On the one hand, his niece was imploring
him to pardon her husband; on the other were the
leaders, insisting that he stand to his plain duty as
chief magistrate of the State, and place no further
bar to Clayton's execution. Duty won in the
struggle, and the governor gave his word that he
would not again respite the condemned man. This
was two weeks ago. Mrs. Clayton now said:

"Now that you have given your word, my last
hope is gone, for I know you will never go back
from it. But you have done the best you could for
John, and I have no reproaches for you. You love
him, and you love me, and we both know that if you
could honorably save him, you would do it. I will
go to him now, and be what help I can to him, and
get what comfort I may out of the few days that are
left to us before the night comes which will have no
end for me in life. You will be with me that day?
You will not let me bear it alone?"

"I will take you to him myself, poor child, and I will be near you to the last."

By the governor's command, Clayton was now allowed every indulgence he might ask for which could interest his mind and soften the hardships of his imprisonment. His wife and child spent the days with him; I was his companion by night. He was removed from the narrow cell which he had occupied during such a dreary stretch of time, and given the chief warden's roomy and comfortable quarters. His mind was always busy with the catastrophe of his life, and with the slaughtered inventor, and he now took the fancy that he would like to have the telelectroscope and divert his mind with it. He had his wish. The connection was made with the international telephone-station, and day by day, and night by night, he called up one corner of the globe after another, and looked upon its life, and studied its strange sights, and spoke with its people, and realized that by grace of this marvelous instrument he was almost as free as the birds of the air, although a prisoner under locks and bars. He seldom spoke, and I never interrupted him when he was absorbed in this amusement. I sat in his parlor and read and smoked, and the nights were very quiet and reposefully sociable, and I found them pleasant. Now and then I would hear him say, "Give me Yedo"; next, "Give me Hong-Kong"; next, "Give me Melbourne." And I smoked on, and read in comfort, while he wandered about the remote under-world, where the sun was shining in the sky, and the people were at their daily work. Sometimes the talk that came from those far regions through the microphone attachment interested me, and I listened.

Yesterday — I keep calling it yesterday, which is quite natural, for certain reasons — the instrument remained unused, and that, also, was natural, for it was the eve of the execution-day. It was spent in tears and lamentations and farewells. The governor and the wife and child remained until a quarter past eleven at night, and the scenes I witnessed were pitiful to see. The execution was to take place at four in the morning. A little after eleven a sound of hammering broke out upon the still night, and there was a glare of light, and the child cried out, "What is that, papa?" and ran to the window before she could be stopped, and clapped her small hands, and said: " Oh, come and see, mama — such a pretty thing they are making!" The mother knew — and fainted. It was the gallows!

She was carried away to her lodging, poor woman, and Clayton and I were alone — alone, and thinking, brooding, dreaming. We might have been statues, we sat so motionless and still. It was a wild night, for winter was come again for a moment, after the habit of this region in the early spring. The sky was starless and black, and a strong wind was blowing from the lake. The silence in the room was so deep that all outside sounds seemed exag-

gerated by contrast with it. These sounds were
fitting ones; they harmonized with the situation and
the conditions: the boom and thunder of sudden
storm-gusts among the roofs and chimneys, then the
dying down into moanings and wailings about the
eaves and angles; now and then a gnashing and
lashing rush of sleet along the window-panes; and
always the muffled and uncanny hammering of the
gallows-builders in the courtyard. After an age of
this, another sound — far off, and coming smothered
and faint through the riot of the tempest — a bell
tolling twelve! Another age, and it tolled again.
By and by, again. A dreary, long interval after
this, then the spectral sound floated to us once more
— one, two, three; and this time we caught our
breath: sixty minutes of life left!

Clayton rose, and stood by the window, and
looked up into the black sky, and listened to the
thrashing sleet and the piping wind; then he said:
" That a dying man's last of earth should be — this!"
After a little he said: " I must see the sun again —
the sun!" and the next moment he was feverishly
calling: " China! Give me China — Peking!"

I was strangely stirred, and said to myself: " To
think that it is a mere human being who does this
unimaginable miracle — turns winter into summer,
night into day, storm into calm, gives the freedom
of the great globe to a prisoner in his cell, and the
sun in his naked splendor to a man dying in
Egyptian darkness!"

I was listening.

"What light! what brilliancy! what radiance! . . .
This is Peking?"

"Yes."

"The time?"

"Mid-afternoon."

"What is the great crowd for, and in such
gorgeous costumes? What masses and masses of
rich color and barbaric magnificence! And how
they flash and glow and burn in the flooding sun-
light! What *is* the occasion of it all?"

"The coronation of our new emperor — the
Czar."

"But I thought that that was to take place
yesterday."

"This *is* yesterday — to you."

"Certainly it is. But my mind is confused, these
days; there are reasons for it. . . Is this the beginning of the procession?"

"Oh, no; it began to move an hour ago."

"Is there much more of it still to come?"

"Two hours of it. Why do you sigh?"

"Because I should like to see it all."

"And why can't you?"

"I have to go — presently."

"You have an engagement?"

After a pause, softly: "Yes." After another
pause: "Who are these in the splendid pavilion?"

"The imperial family, and visiting royalties from
here and there and yonder in the earth."

19E

" And who are those in the adjoining pavilions to the right and left?"

" Ambassadors and their families and suites to the right; unofficial foreigners to the left."

" If you will be so good, I —"

Boom! That distant bell again, tolling the half-hour faintly through the tempest of wind and sleet. The door opened, and the governor and the mother and child entered — the woman in widow's weeds! She fell upon her husband's breast in a passion of sobs, and I — I could not stay; I could not bear it. I went into the bedchamber, and closed the door. I sat there waiting — waiting — waiting, and listening to the rattling sashes and the blustering of the storm. After what seemed a long, long time, I heard a rustle and movement in the parlor, and knew that the clergyman and the sheriff and the guard were come. There was some low-voiced talking; then a hush; then a prayer, with a sound of sobbing; presently, footfalls — the departure for the gallows; then the child's happy voice: " Don't cry *now*, mama, when we've got papa again, and taking him home."

The door closed; they were gone. I was ashamed: I was the only friend of the dying man that had no spirit, no courage. I stepped into the room, and said I would be a man and would follow. But we are made as we are made, and we cannot help it. I did not go.

I fidgeted about the room nervously, and presently

went to the window, and softly raised it, — drawn
by that dread fascination which the terrible and the
awful exert,— and looked down upon the courtyard.
By the garish light of the electric lamps I saw the
little group of privileged witnesses, the wife crying
on her uncle's breast, the condemned man standing
on the scaffold with the halter around his neck, his
arms strapped to his body, the black cap on his
head, the sheriff at his side with his hand on the
drop, the clergyman in front of him with bare head
and his book in his hand.

" *I am the resurrection and the life —*"

I turned away. I could not listen; I could not
look. I did not know whither to go or what to do.
Mechanically, and without knowing it, I put my eye
to that strange instrument, and there was Peking
and the Czar's procession! The next moment I was
leaning out of the window, gasping, suffocating,
trying to speak, but dumb from the very imminence
of the necessity of speaking. The preacher could
speak, but I, who had such need of words —

"*And may God have mercy upon your soul.
Amen.*"

The sheriff drew down the black cap, and laid his
hand upon the lever. I got my voice.

" Stop, for God's sake! The man is innocent.
Come here and see Szczepanik face to face!"

Hardly three minutes later the governor had my
place at the window, and was saying:

" Strike off his bonds and set him free!"

Three minutes later all were in the parlor again. The reader will imagine the scene; I have no need to describe it. It was a sort of mad orgy of joy.

A messenger carried word to Szczepanik in the pavilion, and one could see the distressed amazement dawn in his face as he listened to the tale. Then he came to his end of the line, and talked with Clayton and the governor and the others; and the wife poured out her gratitude upon him for saving her husband's life, and in her deep thankfulness she kissed him at twelve thousand miles' range.

The telelectrophonoscopes of the globe were put to service now, and for many hours the kings and queens of many realms (with here and there a reporter) talked with Szczepanik, and praised him; and the few scientific societies which had not already made him an honorary member conferred that grace upon him.

How had he come to disappear from among us? It was easily explained. He had not grown used to being a world-famous person, and had been forced to break away from the lionizing that was robbing him of all privacy and repose. So he grew a beard, put on colored glasses, disguised himself a little in other ways, then took a fictitious name, and went off to wander about the earth in peace.

Such is the tale of the drama which began with an inconsequential quarrel in Vienna in the spring of 1898, and came near ending as a tragedy in the spring of 1904.   MARK TWAIN.

II

Correspondence of the " London Times."

CHICAGO, April 5, 1904.

TO-DAY, by a clipper of the Electric Line, and the latter's Electric Railway connections, arrived an envelope from Vienna, for Captain Clayton, containing an English farthing. The receiver of it was a good deal moved. He called up Vienna, and stood face to face with Mr. K., and said:

" I do not need to say anything; you can see it all in my face. My wife has the farthing. Do not be afraid — she will not throw it away."   M. T.

III

Correspondence of the " London Times."

CHICAGO, April 23, 1904.

NOW that the after developments of the Clayton case have run their course and reached a finish, I will sum them up. Clayton's romantic escape from a shameful death steeped all this region in an enchantment of wonder and joy — during the proverbial nine days. Then the sobering process followed, and men began to take thought, and to say: " But *a man was killed*, and Clayton killed him." Others replied: " That is true: we have been overlooking that important detail; we have been led away by excitement."

The feeling soon became general that Clayton ought to be tried again. Measures were taken accordingly, and the proper representations conveyed to Washington; for in America, under the new paragraph added to the Constitution in 1899, second trials are not State affairs, but national, and must be tried by the most august body in the land — the Supreme Court of the United States. The justices were, therefore, summoned to sit in Chicago. The session was held day before yesterday, and was opened with the usual impressive formalities, the nine judges appearing in their black robes, and the new chief justice (Lemaitre) presiding. In opening the case, the chief justice said:

"It is my opinion that this matter is quite simple. The prisoner at the bar was charged with murdering the man Szczepanik; he was tried for murdering the man Szczepanik; he was fairly tried, and justly condemned and sentenced to death for murdering the man Szczepanik. It turns out that the man Szczepanik was not murdered at all. By the decision of the French courts in the Dreyfus matter, it is established beyond cavil or question that the decisions of courts are permanent and cannot be revised. We are obliged to respect and adopt this precedent. It is upon precedents that the enduring edifice of jurisprudence is reared. The prisoner at the bar has been fairly and righteously condemned to death for the murder of the man Szczepanik, and, in my opinion, there is but one course to pursue in the matter: he must be hanged."

Mr. Justice Crawford said:

" But, your Excellency, he was pardoned on the scaffold for that."

" The pardon is not valid, and cannot stand, because he was pardoned for killing a man whom he had not killed. A man cannot be pardoned for a crime which he has not committed; it would be an absurdity."

" But, your Excellency, he did kill a man."

" That is an extraneous detail; we have nothing to do with it. The court cannot take up this crime until the prisoner has expiated the other one."

Mr. Justice Halleck said:

" If we order his execution, your Excellency, we shall bring about a miscarriage of justice; for the governor will pardon him again."

" He will not have the power. He cannot pardon a man for a crime which he has not committed. As I observed before, it would be an absurdity."

After a consultation, Mr. Justice Wadsworth said:

" Several of us have arrived at the conclusion, your Excellency, that it would be an error to hang the prisoner for killing Szczepanik, but only for killing the other man, since it is proven that he did not kill Szczepanik."

" On the contrary, it is proven that he *did* kill Szczepanik. By the French precedent, it is plain that we must abide by the finding of the court."

" But Szczepanik is still alive."

" So is Dreyfus."

In the end it was found impossible to ignore or

get around the French precedent.   There could be
but one result: Clayton was delivered over to the
executioner.   It made an immense excitement; the
State rose as one man and clamored for Clayton's
pardon and re-trial.   The governor issued the
pardon, but the Supreme Court was in duty bound
to annul it, and did so, and poor Clayton was
hanged yesterday.   The city is draped in black, and,
indeed, the like may be said of the State.   All
America is vocal with scorn of " French justice,"
and of the malignant little soldiers who invented it
and inflicted it upon the other Christian lands.

AT THE APPETITE CURE

THIS establishment's name is Hochberghaus. It is in Bohemia, a short day's journey from Vienna, and being in the Austrian empire is, of course, a health resort. The empire is made up of health resorts; it distributes health to the whole world. Its waters are all medicinal. They are bottled and sent throughout the earth; the natives themselves drink beer. This is self-sacrifice, apparently — but outlanders who have drunk Vienna beer have another idea about it. Particularly the Pilsener which one gets in a small cellar up an obscure back lane in the First Bezirk — the name has escaped me, but the place is easily found: You inquire for the Greek church; and when you get to it, go right along by — the next house is that little beer-mill. It is remote from all traffic and all noise; it is always Sunday there. There are two small rooms, with low ceilings supported by massive arches; the arches and ceilings are whitewashed, otherwise the rooms would pass for cells in the dungeons of a bastile. The furniture is plain and cheap, there is no ornamentation anywhere; yet it is a heaven for the self-sacrificers, for the beer there is incomparable; there

is nothing like it elsewhere in the world. In the first
room you will find twelve or fifteen ladies and gentlemen of civilian quality; in the other one a dozen
generals and ambassadors. One may live in Vienna
many months and not hear of this place; but having
once heard of it and sampled it the sampler will
afterward infest it.

However, this is all incidental — a mere passing
note of gratitude for blessings received — it has
nothing to do with my subject. My subject is health
resorts. All unhealthy people ought to domicile
themselves in Vienna, and use that as a base,
making flights from time to time to the outlying
resorts, according to need. A flight to Marien-
bad to get rid of fat; a flight to Carlsbad to get
rid of rheumatism; a flight to Kaltenleutgeben to
take the water cure and get rid of the rest of the
diseases. It is all so handy. You can stand in
Vienna and toss a biscuit into Kaltenleutgeben,
with a twelve-inch gun. You can run out thither
at any time of the day; you go by the phenom-
enally slow trains, and yet inside of an hour you
have exchanged the glare and swelter of the city
for wooded hills, and shady forest paths, and soft
cool airs, and the music of birds, and the repose
and peace of paradise.

And there are plenty of other health resorts at
your service and convenient to get at from Vienna;
charming places, all of them; Vienna sits in the
center of a beautiful world of mountains with now

and then a lake and forests; in fact, no other city is so fortunately situated.

There are abundance of health resorts, as I have said. Among them this place — Hochberghaus. It stands solitary on the top of a densely wooded mountain, and is a building of great size. It is called the Appetite Anstallt, and people who have lost their appetites come here to get them restored. When I arrived I was taken by Professor Haimberger to his consulting-room and questioned:

" It is six o'clock.   When did you eat last? "

" At noon."

" What did you eat?"

" Next to nothing."

" What was on the table?"

" The usual things."

" Chops, chickens, vegetables, and so on?"

" Yes; but don't mention them — I can't bear it."

" Are you tired of them?"

" Oh, utterly.   I wish I might never hear of them again."

" The mere sight of food offends you, does it? "

" More, it revolts me."

The doctor considered awhile, then got out a long menu and ran his eye slowly down it.

" I think," said he, " that what you need to eat is — but here, choose for yourself."

I glanced at the list, and my stomach threw a handspring.   Of all the barbarous layouts that were ever contrived, this was the most atrocious. At the top stood "tough, underdone, overdue tripe, garnished with garlic "; half-way down the bill stood "young cat; old cat; scrambled cat "; at the bottom stood " sailor-boots, softened with tallow — served raw." The wide intervals of the bill were packed with dishes calculated to insult a cannibal. I said:

" Doctor, it is not fair to joke over so serious a case as mine. I came here to get an appetite, not to throw away the remnant that's left."

He said gravely: " I am not joking, why should I joke?"

" But I can't eat these horrors."

" Why not?"

He said it with a naïveté that was admirable, whether it was real or assumed.

" Why not? Because — why, doctor, for months I have seldom been able to endure anything more substantial than omelettes and custards. These unspeakable dishes of yours —"

" Oh, you will come to like them. They are very good. And you *must* eat them. It is the rule of the place, and is strict. I cannot permit any departure from it."

I said smiling: " Well, then, doctor, you will have to permit the departure of the patient. I am going."

He looked hurt, and said in a way which changed the aspect of things:

" I am sure you would not do me that injustice. I accepted you in good faith — you will not shame that confidence. This appetite-cure is my whole living. If you should go forth from it with the sort of appetite which you now have, it could become known, and you can see, yourself, that people would say my cure failed in your case and hence can fail in other cases. You will not go; you will not do me this hurt."

I apologized and said I would stay.

" That is right. I was sure you would not go; it would take the food from my family's mouths."

" Would they mind that? Do they eat these fiendish things?"

" They? My family? " His eyes were full of gentle wonder. "Of course not."

" Oh, they don't! Do you?"

" Certainly not."

" I see. It's another case of a physician who doesn't take his own medicine."

" I don't need it. It is six hours since you lunched. Will you have supper now — or later?"

" I am not hungry, but now is as good a time as any, and I would like to be done with it and have it off my mind. It is about my usual time, and regularity is commanded by all the authorities. Yes, I will try to nibble a little now — I wish a light horsewhipping would answer instead."

The professor handed me that odious menu.

" Choose — or will you have it later?"

"Oh, dear me, show me to my room; I forgot your hard rule."

"Wait just a moment before you finally decide. There is another rule. If you choose now, the order will be filled at once; but if you wait, you will have to await my pleasure. You cannot get a dish from that entire bill until I consent."

"All right. Show me to my room, and send the cook to bed; there is not going to be any hurry."

The professor took me up one flight of stairs and showed me into a most inviting and comfortable apartment consisting of parlor, bedchamber, and bathroom.

The front windows looked out over a far-reaching spread of green glades and valleys, and tumbled hills clothed with forests — a noble solitude unvexed by the fussy world. In the parlor were many shelves filled with books. The professor said he would now leave me to myself; and added:

"Smoke and read as much as you please, drink all the water you like. When you get hungry, ring and give your order, and I will decide whether it shall be filled or not. Yours is a stubborn, bad case, and I think the first fourteen dishes in the bill are each and all too delicate for its needs. I ask you as a favor to restrain yourself and not call for them."

"Restrain myself, is it? Give yourself no uneasiness. You are going to save money by me. The idea of coaxing a sick man's appetite back with this buzzard-fare is clear insanity."

I said it with bitterness, for I felt outraged by this calm, cold talk over these heartless new engines of assassination. The doctor looked grieved, but not offended. He laid the bill of fare on the commode at my bed's head, " so that it would be handy," and said:

" Yours is not the worst case I have encountered, by any means; still it is a bad one and requires robust treatment; therefore I shall be gratified if you will restrain yourself and skip down to No. 15 and begin with that."

Then he left me and I began to undress, for I was dog-tired and very sleepy. I slept fifteen hours and woke up finely refreshed at ten the next morning. Vienna coffee! It was the first thing I thought of — that unapproachable luxury — that sumptuous coffee-house coffee, compared with which all other European coffee and all American hotel coffee is mere fluid poverty. I rang, and ordered it; also Vienna bread, that delicious invention. The servant spoke through the wicket in the door and said — but you know what he said. He referred me to the bill of fare. I allowed him to go — I had no further use for him.

After the bath I dressed and started for a walk, and got as far as the door. It was locked on the outside. I rang and the servant came and explained that it was another rule. The seclusion of the patient was required until after the first meal. I had not been particularly anxious to get out before; but it was different now. Being locked in makes a person wishful to get out. I soon began to find it difficult to put in the time. At two o'clock I had been twenty-six hours without food. I had been growing hungry for some time; I recognized that I was not only hungry now, but hungry with a strong adjective in front of it. Yet I was not hungry enough to face the bill of fare.

I must put in the time somehow. I would read and smoke. I did it; hour by hour. The books were all of one breed — shipwrecks; people lost in deserts; people shut up in caved-in mines; people starving in besieged cities. I read about all the revolting dishes that ever famishing men had stayed their hunger with. During the first hours these things nauseated me; hours followed in which they did not so affect me; still other hours followed in which I found myself smacking my lips over some tolerably infernal messes. When I had been without food forty-five hours I ran eagerly to the bell and ordered the second dish in the bill, which was a sort of dumplings containing a compost made of caviar and tar.

It was refused me. During the next fifteen hours I visited the bell every now and then and ordered a dish that was further down the list. Always a refusal. But I was conquering prejudice after prejudice, right along; I was making sure progress; I was creeping up on No. 15 with deadly certainty, and my heart beat faster and faster, my hopes rose higher and higher.

At last when food had not passed my lips for sixty hours, victory was mine, and I ordered No. 15:

" Soft-boiled spring chicken — in the egg; six dozen, hot and fragrant!"

In fifteen minutes it was there; and the doctor along with it, rubbing his hands with joy. He said with great excitement:

" It's a cure, it's a cure! I knew I could do it. Dear sir, my grand system never fails — never. You've got your appetite back — you know you have; say it and make me happy."

" Bring on your carrion — I can eat anything in the bill!"

" Oh, this is noble, this is splendid — but I knew I could do it, the system never fails. How are the birds?"

" Never was anything so delicious in the world; and yet as a rule I don't care for game. But don't interrupt me, don't — I can't spare my mouth, I really can't."

Then the doctor said:

" The cure is perfect. There is no more doubt nor danger. Let the poultry alone; I can trust you with a beefsteak, now."

The beefsteak came — as much as a basketful of it — with potatoes, and Vienna bread and coffee; and I ate a meal then that was worth all the costly preparation I had made for it. And dripped tears of gratitude into the gravy all the time — gratitude

20E

to the doctor for putting a little plain common sense into me when I had been empty of it so many, many years.

II

· Thirty years ago Haimberger went off on a long voyage in a sailing-ship. There were fifteen passengers on board. The table-fare was of the regulation pattern of the day: At 7 in the morning, a cup of bad coffee in bed; at 9, breakfast: bad coffee, with condensed milk; soggy rolls, crackers, salt fish; at 1 P. M., luncheon: cold tongue, cold ham, cold corned beef, soggy cold rolls, crackers; 5 P. M., dinner: thick pea soup, salt fish, hot corned beef and sauerkraut, boiled pork and beans, pudding; 9 till 11 P. M., supper: tea, with condensed milk, cold tongue, cold ham, pickles, sea biscuit, pickled oysters, pickled pig's feet, grilled bones, golden buck.

At the end of the first week eating had ceased, nibbling had taken its place. The passengers came to the table, but it was partly to put in the time, and partly because the wisdom of the ages commanded them to be regular in their meals. They were tired of the coarse and monotonous fare, and took no interest in it, had no appetite for it. All day and every day they roamed the ship half hungry, plagued by their gnawing stomachs, moody, untalkative, miserable. Among them were three confirmed dyspeptics. These became shadows in the course of three weeks. There was also a bedridden invalid;

he lived on boiled rice; he could not look at the regular dishes.

Now came shipwreck and life in open boats, with the usual paucity of food. Provisions ran lower and lower. The appetites improved, then. When nothing was left but raw ham and the ration of that was down to two ounces a day per person, the appetites were perfect. At the end of fifteen days the dyspeptics, the invalid and the most delicate ladies in the party were chewing sailor-boots in ecstasy, and only complaining because the supply of them was limited. Yet these were the same people who couldn't endure the ship's tedious corned beef and sauerkraut and other crudities. They were rescued by an English vessel. Within ten days the whole fifteen were in as good condition as they had been when the shipwreck occurred.

" They had suffered no damage by their adventure," said the professor. "Do you note that?"

" Yes."

" Do you note it well?"

" Yes — I think I do."

" But you don't. You hesitate. You don't rise to the importance of it. I will say it again — with emphasis —*not one of them suffered any damage.*"

" Now I begin to see. Yes, it was indeed remarkable."

" Nothing of the kind. It was perfectly natural. There was no reason why they should suffer damage.

They were undergoing Nature's Appetite Cure, the best and wisest in the world.''

"Is that where you got your idea?''

"That is where I got it.''

"It taught those people a valuable lesson.''

"What makes you think that?''

"Why shouldn't I? You seem to think it taught you one.''

"That is nothing to the point. I am not a fool.''

"I see. Were they fools?''

"They were human beings.''

"Is it the same thing?''

"Why do you ask? You know it yourself. As regards his health — and the rest of the things — the average man is what his environment and his superstitions have made him; and their function is to make him an ass. He can't add up three or four new circumstances together and perceive what they mean; it is beyond him. He is not capable of observing for himself. He has to get everything at second-hand. If what are miscalled the lower animals were as silly as man is, they would all perish from the earth in a year.''

"Those passengers learned no lesson, then?''

"Not a sign of it. They went to their regular meals in the English ship, and pretty soon they were nibbling again — nibbling, appetiteless, disgusted with the food, moody, miserable, half hungry, their outraged stomachs cursing and swearing and whining and supplicating all day long. And in vain, for they were the stomachs of fools."

" Then as I understand it, your scheme is —"

" Quite simple. Don't eat till you are hungry. If the food fails to taste good, fails to satisfy you, rejoice you, comfort you, don't eat again until you are *very* hungry. Then it will rejoice you — and do you good, too."

" And I observe no regularity, as to hours?"

" When you are conquering a bad appetite — no. After it is conquered, regularity is no harm, so long as the appetite remains good. As soon as the appetite wavers, apply the corrective again — which is starvation, long or short according to the needs of the case."

" The best diet, I suppose — I mean the whole-somest ——"

" All diets are wholesome. Some are wholesomer than others, but all the ordinary diets are wholesome enough for the people who use them. Whether the food be fine or coarse, it will taste good and it will nourish if a watch be kept upon the appetite and a little starvation introduced every time it weakens. Nansen was used to fine fare, but when his meals were restricted to bear-meat months at a time he suffered no damage and no discomfort, because his appetite was kept at par through the difficulty of getting his bear-meat regularly."

" But doctors arrange carefully considered and delicate diets for invalids."

20*.*.

" They can't help it. The invalid is full of inherited superstitions and won't starve himself. He
believes it would certainly kill him."

" It would weaken him, wouldn't it?"

" Nothing to hurt. Look at the invalids in our
shipwreck. They lived fifteen days on pinches of
raw ham, a suck at sailor-boots, and general
starvation. It weakened them, but it didn't hurt
them. It put them in fine shape to eat heartily of
hearty food and build themselves up to a condition
of robust health. But they did not perceive that;
they lost their opportunity; they remained invalids;
it served them right. Do you know the tricks that
the health-resort doctors play?"

" What is it?"

" My system disguised — covert starvation.
Grape-cure, bath-cure, mud-cure — it is all the same.
The grape and the bath and the mud make a show
and do a trifle of the work — the real work is done
by the surreptitious starvation. The patient accustomed to four meals and late hours — at both
ends of the day — now consider what he has to do
at a health resort. He gets up at 6 in the morning.
Eats one egg. Tramps up and down a promenade
two hours with the other fools. Eats a butterfly.
Slowly drinks a glass of filtered sewage that smells
like a buzzard's breath. Promenades another two
hours, but alone; if you speak to him he says
anxiously, ' My water ! — I am walking off my
water ! — please don't interrupt,' and goes stumping

HE EATS A BUTTERFLY

along again. Eats a candied rose-leaf. Lies at rest
in the silence and solitude of his room for hours;
mustn't speak, mustn't read, mustn't smoke. The
doctor comes and feels of his heart, now, and his
pulse, and thumps his breast and his back and his
stomach, and listens for results through a penny
flageolet; then orders the man's bath — half a degree,
Réaumur, cooler than yesterday. After the bath,
another egg. A glass of sewage at 3 or 4 in the
afternoon, and promenade solemnly with the other
freaks. Dinner at 6 — half a doughnut and a cup
of tea. Walk again. Half-past 8, supper — more
butterfly; at 9, to bed. Six weeks of this régime
— think of it. It starves a man out and puts him in
splendid condition. It would have the same effect
in London, New York, Jericho — anywhere."

"How long does it take to put a person in condition here?"

"It ought to take but a day or two; but in fact
it takes from one to six weeks, according to the
character and mentality of the patient."

"How is that?"

"Do you see that crowd of women playing foot-
ball, and boxing, and jumping fences yonder? They
have been here six or seven weeks. They were
spectral poor weaklings when they came. They
were accustomed to nibbling at dainties and delicacies
at set hours four times a day, and they had no
appetite for anything. I questioned them, and then
locked them into their rooms, the frailest ones to

T***

starve nine or ten hours, the others twelve or fifteen.
Before long they began to beg; and indeed they
suffered a good deal. They complained of nausea,
headache, and so on. It was good to see them eat
when the time was up. They could not remember
when the devouring of a meal had afforded them
such rapture — that was their word. Now, then,
that ought to have ended their cure, but it didn't.
They were free to go to any meals in the house, and
they chose their accustomed four. Within a day or
two I had to interfere. Their appetites were
weakening. I made them knock out a meal. That
set them up again. Then they resumed the four. I
begged them to learn to knock out a meal themselves,
without waiting for me. Up to a fortnight ago they
couldn't; they really hadn't manhood enough; but
they were gaining it, and now I think they are safe.
They drop out a meal every now and then of their
own accord. They are in fine condition now, and
they might safely go home, I think, but their confidence is not quite perfect yet, so they are waiting
awhile."

"Other cases are different?"

"Oh, yes. Sometimes a man learns the whole
trick in a week. Learns to regulate his appetite and
keep it in perfect order. Learns to drop out a meal
with frequency and not mind it."

"But why drop the entire meal out? Why not a
part of it?"

"It's a poor device, and inadequate. If the

stomach doesn't call vigorously — with a shout, as you may say — it is better not to pester it but just give it a real rest. Some people can eat more meals than others, and still thrive. There are all sorts of people, and all sorts of appetites. I will show you a man presently who was accustomed to nibble at eight meals a day. It was beyond the proper gait of his appetite by two. I have got him down to six a day, now, and he is all right, and enjoys life. How many meals do you effect per day?"

" Formerly — for twenty-two years — a meal and a half; during the past two years, two and a half: coffee and a roll at 9, luncheon at 1, dinner at 7:30 or 8."

" Formerly a meal and a half — that is, coffee and a roll at 9, dinner in the evening, nothing between — is that it?"

" Yes."

" Why did you add a meal?"

" It was the family's idea. They were uneasy. They thought I was killing myself."

" You found a meal and a half per day enough, all through the twenty-two years?"

" Plenty."

" Your present poor condition is due to the extra meal. Drop it out. You are trying to eat oftener than your stomach demands. You don't gain, you lose. You eat less food now, in a day, on two and a half meals, than you formerly ate on one and a half."

"True — a good deal less; for in those old days my dinner was a very sizable thing."

"Put yourself on a single meal a day, now — dinner — for a few days, till you secure a good, sound, regular, trustworthy appetite, then take to your one and a half permanently, and don't listen to the family any more. When you have any ordinary ailment, particularly of a feverish sort, eat nothing at all during twenty-four hours. That will cure it. It will cure the stubbornest cold in the head, too. No cold in the head can survive twenty-four hours on modified starvation."

"I know it. I have proved it many a time."

IN MEMORIAM

OLIVIA SUSAN CLEMENS

DIED AUGUST 18, 1896; AGED 24

IN a fair valley — oh, how long ago, how long ago!
  Where all the broad expanse was clothed in vines
And fruitful fields and meadows starred with flowers,
And clear streams wandered at their idle will,
And still lakes slept, their burnished surfaces
A dream of painted clouds, and soft airs
Went whispering with odorous breath,
And all was peace — in that fair vale,
Shut from the troubled world, a nameless hamlet
    drowsed.

  Hard by, apart, a temple stood;
And strangers from the outer world
Passing, noted it with tired eyes,
And seeing, saw it not:
A glimpse of its fair form — an answering momen-
    tary thrill —
And they passed on, careless and unaware.

They could not know the cunning of its make;
They could not know the secret shut up in its heart;
Only the dwellers of the hamlet knew:

They knew that what seemed brass was gold;
What marble seemed, was ivory;
The glories that enriched the milky surfaces —
The trailing vines, and interwoven flowers,
And tropic birds awing, clothed all in tinted fire —
They knew for what they were, not what they
    seemed:
Encrustings all of gems, not perishable splendors of
    the brush.
They knew the secret spot where one must stand —
They knew the surest hour, the proper slant of
    sun —
To gather in, unmarred, undimmed,
The vision of the fane in all its fairy grace,
A fainting dream against the opal sky.
    And more than this.   They knew
That in the temple's inmost place a spirit dwelt,
Made all of light!
    For glimpses of it they had caught
Beyond the curtains when the priests
That served the altar came and went.

    All loved that light and held it dear
That had this partial grace;
But the adoring priests alone who lived
By day and night submerged in its immortal glow
Knew all its power and depth, and could appraise
    the loss
If it should fade and fail and come no more.

    All this was long ago — so long ago!

The light burned on; and they that worship'd it,
And they that caught its flash at intervals and held
   it dear,
Contented lived in its secure possession.   Ah,
How long ago it was!
                     And then when they
Were nothing fearing, and God's peace was in the
   air,
And none was prophesying harm —
The vast disaster fell:
Where stood the temple when the sun went down,
Was vacant desert when it rose again!

   Ah, yes! 'Tis ages since it chanced!
                  So long ago it was,
That from the memory of the hamlet-folk the Light
   has passed —
They scarce believing, now, that once it was,
Or, if believing, yet not missing it,
And reconciled to have it gone.

   Not so the priests!   Oh, not so
The stricken ones that served it day and night,
Adoring it, abiding in the healing of its peace:
They stand, yet, where erst they stood
Speechless in that dim morning long ago;
And still they gaze, as then they gazed,
And murmur, " It will come again;
It knows our pain — it knows — it knows —
Ah, surely it will come again."

                            S. L. C.

LAKE LUCERNE, August 18, 1897.

MARK TWAIN

A BIOGRAPHICAL SKETCH

By SAMUEL E. MOFFETT

IN 1835 the creation of the Western empire of
America had just begun. In the whole region
west of the Mississippi, which now contains 21,-
000,000 people — nearly twice the entire population of the United States at that time — there were
less than half a million white inhabitants. There
were only two states beyond the great river, Louisiana and Missouri. There were only two considerable groups of population, one about New
Orleans, the other about St. Louis. If we omit
New Orleans, which is east of the river, there was
only one place in all that vast domain with any
pretension to be called a city. That was St.
Louis, and that metropolis, the wonder and pride
of all the Western country, had no more than
10,000 inhabitants.

It was in this frontier region, on the extreme fringe
of settlement " that just divides the desert from the
sown," that Samuel Langhorne Clemens was born,
November 30, 1835, in the hamlet of Florida, Missouri. His parents had come there to be in the

thick of the Western boom, and by a fate for which no lack of foresight on their part was to blame, they found themselves in a place which succeeded in accumulating 125 inhabitants in the next sixty years. When we read of the westward sweep of population and wealth in the United States, it seems as if those who were in the van of that movement must have been inevitably carried on to fortune. But that was a tide full of eddies and back currents, and Mark Twain's parents possessed a faculty for finding them that appears nothing less than miraculous. The whole Western empire was before them where to choose. They could have bought the entire site of Chicago for a pair of boots. They could have taken up a farm within the present city limits of St. Louis. What they actually did was to live for a time in Columbia, Kentucky, with a small property in land, and six inherited slaves, then to move to Jamestown, on the Cumberland plateau of Tennessee, a place that was then no farther removed from the currents of the world's life than Uganda, but which no resident of that or any other part of Central Africa would now regard as a serious competitor, and next to migrate to Missouri, passing St. Louis and settling first in Florida, and afterward in Hannibal. But when the whole map was blank the promise of fortune glowed as rosily in these regions as anywhere else. Florida had great expectations when Jackson was President. When John Marshall Clemens took up 80,000 acres of land in Tennessee, he thought he had established his children as territorial magnates. That phantom vision of wealth furnished later one of the motives of "The Gilded Age." It conferred no other benefit.

If Samuel Clemens missed a fortune he inherited good blood. On both sides his family had been settled in the South since early colonial times. His father, John Marshall Clemens, of Virginia, was a descendant of Gregory Clemens, who became one of the judges that condemned Charles I. to death, was excepted from the amnesty after the Restoration in consequence, and lost his head. A cousin of John M. Clemens, Jeremiah Clemens, represented Alabama in the United States Senate from 1849 to 1853.

Through his mother, Jane Lampton (Lambton), the boy was descended from the Lambtons of Durham, whose modern English representatives still possess the lands held by their ancestors of the same name since the twelfth century. Some of her forbears on the maternal side, the Montgomerys, went with Daniel Boone to Kentucky, and were in the thick of the romantic and tragic events that accompanied the settlement of the "Dark and Bloody Ground," and she herself was born there twenty-nine years after the first log cabin was built within the limits of the present commonwealth. She was one of the earliest, prettiest, and brightest of the many belles that have given Kentucky such an enviable reputation as a nursery of fair women, and her vivacity and wit left no doubt in the minds of her friends concerning the source of her son's genius.

John Marshall Clemens, who had been trained for the bar in Virginia, served for some years as a magistrate at Hannibal, holding for a time the position of county judge. With his death, in March, 1847, Mark Twain's formal education came to an end, and his education in real life began. He had always been a delicate boy, and his father, in consequence, had been lenient in the matter of enforcing attendance at school, although he had been profoundly anxious that his children should be well educated. His wish was fulfilled, although not in the way he had expected. It is a fortunate thing for literature that Mark Twain was never ground into smooth uniformity under the scholastic emery wheel. He has made the world his university, and in men, and books, and strange places, and all the phases of an infinitely varied life, has built an education broad and deep, on the foundations of an undisturbed individuality.

His high school was a village printing-office, where his elder brother Orion was conducting a newspaper. The thirteen-year-old boy served in all capacities, and in the occasional absences of his chief he reveled in personal journalism, with original illustrations hacked on wooden blocks with a jackknife, to an extent that riveted the town's attention, " but not its admiration," as his brother plaintively confessed. The editor spoke with feeling, for he had to take the consequences of these exploits on his return.

From his earliest childhood young Clemens had been of an adventurous disposition. Before he was thirteen, he had been extracted three times from the Mississippi, and six times from Bear Creek, in a substantially drowned condition, but his mother, with the high confidence in his future that never deserted her, merely remarked: " People who are born to be hanged are safe in the water." By 1853 the Hannibal tether had become too short for him. He disappeared from home and wandered from one Eastern printing-office to another. He saw the World's Fair at New York, and other marvels, and supported himself by setting type. At the end of this *Wanderjahr* financial stress drove him back to his family. He lived at St. Louis, Muscatine, and Keokuk until 1857, when he induced the great Horace Bixby to teach him the mystery of steamboat piloting. The charm of all this warm, indolent existence in the sleepy river towns has colored his whole subsequent life. In "Tom Sawyer," "Huckleberry Finn," "Life on the Mississippi," and "Pudd'nhead Wilson," every phase of that vanished estate is lovingly dwelt upon.

Native character will always make itself felt, but one may wonder whether Mark Twain's humor would have developed in quite so sympathetic and buoyant a vein if he had been brought up in Ecclefechan instead of in Hannibal, and whether Carlyle might not have been a little more human if he had spent his boyhood in Hannibal instead of in Ecclefechan.

A Mississippi pilot in the later fifties was a personage of imposing grandeur. He was a miracle of attainments; he was the absolute master of his boat while it was under way, and just before his fall he commanded a salary precisely equal to that earned at that time by the Vice-President of the United States or a Justice of the Supreme Court. The best proof of the superlative majesty and desirability of his position is the fact that Samuel Clemens deliberately subjected himself to the incredible labor necessary to attain it — a labor compared with which the efforts needed to acquire the degree of Doctor of Philosophy at a University are as light as a summer course of modern novels. To appreciate the full meaning of a pilot's marvelous education, one must read the whole of "Life on the Mississippi," but this extract may give a partial idea of a single feature of that training — the cultivation of the memory:

"First of all, there is one faculty which a pilot must incessantly cultivate until he has brought it to absolute perfection. Nothing short of perfection will do. That faculty is memory. He cannot stop with merely thinking a thing is so and so; he must *know* it; for this is eminently one of the exact sciences. With what scorn a pilot was looked upon, in the old times, if he ever ventured to deal in that feeble phrase 'I think,' instead of the vigorous one 'I know!' One cannot easily realize what a tremendous thing it is to know every trivial detail of

twelve hundred miles of river, and know it with
absolute exactness. If you will take the longest
street in New York, and travel up and down it,
conning its features patiently until you know every
house, and window, and door, and lamp-post, and
big and little sign by heart, and know them so
accurately that you can instantly name the one
you are abreast of when you are set down at
random in that street in the middle of an inky
black night, you will then have a tolerable notion
of the amount and the exactness of a pilot's knowledge who carries the Mississippi River in his head.
And then, if you will go on until you know every
street crossing, the character, size, and position of
the crossing-stones, and the varying depth of mud
in each of those numberless places, you will have
some idea of what the pilot must know in order to
keep a Mississippi steamer out of trouble. Next, if
you will take half of the signs in that long street and
change their places once a month, and still manage to
know their new positions accurately on dark nights,
and keep up with these repeated changes without
making any mistakes, you will understand what is
required of a pilot's peerless memory by the fickle
Mississippi.

"I think a pilot's memory is about the most
wonderful thing in the world. To know the Old
and New Testaments by heart, and be able to recite
them glibly, forward or backward, or begin at random
anywhere in the book and recite both ways, and

never trip or make a mistake, is no extravagant mass of knowledge, and no marvelous facility, compared to a pilot's massed knowledge of the Mississippi, and his marvelous facility in handling it. . .

" And how easily and comfortably the pilot's memory does its work; how placidly effortless is its way; how *unconsciously* it lays up its vast stores, hour by hour, day by day, and never loses or mislays a single valuable package of them all! Take an instance. Let a leadsman say: ' Half twain! half twain! half twain! half twain! half twain!' until it becomes as monotonous as the ticking of a clock; let conversation be going on all the time, and the pilot be doing his share of the talking, and no longer consciously listening to the leadsman; and in the midst of this endless string of half twains let a single ' quarter twain!' be interjected, without emphasis, and then the half twain cry go on again, just as before: two or three weeks later that pilot can describe with precision the boat's position in the river when that quarter twain was uttered, and give you such a lot of head marks, stern marks, and side marks to guide you that you ought to be able to take the boat there and put her in that same spot again yourself! The cry of ' Quarter twain ' did not really take his mind from his talk, but his trained faculties instantly photographed the bearings, noted the change of depth, and laid up the important details for future reference without requiring any assistance from him in the matter."

21*₀*₀

Young Clemens went through all that appalling training, stored away in his head the bewildering mass of knowledge a pilot's duties required, received the license that was the diploma of the river university, entered into regular employment, and regarded himself as established for life, when the outbreak of the Civil War wiped out his occupation at a stroke, and made his weary apprenticeship a useless labor. The commercial navigation of the lower Mississippi was stopped by a line of fire, and black, squat gunboats, their sloping sides plated with railroad iron, took the place of the gorgeous white side-wheelers, whose pilots had been the envied aristocrats of the river towns. Clemens was in New Orleans when Louisiana seceded, and started North the next day. The boat ran a blockade every day of her trip, and on the last night of the voyage the batteries at the Jefferson barracks, just below St. Louis, fired two shots through her chimneys.

Brought up in a slaveholding atmosphere, Mark Twain naturally sympathized at first with the South. In June he joined the Confederates in Ralls County, Missouri, as a Second Lieutenant under General Tom Harris. His military career lasted for two weeks. Narrowly missing the distinction of being captured by Colonel Ulysses S. Grant, he resigned, explaining that he had become "incapacitated by fatigue" through persistent retreating. In his subsequent writings he has always treated his brief experience of warfare as a burlesque episode, although the official reports and correspondence of the Confederate commanders speak very respectfully of the work of the raw countrymen of the Harris Brigade. The elder Clemens brother, Orion, was *persona grata* to the Administration of President Lincoln, and received in consequence an appointment as the first Secretary of the new Territory of Nevada. He offered his speedily reconstructed junior the position of private secretary to himself, " with nothing to do and no salary." The two crossed the plains in the overland coach in eighteen days — almost precisely the time it will take to go from New York to Vladivostok when the Trans-Siberian Railway is finished.

A year of variegated fortune hunting among the silver mines of the Humboldt and Esmeralda regions followed. Occasional letters written during this time to the leading newspaper of the Territory, the Virginia City *Territorial Enterprise*, attracted the attention of the proprietor, Mr. J. T. Goodman, a man of keen and unerring literary instinct, and he offered the writer the position of local editor on his staff. With the duties of this place were combined those of legislative correspondent at Carson City, the capital. The work of young Clemens created a sensation among the lawmakers. He wrote a weekly letter, spined with barbed personalities. It appeared every Sunday, and on Mondays the legislative business was obstructed with the complaints of members who rose to questions of privilege, and expressed their opinion of the correspondent with

T*₊*₊

acerbity. This encouraged him to give his letters more individuality by signing them. For this purpose he adopted the old Mississippi leadsman's call for two fathoms (twelve feet)—"Mark Twain."

At that particular period dueling was a passing fashion on the Comstock. The refinements of Parisian civilization had not penetrated there, and a Washoe duel seldom left more than one survivor. The weapons were always Colt's navy revolvers — distance, fifteen paces; fire and advance; six shots allowed. Mark Twain became involved in a quarrel with Mr. Laird, the editor of the Virginia *Union*, and the situation seemed to call for a duel. Neither combatant was an expert with the pistol, but Mark Twain was fortunate enough to have a second who was. The men were practicing in adjacent gorges, Mr. Laird doing fairly well, and his opponent hitting everything but the mark. A small bird lit on a sage bush thirty yards away, and Mark Twain's second fired and knocked off its head. At that moment the enemy came over the ridge, saw the dead bird, observed the distance, and learned from Gillis, the humorist's second, that the feat had been performed by Mark Twain, for whom such an exploit was nothing remarkable. They withdrew for consultation, and then offered a formal apology, after which peace was restored, leaving Mark Twain with the honors of war.

However, this incident was the means of effecting another change in his life. There was a new law which prescribed two years' imprisonment for any one who should send, carry, or accept a challenge. The fame of the proposed duel had reached the capital, eighteen miles away, and the governor wrathfully gave orders for the arrest of all concerned, announcing his intention of making an example that would be remembered. A friend of the duelists heard of their danger, outrode the officers of the law, and hurried the parties over the border into California.

Mark Twain found a berth as city editor of the San Francisco *Morning Call*, but he was not adapted to routine newspaper work, and in a couple of years he made another bid for fortune in the mines. He tried the " pocket mines " of California, this time, at Jackass Gulch, in Calaveras County, but was fortunate enough to find no pockets. Thus he escaped the hypnotic fascination that has kept some intermittently successful pocket miners willing prisoners in Sierra cabins for life, and in three months he was back in San Francisco, penniless, but in the line of literary promotion. He wrote letters for the Virginia *Enterprise* for a time, but tiring of that, welcomed an assignment to visit Hawaii for the Sacramento *Union*, and write about the sugar interests. It was in Honolulu that he accomplished one of his greatest feats of " straight newspaper work." The clipper *Hornet* had been burned on " the line," and when the skeleton survivors arrived, after a passage of forty-three days in an open boat on ten days' provisions, Mark Twain gathered their stories, worked all day and all night, and threw a complete account of the horror aboard a schooner that had already cast off. It was the only full account that reached California, and it was not only a clean " scoop " of unusual magnitude, but an admirable piece of literary art. The *Union* testified its appreciation by paying the correspondent ten times the current rates for it.

After six months in the Islands, Mark Twain returned to California, and made his first venture upon the lecture platform. He was warmly received, and delivered several lectures with profit. In 1867 he went East by way of the Isthmus, and joined the Quaker City excursion to Europe and the Holy Land, as correspondent of the *Alta California*, of San Francisco. During this tour of five or six months the party visited the principal ports of the Mediterranean and the Black Sea. From this trip grew " The Innocents Abroad," the creator of Mark Twain's reputation as a literary force of the first order. " The Celebrated Jumping Frog of Calaveras County " had preceded it, but " The Innocents " gave the author his first introduction to international literature. A hundred thousand copies were sold the first year, and as many more later.

Four years of lecturing followed — distasteful, but profitable. Mark Twain always shrank from the public exhibition of himself on the platform, but he was a popular favorite there from the first. He was one of a little group, including Henry Ward Beecher and two or three others, for whom every lyceum committee in the country was bidding, and whose capture at any price insured the success of a lecture course.

The Quaker City excursion had a more important result than the production of "The Innocents Abroad." Through her brother, who was one of the party, Mr. Clemens became acquainted with Miss Olivia L. Langdon, the daughter of Jervis Langdon, of Elmira, New York, and this acquaintance led, in February, 1870, to one of the most ideal marriages in literary history.

Four children came of this union. The eldest, Langdon, a son, was born in November, 1870, and died in 1872. The second, Susan Olivia, a daughter, was born in the latter year, and lived only twenty-four years, but long enough to develop extraordinary mental gifts and every grace of character. Two other daughters, Clara Langdon and Jean, were born in 1874 and 1880, respectively, and still live (1899).

Mark Twain's first home as a man of family was in Buffalo, in a house given to the bride by her father as a wedding present. He bought a third interest in a daily newspaper, the Buffalo *Express*, and joined its staff. But his time for jogging in harness was past. It was his last attempt at regular newspaper work, and a year of it was enough. He had become assured of a market for anything he might produce, and he could choose his own place and time for writing.

There was a tempting literary colony at Hartford;

the place was steeped in an atmosphere of antique peace and beauty, and the Clemens family were captivated by its charm. They moved there in October, 1871, and soon built a house which was one of the earliest fruits of the artistic revolt against the mid-century Philistinism of domestic architecture in America. For years it was an object of wonder to the simple-minded tourist. The facts that its rooms were arranged for the convenience of those who were to occupy them, and that its windows, gables, and porches were distributed with an eye to the beauty, comfort, and picturesqueness of that particular house, instead of following the traditional lines laid down by the carpenters and contractors who designed most of the dwellings of the period, distracted the critics, and gave rise to grave discussions in the newspapers throughout the country of " Mark Twain's practical joke."

The years that followed brought a steady literary development. " Roughing It," which was written in 1872, and scored a success hardly second to that of " The Innocents," was, like that, simply a humorous narrative of personal experiences, variegated by brilliant splashes of description; but with " The Gilded Age," which was produced in the same year, in collaboration with Mr. Charles Dudley Warner, the humorist began to evolve into the philosopher. " Tom Sawyer," appearing in 1876, was a veritable manual of boy nature, and its sequel, " Huckleberry Finn," which was published nine years later, was not only an advanced treatise in the same science, but a most moving study of the workings of the untutored human soul, in boy and man. "The Prince and the Pauper," 1882, "A Connecticut Yankee at King Arthur's Court" (1890), and "Pudd'nhead Wilson" (first published serially in 1893-94), were all alive with a comprehensive and passionate sympathy to which their humor was quite subordinate, although Mark Twain never wrote, and probably never will write, a book that could be read without laughter. His humor is as irrepressible as Lincoln's, and like that, it bubbles out on the most solemn occasions; but still, again like Lincoln's, it has a way of seeming, in spite of the surface incongruity, to belong there. But it was in the "Personal Recollections of Joan of Arc," whose anonymous serial publication in 1894-95 betrayed some critics of reputation into the absurdity of attributing it to other authors, notwithstanding the characteristic evidences of its paternity that obtruded themselves on every page, that Mark Twain became most distinctly a prophet of humanity. Here, at last, was a book with nothing ephemeral about it — one that will reach the elemental human heart as well among the flying machines of the next century, as it does among the automobiles of to-day, or as it would have done among the stage coaches of a hundred years ago.

And side by side with this spiritual growth had come a growth in knowledge and in culture. The

Mark Twain of " The Innocents," keen-eyed, quick
of understanding, and full of fresh, eager interest in
all Europe had to show, but frankly avowing that he
" did not know what in the mischief the Renaissance
was," had developed into an accomplished scholar
and a man of the world for whom the globe had few
surprises left.   The Mark Twain of 1895 might con-
ceivably have written " The Innocents Abroad,"
although it would have required an effort to put himself in the necessary frame of mind, but the Mark
Twain of 1869 could no more have written " Joan
of Arc " than he could have deciphered the Maya
hieroglyphics.

In 1873 the family spent some months in England
and Scotland, and Mr. Clemens lectured for a few
weeks in London.   Another European journey
followed in 1878.

" A Tramp Abroad " was the result of this
tour, which lasted eighteen months.   " The Prince
and the Pauper," " Life on the Mississippi," and
" Huckleberry Finn " appeared in quick succes-
sion in 1882, 1883, and 1885.   Considerably more
amusing than anything the humorist ever wrote was
the fact that the trustees of some village libraries in
New England solemnly voted that " Huckleberry
Finn," whose power of moral uplift has hardly been
surpassed by any book of our time, was too demoral-
izing to be allowed on their shelves.

All this time fortune had been steadily favorable,
and Mark Twain had been spoken of by the press,

sometimes with admiration, as an example of the financial success possible in literature, and sometimes with uncharitable envy, as a haughty millionaire, forgetful of his humble friends.   But now began the series of unfortunate investments that swept away the accumulations of half a lifetime of hard work, and left him loaded with debts incurred by other men.   In 1885 he financed the publishing house of Charles L. Webster & Company in New York.   The firm began business with the prestige of a brilliant *coup*.   It secured the publication of the Memoirs of General Grant, which achieved a sale of more than 600,000 volumes.   The first check received by the Grant heirs was for $200,000, and this was followed a few months later by one for $150,000. These are the largest checks ever paid for an author's work on either side of the Atlantic.   Meanwhile, Mr. Clemens was spending great sums on a type-setting machine of such seductive ingenuity as to captivate the imagination of everybody who saw it. It worked to perfection, but it was too complicated and expensive for commercial use, and after sinking a fortune in it between 1886 and 1889, Mark Twain had to write off the whole investment as a dead loss.

On top of this the publishing house, which had been supposed to be doing a profitable business, turned out to have been incapably conducted, and all the money that came into its hands was lost. Mark Twain contributed $65,000 in efforts to save its life, but to no purpose, and when it finally failed, he found that it had not only absorbed everything he had put in, but had incurred liabilities of $96,000, of which less than one-third was covered by assets.

He could easily have avoided any legal liability for the debts, but as the credit of the company had been based largely upon his name, he felt bound in honor to pay them. In 1895-96 he took his wife and second daughter on a lecturing tour around the world, wrote "Following the Equator," and cleared off the obligations of the house in full.

The years 1897, 1898, and 1899 were spent in England, Switzerland, and Austria. Vienna took the family to its heart, and Mark Twain achieved such a popularity among all classes there as is rarely won by a foreigner anywhere. He saw the manufacture of a good deal of history in that time. It was his fortune, for instance, to be present in the Austrian Reichsrath on the memorable occasion when it was invaded by sixty policemen, and sixteen refractory members were dragged roughly out of the hall. That momentous event in the progress of parliamentary government profoundly impressed him.

Mark Twain, although so characteristically American in every fiber, does not appeal to Americans alone, nor even to the English-speaking race. His work has stood the test of translation into French, German, Russian, Italian, Swedish, Norwegian, and Magyar. That is pretty good evidence that it possesses the universal quality that marks the master.

Another evidence of its fidelity to human nature is the readiness with which it lends itself to dramatization. " The Gilded Age," " Tom Sawyer," " The Prince and the Pauper," and "Pudd'nhead Wilson " have all been successful on the stage.

In the thirty-eight years of his literary activity Mark Twain has seen generation after generation of " American humorists " rise, expand into sudden popularity, and disappear, leaving hardly a memory behind. If he has not written himself out like them, if his place in literature has become every year more assured, it is because his " humor " has been something radically different from theirs. It has been irresistibly laughter-provoking, but its sole end has never been to make people laugh. Its more important purpose has been to make them think and feel. And with the progress of the years Mark Twain's own thoughts have become finer, his own feelings deeper and more responsive. Sympathy with the suffering, hatred of injustice and oppression, and enthusiasm for all that tends to make the world a more tolerable place for mankind to live in, have grown with his accumulating knowledge of life as it is. That is why Mark Twain has become a classic, not only at home, but in all lands whose people read and think about the common joys and sorrows of humanity.

22E